THE ACADEMIC SABBATICAL

THE ACADEMIC SABBATICAL

A Voyage of Discovery

Edited by

Timothy Sibbald
Victoria Handford

University of Ottawa Press
2022

 Les **Presses** de l'Université d'Ottawa
University of Ottawa **Press**

The University of Ottawa Press (UOP) is proud to be the oldest of the francophone university presses in Canada and the oldest bilingual university publisher in North America. Since 1936, UOP has been enriching intellectual and cultural discourse by producing peer-reviewed and award-winning books in the humanities and social sciences, in French and in English.

www.press.uottawa.ca

Library and Archives Canada Cataloguing in Publication

Title: The academic sabbatical : a voyage of discovery / edited by Timothy M. Sibbald, Victoria Handford.
Names: Sibbald, Timothy, 1966- editor. | Handford, Victoria, 1957- editor.
Series: Education (University of Ottawa)
Description: Series statement: Education |
  Includes bibliographical references and index.
Identifiers: Canadiana (print) 20210358726 | Canadiana (ebook) 20210358750 |
  ISBN 9780776633206 (hardcover) | ISBN 9780776633190 (softcover) |
  ISBN 9780776629674 (PDF) | ISBN 9780776629681 (EPBU)
Subjects: LCSH: College teachers—Leaves of absence. | LCSH: Sabbatical leave.
Classification: LCC LB2335.8 .A23 2022 | DDC 378.1/21—dc23

Legal Deposit: Second Quarter 2022
Library and Archives Canada

© Timothy Sibbald and Victoria Handford 2022

Creative Commons Open Access Licence

Production Team
Copy editing   Robbie McCaw
Proofreading   Michael Waldin
Typesetting   Nord Compo
Cover design   Édiscript enr.

Cover Image
Carolyn Charbonneau

Attribution-Non-Commercial-Share Alike 4.0 International (CC BY-NC-ND 4.0)

By virtue of this licence you are free to:

Share—copy and redistribute the material in any medium or format

Attribution—You must give appropriate credit, provide a link to the license, and indicate if changes were made. You may do so in any reasonable manner, but not in any way that suggests the licensor endorses you or your use.

Non-Commercial—You may not use the material for commercial purposes.

No Derivatives—If you remix, transform, or build upon the material, you may not distribute the modified material.

No additional restrictions—You may not apply legal terms or technological measures that legally restrict others from doing anything the license permits.

The University of Ottawa Press gratefully acknowledges the support extended to its publishing list by the Government of Canada, the Canada Council for the Arts, the Ontario Arts Council, the Social Sciences and Humanities Research Council and the Canadian Federation for the Humanities and Social Sciences through the Awards to Scholarly Publications Program, and by the University of Ottawa.

  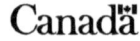

About the Cover Photo

The cover photo, by Carolyn Charbonneau, serves as a metaphor for sabbatical experiences. The image displays calm, reflective characteristics that are analogous to components of sabbaticals. The shades of green, the forest, and the water, serve as metaphors of renewal and growth.

The large rock represents many obstacles present in academia, hiding and obscuring the possibilities beyond it. Opportunities surface, sometimes in the moment. They may reveal themselves as one moves through the sabbatical waters and around the rock. Yet, the more one peers into the distance trying to envision what may be around the rock, the more one notices a loss of clarity. It invites curiosity while recognizing the need for a plan for the sabbatical voyage of discovery.

Table of Contents

Acknowledgements... ix

Introduction.. 1

1 Sabbaticals—The Gift of Time! A Thematic Literature Review
Shelleyann Scott and Donald E. Scott 13

Section 1: The First Sabbatical Experience

2 Not All That Shines Is Gold: What I Learned during My Sabbatical Year
María del Carmen Rodríguez de France 41

3 The Voyage Continues: Navigating Discovery between Two Sabbaticals
Susan Eliott-Johns 47

4 The Sabbatical Voyage: A Triptych of Renewal, Reflection, and Research
Victoria (Tory) Handford 71

5 (Re)Discovering Academia through a Sabbatical
Timothy Sibbald 89

Section 2: First Sabbaticals with Significant Travel

6 Life on the Two Sides of the Pond
Anahit Armenakyan 105

7 Academic Sabbatical Journey: The Crossovers between Research and Cultures
Pei-Ying Lin 129

8 Place Making
Lee Anne Block 139

Section 3: Perspective Based on More Than One Sabbatical

9 Practitioner Study Leave and Academic Sabbaticals: An Unsettling Reflection of Both
Lloyd Kornelsen 155

10 Sabbatical Tales: Expectations and Experiences
Cecile Badenhorst, Antoinette Doyle, Jackie Hesson, Xuemei Li, Heather McLeod, Sharon Penney, and Gabrielle Young 165

11 The Academic Sabbatical as a Voyage of Discovery: What *Really* Counts
Merridee Bujaki 185

12 Sabbaticals in a Research-Intensive University: Supports, Tensions, and Outcomes
Donald E. Scott and Shelleyann Scott 205

Conclusion 227

Contributors 239
Index 245

Acknowledgements

Contributing authors are the essence of any edited book. Our authors are no exception and we thank them for their support of this effort. All the authors are in Canadian universities and represent several disciplines within those institutions. Each has added important tones and themes to this study of sabbaticals, a unique feature of academic life.

Within this book, there is a smaller group of authors who have contributed chapters to our earlier edited books. Those books related to tenure-track and tenure experiences in Canadian universities (Sibbald & Handford, 2017, 2020). We would like to acknowledge their contribution as forming a remarkable longitudinal collection of narratives. To the chapter authors, we say "thank you for your engagement, your belief in this longitudinal project, and your aspirational goals, individually and collectively, to 'tell the story' and tell it well." Editing a collection is a dialogue with authors, and they have surely been our keel as we welcomed authors who were new to what is now a series of books.

The University of Ottawa Press continues to support us with encouragement, thorough critique, and via ongoing conversations that have resulted in ever deeper and nuanced understandings of both the editing and the publishing process as seen through the lens of a publisher. The press took a risk with us as early-career academics and novice editors back in 2014. Thank you for your willingness to work with us. In a myriad of ways, you have fostered our growth as editors.

We proposed this book prior to the pandemic of 2020, but the authors drafted chapters and their work has been edited as the pandemic progressed. The effort represents a phenomenal dedication to this academic endeavour. All of us—editors, authors, publishers—have found focus challenging as work routines have been disrupted, with corresponding fluctuations in motivation. Additionally, stark global events have juxtaposed with the analysis of sabbaticals—it surely was an unusual happenstance. As we watch the beginning of vaccine rollouts, we know public-health efforts will improve the global situation, but it will take time. We can only wonder if the full range of sabbatical experiences will return, or if our book will serve for comparative studies of how the pandemic instigated permanent changes for academics.

References

Sibbald, T. M., & Handford, V. (Eds.). (2017). *The academic gateway: Understanding the journey to tenure.* University of Ottawa Press.

Sibbald, T. M., & Handford, V. (Eds.). (2020). *Beyond the academic gateway: Looking back on the tenure-track journey.* University of Ottawa Press.

Introduction

Sabbaticals are important to faculty and to higher education for a great many reasons, as this book reveals. There is evidence in this volume of significant productivity in terms of research and dissemination, as well as program development, dedication to graduate students, and intellectual sharing among professors. Research and dissemination are foundational to higher education, and the evidence in this book is clear: Sabbaticals build stronger and deeper academic connections. We see this book as a collection of narratives about the academic sabbatical, but also as a collective voice that, like a flower arrangement, is enriched by the diverse experiences and perspectives our authors share in their chapters. In the end, we have an entire sabbatical garden.

Historical Emergence of Sabbaticals

Initially, we thought the history of sabbaticals was straightforward—sabbaticals began in the mid-1800s, with Harvard University being identified as the instigator of this benefit. It was a strategy to attract faculty to an institution. As we considered this academic origin story, questions arose about the beginnings of the concept of the sabbatical itself; why it was rapidly adopted across many institutions, and whether its value extends beyond attracting faculty. Our exploration of the possible roots of sabbatical are connected to agricultural and religious notions of lying fallow, rest, reflection, and renewal. This approach made one thing apparent: We are not scholars of agricultural history or religious histories! We are simply scholars of education doing our best to make sense of the academic sabbatical.

Much of religion and agriculture collocate in ways we may only vaguely recall. "For it was agriculture that allowed the settled division of labour which produced the classes that codified our religions, and in explaining their deeper intents, religious writers used metaphor from the main occupation of their day, agriculture" (Falvey, 2005, p. 2). Both agriculture and religion share concepts of rest, renewal, and sustainability. We will briefly explore these origins and shared beliefs.

Agricultural Origins

The tradition of sabbatical has some important roots in agricultural fallowing, a process for ensuring sustained productivity in crops that has been in use at least since the Bronze Age (Bakels, 2009). Fallowing likely began as part of a strategy to address the depletion of nutrients in soil that can happen over time when there is continuous planting of few crops. Soil nutrients are known to deplete when not replenished. Before chemical fertilizers, farmers would shift cultivation to different locations to take advantage of better soil conditions. In time, the availability of space became an issue. The practice of fallowing individual plots (i.e., letting a growing area lie dormant for a time) was used and a variety of fallowing techniques emerged (Gleave, 1996). Fallowing also occurred in pharaonic Egypt as a pragmatic need to give soil time to recover from flooding or deficient water (Butzer, 1984). The variety and timing for fallowing is not consistent and varies according to the conditions of the soil and demands placed on the soil by the crops (Gleave, 1996), which is consistent with the historical record. Agriculture and farming were important to changes in our stories as a human race. While many cultures continued with hunting and gathering, other cultures chose to gather in a region and learned to use the resources that were nearby to develop and sustain a lifestyle (Diamond, 1997).

Religious Origins

The agrarian usage of laying fallow, rest, restoration, or renewal of land appears to have either preceded, migrated from, or paralleled the application of the same principle to humans. Its occurrence with humans is evident in the records of various religions, but, while there is clearly a parallel, the details of how that transition took place is not clear. World religions are thousands of years old. It makes sense that texts used to describe concepts of sustainability are tied to agricultural images and practices as these understandings were familiar, and connected to survival itself. In particular, the application of the principle to humans clearly developed some standardization of practice with regular intervals that do not parallel agrarian applications.

We will venture to demonstrate some connection without attempting an in-depth interpretation. A detailed accounting of the religious underpinnings of the Sabbath and its interpretation for the sabbatical can be found in Kimball (1978), Endres (2001), and Burton (2010).

Judaism

The concept of a sabbatical developed to parallel the ancient Hebrew practice of the Sabbath and linked directly to agricultural practices. The Hebrew scriptures in the Bible address sabbatical several times. Genesis is the very first mention of sabbatical (Genesis 2:2–3), where the seventh day is one of rest, and includes values of holiness and spiritual renewal. Sabbatical also is part of the Ten Commandments (Exodus 20:2–17; Deuteronomy 5:6–21). Depending on the version of the Bible, it may appear as the fifth, fourth, or third commandment, but its presence is constant. For some, these commandments were written "with the finger of God" (Exodus 31:18; Deuteronomy 9:10). Multiple biblical references occur, making the presence of a Sabbath, or *shmita*, a Sabbath year, far more than a passing idea.

The book of Jeremiah references a freeing of individuals from servitude after seven years (Jeremiah 34:13–14: "At the end of seven years ye shall let go every man his brother that is a Hebrew, that hath been sold unto thee, and hath served thee six years, thou shalt let him go free from thee"). In the end, there are a great many references to the Sabbath and the concept of sabbatical as periods of rest, reflection, and renewal.

Islam

The Quran also identifies Sabbath rest with Jumu'ah, the Friday prayer. While not a full day of rest, there is a nonwork element to this time. The Jumu'ah occurs weekly (every seven days) and is a time to step out of daily work tasks and engage with sacred elements.

Christianity
The same principle arises in the idea that one works six days of the week and rests and worships on the seventh.

Non-Religious Practices
The notion of working six days and resting on the seventh has had cultural influence as a societal norm that goes beyond the details of specific religions. For example, in Canada the Lord's Day Act embedded the religious notion until it was struck down as contravening the Charter of Rights and Freedoms in 1985.[1] The period when the Act was in force aligns with many older people's childhood experiences of when stores were closed on Sundays—a day of rest. Older individuals in North American and European communities recollect those days were quiet, with less traffic and more focus on family. There was, in our experience, some societal coherence in sharing a common experience of rest from work and routine on the seventh day.

Concluding the Historical Emergence
For individuals, sabbaticals arise according to when they were hired, whether they choose to take a sabbatical, along with any deferrals or delays that may take place. Sabbaticals do not occur simultaneously for all, but there is a sense of a common experience. The common experience is recognition of the change of pace that arises because sabbaticals often include flexible hours and change of routine. It is a common experience lacking significant details.

The agricultural notion of leaving fields to fallow may be a better parallel, but the agrarian details are not common knowledge. For instance, it does not mean ignoring the fields. There is, as we understand it, a need for ploughing and harrowing the fields to keep them arable. There is a need for organic material to be tilled into the soil, which as it denatures reduces viability of pathogens that can harm crops.

While the religious and agricultural history is informative about the origin of the concept of sabbatical, it is more germane to investigate sabbatical in the modern academy. Endres (2001) follows the parallel, arguing that the Bible does not demand that the farmer return to the field in year eight or provide evidence of a fallow year being productive—a point that does not help clarify the current understanding of the academic sabbatical. The use of parallels ultimately loses clarity, and does not provide a fundamental conceptualization of sabbaticals that can resolve questions such as whether they are a privilege or a right in the academy (Otto & Kroth, 2011).

Academic Sabbaticals

From the inception of this book, there has been an unusual tension. From the earliest days it was clear that the sabbatical has received little attention as an academic topic (Carraher et al., 2014; Flaspohler, 2009). A literature review conducted for the book proposal revealed a small body of scholarship about sabbaticals, but much more could be done. The literature has been described as "atheoretical" (Carraher et al., 2014, p. 296), filled with many anecdotal accounts. Yet anecdotal accounts provide qualitative details. Burton (2010), for example, highlights how muddy the process of beginning a sabbatical can be.

The lack of literature is surprising given sabbaticals have existed for nearly a century and a half. Kang and Miller (1999) explain that the academic sabbatical began in 1880, in the United States, after a decade of experiments using leaves of absences. It began at one institution and slowly expanded; in 1930, there were 178 institutions offering sabbaticals. Bennett and Scroggs (1932) reported a rate of 48 percent of universities offering sabbaticals based on a sample in or about 1932. Daugherty (1980) reported that in 1972 the occurrence was 64 percent of regionally accredited two- and four-year institutions that had sabbaticals, and that the figure had increased to 73 percent in 1979. By 1982, all the universities studied had sabbatical programs (Kang and Miller, 1999).

Despite the progressive history of adoption there were challenges finding academics who were interested in writing about their sabbatical experiences. The number of faculty who take sabbaticals is low. Numerically, if every eligible faculty member took a sabbatical every seven years (or a half sabbatical after three or four years) then, on average, one-seventh (=1 year per 7 years or 0.5 years per 3.5 years) or roughly 14 percent of faculty would be on sabbatical in any given year. However, the actual rate reported (see table 1) is 3.8 percent, with 68 percent of sabbaticals being one semester as opposed to a year (Kang & Miller, 1999). Weintraub (2008) mentions a 5 percent cap on sabbaticals granted in any given year in some institutions. Flaspohler (2009) cites a statistic from 1979 that only 35 percent of academic librarians eligible for a sabbatical took advantage of it. This figure represents one-third of the 14 percent who are eligible, resulting in an overall rate of sabbatical taking of 4.9 percent, consistent with other figures.

Boening (1996) gives substantial details about sabbatical rates at the University of Alabama based on a ten-year period, from 1986 to 1996, when the Faculty of Arts and Science had requests of 6.3 percent per year and approved 5.4 percent per year, while the Faculty of Education had the lowest percentage approved, at 2.9 percent per year. These figures pool semester sabbaticals with full-year sabbaticals. Distinguishing the two types of sabbaticals, one-semester sabbaticals were requested at a rate of 8.1 percent per year, with 6.5 percent per year approved, while one-year sabbaticals had a request rate of 1.7 percent per year and 1.4 percent per year were approved. (This is an 82 percent rate of one-semester sabbaticals and contrasts with the 68 percent figure Kang and Miller reported.)

Table 1
Reported rates of sabbaticals

Academic discipline	Sabbaticals requested by type and approval			
	One year		One semester	
	Requested	Approved	Requested	Approved
Arts and Science	8.1%	6.5%	1.7%	1.4%
Education		2.9%		
Library Science		4.9%		

Easteal and Westmarland (2010) argue that the low rate of sabbatical taking arises because faculty do not have equivalent capacities for activities or access to sabbaticals. They propose addressing the inequalities of access by using virtual sabbaticals to promote international travel and collaboration opportunities. This may be valid but contrasts with Weintraub (2008), who indicates she did not apply for a sabbatical because she could not identify a focal purpose. Additionally, it contrasts with Brazeau and Van Tyle (2006), who claim sabbaticals are underutilized in professional schools, such as in schools of pharmacy. In other words, there are multiple explanations for the low rate of sabbaticals, but the rate is historically and consistently low.

In addition to the low sabbatical rate, among faculty who have taken sabbaticals there seemed to be reluctance to write about them—we wondered if sabbaticals caused academics to focus within their own area of study and avoid broader academic thinking and scholarship or if there was something else taking place. We had to extend our efforts, and, in the end, it took roughly double the time we expected to gather a representative group of authors for the chapters in this book. The existence of this tension—a lack of scholarship, but also a struggle to engage scholars in an area needing scholarship—served to reinforce the view that this book would address both the need for scholarship and the need to understand the tension.

In the context of academia, sabbaticals are negotiated structures that provide an option for faculty. With the tripartite model of academia (teaching/research/service), the sabbatical ideally provides a period with no teaching or service roles, so that the academic can focus on their research. Variations of this model exist; for example, alternative foci such as course or program development among bipartite (teaching/service) faculty occur. The application process for a sabbatical, the duration, and amount of financial remuneration during the sabbatical vary as well. Despite the variations, the basic structure is fundamental, is available at most institutions, and seems to be appreciated among academics who take them. Yet the details can include political interactions, student and service commitments that do not easily stop, research dynamics, and myriads of other complexities.

Miller et al. (2012) used stratified international sampling to examine and detail many policies pertaining to sabbaticals and show there are variations. In many instances there is oversight by an administrator, but peer review is also used (Thompson & Louth, 2003; Weintraub, 2008). Miller et al. (2012) take issue with subjectivity and identify a lack of accountability and effectiveness evidence. However, establishing policies of accountability and effectiveness requires that foundational issues are reined in when, as one example, there is no consensus on whether sabbaticals are a privilege or a right (Otto & Kroth, 2011).

Beyond the most cursory description, sabbaticals are a valid option within higher education. They are earned periods of self-directed focused work. This is why we were surprised to find a tension—where the dearth of academic study about sabbaticals was clear but so was the reluctance to provide a written reflection on them. We suspected it might be related to the complexities that arise from the wide variety of personal details, as evident when reading the chapters of this book. However, the commonality and shared sense of what sabbaticals are among academics seemed to defy the tension. We wondered if perhaps there was a sense that when the complexities are removed there might be little left. We also wondered if there may be psychological components where academics, as high achievers, may aim for the stars and decline to write about not reaching them.

Interactions with other academics have highlighted shared experiences within sabbaticals. Many have remarked about an initial stage of putting their feet up and genuinely resting for a week or two. It is not uncommon to hear of a stage, not long after that, when there is a realization that—to achieve everything that was planned—requires becoming focused on their objectives. Others mention travel, including lingering at the destination before or after a conference to gain a deeper experience. While these anecdotal experiences are common, they are not universal, and they most certainly do not define a sabbatical or place its importance within the academic context.

Our aim was to gather a cross-section of experiences and have authors narrate them, along with their reasoning. Our hope was that the self-selection to submit chapters would be a proxy for the range of experiences which academics have. We wanted to see the natural balance that came from narrative accounts about sabbaticals. We feel we have been successful in this endeavour. There are, however, a couple of significant challenges that deserve mention. The first is that academics are loath to make some of their workplace struggles public. It is simple self-preservation, as their places in academia will persist for longer than the writing of a chapter for this book. We were apprised of various issues and will raise them in due course, but they will lack the contextual connection to the authors, to respect their desire for self-preservation.

A second challenge is the relatively small number of academics who have contributed to the literature, which constrains the representation of issues known to exist. We, therefore, aimed for detail of the sabbatical experience and looked for the richness of the experience rather than have multiple authors clarifying the details of any single dimension of sabbatical experiences.

The result achieves several significant outcomes. The individual narratives show a diversity of experiences that promote thoughts about activities that academics might pursue in future sabbaticals. On more than one occasion, there were reflective moments in the editing process. Collectively, the voices show the richness and power of the sabbatical as a structural feature of the academy. And while it is not without its challenges and tensions—it is, without a doubt—sabbaticals are a beneficial and productive tool for academics.

Lastly, this book follows two others, also published by the University of Ottawa Press. *The Academic Gateway: Understanding the Journey to Tenure* (Sibbald & Handford, 2017) and *Beyond the Academic Gateway: Looking Back on the Tenure-Track Journey* (Sibbald & Handford, 2020). The two earlier books along with this book show a progression of academic activity. There is a longitudinal aspect, where six chapters in this book have contributors who were included in the prior two books. This opens a door to a research opportunity where the longitudinal record can be examined, whether by the interested reader or in a more rigorous effort, to address the need for theoretical contributions in the research literature.

Organization of this Book

The contributors to this book are varied in academic disciplines, are at different career stages, and are at different sized, and differently oriented, universities. Organizing within this diversity required attention to the different thematic approaches that academics often pursue. The examination of approaches represents the general nature of the experiences described. It is not an exhaustive or comprehensive review of approaches. This led to sectioning of groups of chapters that fit several themes. Each section includes an introduction, but by way of overview they are: *first sabbaticals, first sabbaticals with significant travel*, and *perspectives of more than one sabbatical*.

The organization is pragmatic, corresponding to significant themes among the chapters. The first section focuses on first sabbatical experiences with limited travel. The experiences include some travel and a chapter where the COVID-19 pandemic removed the opportunity for travel. This section is focused on travel, when feasible, for dissemination of research and attending conferences as opposed to a defining feature of the sabbatical. The second section of the book includes contributions where travel was a defining feature of the sabbatical. The third section includes contributors who have, or are on the verge of, experiences with more than one sabbatical. The authors in this section provide a longer view and have had the additional experience of years after returning from the sabbatical, which doubtlessly contributes to a focused sense of the sabbatical experience within the broader scope of academic endeavour.

Endnote

1   See https://canliiconnects.org/en/summaries/28387

References

Bakels, C. C. (2009). *The western European Loess belt: Agrarian history, 5300 BC–AD 1000*. Springer.

Bennett, H. G., & Scroggs, S. (1932). Sabbatical leave. *The Journal of Higher Education, 3*(4), 196–199.

Boening, C. H. (1996). *Faculty renewal through sabbatical: An analysis of sabbatical application patterns, 1986–1996* [Abstract for unpublished doctoral dissertation]. University of Alabama.

Brazeau, G. A., & Van Tyle, J. H. (2006). Sabbaticals: The key to sharpening our professional skills as educators, scientists, and clinicians. *American Journal of Pharmaceutical Education, 70*(5), 1–4.

Burton, L. D. (2010). Sabbatical (Editorial). *Journal of Research on Christian Education, 19*, 1–6.

Butzer, K. W. (1984). Long-term Nile flood variation and political discontinuities in pharaonic Egypt. In J. D. Clark & S. A. Brandt (Eds.), *From hunters to farmers: The causes and consequences of food production in Africa* (pp. 102–112). University of California Press.

Carraher, S. M., Crocitto, M. M., & Sullivan, S. (2014). A kaleidoscope career perspective on faculty sabbaticals. *Career Development International, 19*(3), 295–313.

Daugherty, H. M. (1980). *Sabbatical leaves in higher education* [Abstract from unpublished doctoral dissertation]. Indiana University.

Diamond, J. (1998). *Guns, germs, and steel: The fates of human societies*. Norton.

Easteal, P., & Westmarland, N. (2010). The virtual sabbatical: A pioneering case study. *Innovative Higher Education, 35*, 297–311.

Endres, T. G. (2001). An examination of the sabbatical year in Leviticus 25 and its implications for academic practice. *Journal of the Association for Communication Administration, 30*, 29–38.

Falvey, L. (2005). *Religion and agriculture: Sustainability in Christianity and Buddhism*. Institute for International Development, Adelaide, Australia.

Flaspohler, M. R. (2009). Librarian sabbatical leaves: Do we need to get out more? *The Journal of Academic Librarianship, 35*(2), 152–161.

Gleave, M. B. (1996). The length of the fallow period in tropical fallow farming systems: A discussion with evidence from Sierra Leone. *The Geographical Journal, 162*(1), 14–24.

Kang, B., & Miller, M. T. (1999). *An overview of the sabbatical leave in higher education: A synopsis of the literature base*. ERIC. https://files.eric.ed.gov/fulltext/ED430471.pdf

Kimball, B. A. (1978). The origin of the Sabbath and its legacy to the modern sabbatical. *The Journal of Higher Education, 49*(4), 303–315.

Miller, M. T., Bai, K., & Newman, R. E. (2012). A critical examination of sabbatical application policies: Implications for academic leaders. *College Quarterly, 15*(2), 1–13.

Otto, L. R., & Kroth, M. (2011). An examination of the benefits and costs of sabbatical leave for general higher education, industry, and professional-technical/community college environments. *Journal of STEM Teacher Development, 48*(3), 22–43.

Sibbald, T. M., & Handford, V. (Eds.). (2017). *The academic gateway: Understanding the journey to tenure.* University of Ottawa Press.

Sibbald, T. M., & Handford, V. (Eds.). (2020). *Beyond the academic gateway: Looking back on the tenure-track journey.* University of Ottawa Press.

Thompson, T. C., & Louth, R. (2003). Radical sabbaticals: Putting yourself in danger. *College Composition and Communication, 55*(1), 147–171.

Weintraub, T. (2008). Sabbatical in paradise. *Community & Junior College Libraries, 14*(3), 153–160.

CHAPTER 1

Sabbaticals—The Gift of Time! A Thematic Literature Review

Shelleyann Scott and Donald E. Scott

In considering sabbaticals, we reviewed the research others have shared in education and in other disciplines. The historical background, and how sabbaticals are conceptualized across the international context, was a priority throughout. This chapter presents a review of the knowledge base as it pertains to the purposes, benefits, problems, and conundrums associated with academic sabbaticals and administrative leaves. This provided us with insights into others' experiences and institutional expectations, as well as founded our narratives in our other chapter in this book (ch. 12).

Scoping the Literature

Even though we have experienced research and scholarship leaves, and given our research interests pertain to leadership and leadership development, sabbatical and research leaves were not a topic we had explored. So, we dutifully delved into the research databases to uncover what others knew and had shared about the mysterious field of sabbaticals. We limited this review to university and industry sabbaticals, and excluded the K–12 sector because of the differences in expectations and outcomes. Keywords such as "sabbatical," "research leave," "scholarship leave," "administrative leave," "higher education," and "university" were used as the entry-level position to investigate research relevant to this topic. What we found intrigued and amazed us. We were intrigued by how much of the literature was more than twenty years old, giving us a glimpse into academe of times gone by. It amazed us just how little was written on this topic, particularly of an empirical nature, although there were several advocatory or personal-experience narratives. For example, the earliest paper we accessed was the *Industrial Relations News* in 1963, which was heavily gender biased, anachronistic, and outlined the pros and cons of executive sabbaticals. The latest papers, published between 2018 and 2020, detailed the constraints experienced in an academic's sabbatical due to the COVID-19 pandemic (Smith, 2020) and others expressed concerns about work-life balance, the intensification of academic work, and job satisfaction (Lakkoju, 2020; Sabagh et al., 2018).

We structured our analysis to explore demographic features, such as the stakeholder group in the paper (e.g., medical clinicians, pharmacists, engineers, etc.), date of publication, and methodology (e.g., empirical, autoethnography, etc.). The thematic analysis included the historical background, stated purposes (both personal and professional), benefits/advantages, problems and conundrums encountered, advice in terms of what to avoid and what to do, and any interesting or unusual notes. Our search included a range of academic databases (e.g., ERIC, ABI/Business Premium Collection, ProQuest, SAGE, and Wiley) and Google Scholar.

It was rather surprising how few empirical studies were found on this topic. There is a definite gap in the academic literature. Indeed, many papers stated that more research was needed, particularly when considering some of the problems and contentions related to sabbaticals. Overall, we were able to access fifty sources (see the appendix) which directly discussed sabbaticals and included themes related to staff and faculty recruitment and/or retention strategies, career advice, faculty-development approaches, stress and burnout, and tax issues surrounding sabbatical expenses. There were several papers where the central focus was on work-life balance, job satisfaction, and well-being that mentioned "leaves" as strategies for amelioration. Additionally, eleven papers discussed aspects of academic teaching or graduate supervision regarding the intensity of academic responsibilities, which highlights the importance of sabbaticals, but these do not explicitly reference sabbaticals.

A range of methodologies were found in the papers on sabbaticals (see the appendix) including surveys, autoethnographies, opinion or advice papers, literature reviews, narratives, case studies, mixed methodologies, policy analyses, methodological and instrument design, legal analysis, and a few that were unclear. Various academic disciplines were represented, including business, counselling, educational leadership, legal fields, medicine, nursing, pharmacy, and science. The appendix summarizes the range of methodologies encountered.

We also read six papers related to administrative leaves or sabbaticals for administrators. Miller and his colleagues appeared to be the most consistent authors who systematically researched sabbaticals, and Miller's administrative roles (as faculty associate dean and dean) offer interesting insights into administrative, institutional, and accountability considerations (refer to: Bai & Miller, 1998, 1999; Miller, 2002; Miller & Bai, 2006; Miller, Bai, & Newman, 2012; Miller & Pikowsky, 2010).

Historical Background

It was fascinating to learn the term "sabbatical" had its roots in Jewish tradition (i.e., Mosaic Law) and derived from the word "sabbath"—a day of rest instituted for contemplation of spiritual matters:

> Six days you shall do your work, *but on the seventh day you shall rest;* that your ox and your donkey *may have rest,* and the son of your servant woman, and the alien, *may be refreshed.* (Exodus 23:12; emphasis added)

Not only did the Mosaic Law specify rest on a sabbath day each week, but also a sabbath year every seven years. Indeed, in the sabbath year the Israelites were prohibited from working the land, which enabled the rejuvenation of the soil by it lying fallow for the year:

> *The Lord spoke to Moses on Mount Sinai, saying, "Speak to the people of Israel and say to them, when you come into the land that I give you, the* land shall keep a Sabbath *to the Lord. For six years you shall sow your field, and for six years you shall prune your vineyard and gather in its fruits,* but in the seventh year there shall be a Sabbath of solemn rest for the land, *a Sabbath to the Lord. You shall not sow your field or prune your vineyard. You shall not reap what grows of itself in your harvest, or gather the grapes of your undressed vine. It*

shall be a year of solemn rest for the land. *The Sabbath of the land shall provide food for you, for yourself and for your male and female slaves and for your hired worker and the sojourner who lives with you, and for your cattle and for the wild animals that are in your land: all its yield shall be for food. . . ."* (Leviticus 25:1–7; emphasis added)

Therefore, the Sabbath represented rest for all—the Israelites, their servants, livestock, and the land. Therefore, modelled from the Jewish Sabbath, an academic sabbatical is a period of rest from teaching and service responsibilities. Sabbaticals were initiated at Harvard University in 1880 by its president, Charles Eliot, as a strategy to lure a pre-eminent scholar to Harvard, and as Sima (2000) stated, "sabbatical leaves have continued as a cherished part of academic life" (p. 67).

Qualification Periods and Nomenclature

Research-intensive and some comprehensive universities in the United States, the United Kingdom, Australia, New Zealand, and Canada offer a sabbatical or research and scholarship leave as part of their workplace agreement (Bai & Miller, 1999; Else, 2015; Gilbert et al., 2007; Spencer et al., 2012). However, the qualification periods, who can access a sabbatical, terms, and accountability for outcomes vary significantly from institution to institution. Gilbert and his colleagues (2007), Bai and Miller (1999), Smith et al. (2016), and Sima (2000) all identified a range of qualification periods of three and/or six years of service, with the period of the sabbatical varying from a semester to a full year on varied pay (e.g., half, full, or 87.5 percent salary, etc.). With the difficulties of "getting away" for an extended period, Wilson (2016) and Pillinger et al. (2019) discussed "mini-sabbaticals" of two- or three-week periods, which they proposed as sufficient to complete a writing project. Originally, only senior research professors were eligible. Over time, more in the professoriate (at lower levels, such as assistant and associate professors) and contract faculty (those with a defined contractual term with different conditions) have become eligible, although many exclude sessional faculty or those in teaching-specialist streams (Gilbert et al., 2007; Bai & Miller, 1999; Miller & Bai, 2006).

Interestingly, Else (2015) noted there has been a change in nomenclature from "sabbatical" to "research and scholarship leave" or "study leave," where the intent, expectations, and outcomes have changed:

> [A]lthough the sabbatical is an "integral" part of academic life, it no longer exists in its true form. In the UK, an increasing number of universities, Warwick among them, now refer to it as "study leave," which in practice does not give people the time and freedom to rest, relax and re-engage with their discipline, he argues . . . that sabbaticals should be viewed as unstructured time in which an academic cannot predict the outcome of his or her research. (p. 44)

This nomenclature change is an important distinction as there has clearly been a shift in the purpose of sabbaticals to ensure faculty members are productive rather than simply taking a break (Else, 2015). Else identified that this change was due to budget concerns, competition in the form of league tables, and notions of efficiency measured through productivity (p. 44). In this chapter, we use the term "sabbatical" in preference to "research and scholarship leave" given its succinctness and commonality in the literature. We recognize there are important political and ideological differences between the two terms, but for the sake of brevity we use sabbatical.

Purposes and Benefits of Sabbaticals

The purposes and benefits of sabbaticals vary considerably, most likely in alignment with universities' and colleges' priorities. Wyman (1973) indicated that, unlike the Sabbath, academic sabbaticals represented important time for increased productivity, yet in this case away from the intense work undertaken on campus. The purposes (see figure 1.1) cited in the literature were categorized as intellectual and academic rejuvenation, reduce or prevent burnout, increase research productivity, teaching and curriculum development, collaborative engagement, skill development and sharing, complete graduate studies, and/or as political rewards and recognition.

Intellectual and academic rejuvenation through engagement with others, research and writing, updating knowledge, and identifying innovations in a discipline and as a visiting fellow were identified as important purposes within academic renewal (Bai & Miller, 1999; Gilbert et al., 2007; Harley, 2005; Hedges, 1999; Leung et al., 2020; Marker, 1983; Sima, 2000). Within the intellectual dimension was reflection time. Reflection time allowed academics to engage with new knowledge (Maranville, 2014), take stock of their research agenda, and decide on new directions.

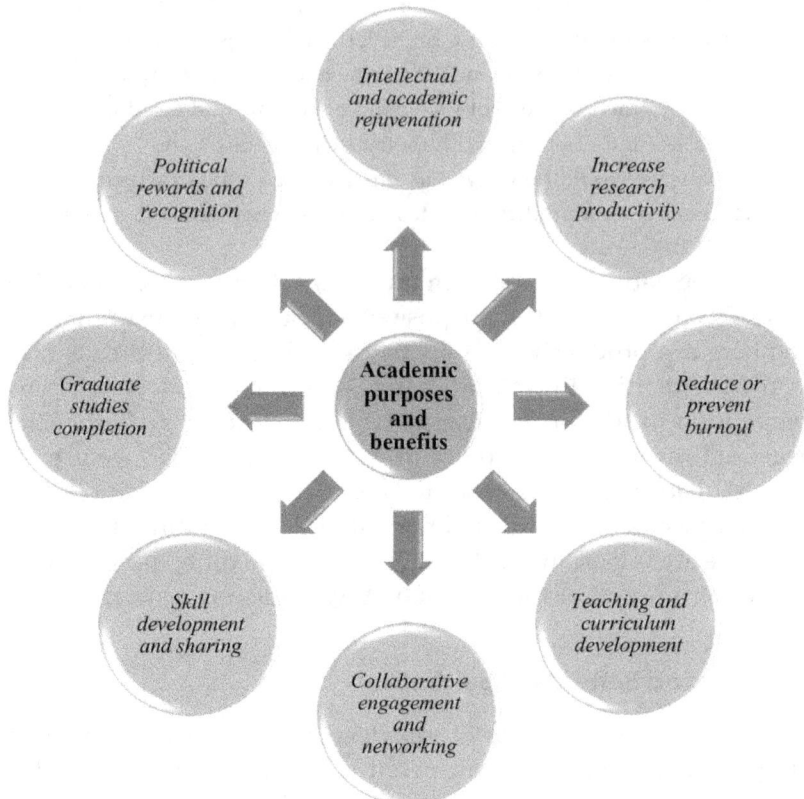

Figure 1.1. *Academic purposes and benefits of sabbaticals.*

Increase research productivity encompassed conducting research, undertaking analysis, establishing individual and collaborative projects, and writing. Research activities have become more important in contemporary research-intensive universities focused on competition, high research metrics, and rankings (Bai & Miller, 1999; Benshoff & Spruill, 2002; Carraher et al., 2014; Eisenberg, 2010; Else, 2015; Gallagher, 2018; Gilbert et al., 2007; June, 2018; Maranville, 2014; Marshall, 2014; Miller & Bai, 2006; Sima, 2000; Smith et al., 2016; Spencer & Kent, 2007; Spencer et al., 2012; Yarmohammadian et al., 2018).

Reduce or prevent burnout directly related to a recognition of the intensity in academic work (Benshoff & Spruill, 2002; Carraher et al., 2014). This concept encompassed preventing burnout, reducing stress (Altmann & Kröll, 2017; Blum, 2007; Leung et al., 2020; Straus

& Sackett, 2015), and retaining faculty (Bai & Miller 1999; Swenty et al., 2011).

Teaching and curriculum development was a very broad category. For example, teaching activities were described in both vague and specific terms. Vague references included "developing teaching" (Benshoff & Spruill, 2002, p. 133); renewed "teaching methods" and becoming "better teachers" (Bai & Miller, 1999, p. 10); "the improvement of teaching" (Bai & Miller, 1998; Marker, 1983, p. 38; Miller & Bai, 2006); "to promote course and curriculum development" (Marker, 1983; Miller & Bai, 2006; Sima, 2000, p. 69); and "engaging in the preparation of teaching materials or other work related to teaching" (Spencer & Kent, 2007, p. 660). More specific references included "teaching workshops," learning "how to teach online," and investigating "other doctoral programs to determine their best practices regarding online teaching" (Marshall, 2012, n.p.).

Collaborative engagement and networking were generally in relation to working with colleagues in other institutions and sometimes in other countries. This included moving to another research site to work with others (Easteal & Westmarland, 2010; Friedman, 2018; Sima, 2000) and to expand professional and research networks (Yarmohammadian et al., 2018).

Skill development and sharing were frequently mentioned in more applied disciplines like science, medicine, nursing, and pharmacy. Skill development included new techniques and discipline-specific processes, as well as technological, administrative, business, academic, and other skills. One aspect of skill development was the understanding that the sabbaticant would share newly acquired skills with colleagues at the home institution (Bai & Miller, 1998; Benshoff & Spruill, 2002; Carraher et al., 2014; Eisenberg, 2010; Friedman, 2018; Hedges, 1999; Kraus, 2018; Leung et al., 2020; Maranville, 2014; Sale, 2013).

Graduate studies completion was mentioned infrequently as this potentially conflicted with an academic being "qualified" for a sabbatical (Sima, 2000). This was leave granted for a faculty member who was struggling or needed dedicated time to complete their doctorate, or engage in a "recognized course of study" (Spencer & Kent, 2007, p. 660). This was more likely to occur in the college context than in university as a doctorate is a prerequisite for most university faculty.

Political rewards and recognition were discussed in relation to academics who had provided superior service and/or leadership

(Blum, 2007; Else, 2015; Harley, 2005; June, 2018; Sale, 2013; Wildman, 2012), which may include service to students (Gilbert et al., 2007) and loyal and long service to the institution (Miller & Bai, 2006; Wildman, 2012). It also included a performance-management dimension wherein it served as an incentive for performance improvement (Bia & Miller, 1999). Conversely, it was to reward research prowess or retain high flyers (Industrial Relations News, 1963; Spencer et al., 2012). A disturbing tone within this dimension was that these sabbaticals were approved through leader discretion, which could potentially be discriminatory or nepotistic.

Overall, everyone espoused the benefits of sabbatical leaves. In fact, the personal-narrative accounts waxed lyrical about the academic benefits of sabbaticals and advocated for their continuation in the face of political pressure to remove such opportunity. Many of the benefits directly aligned with the purposes (see figure 1.1). These included increased research productivity, which is important to all academic institutions; the enhancement of teaching and learning; innovation of curriculum, assessment tasks, and course materials; increases in faculty knowledge and skill development; and partnerships and collaborative research projects that can increase visiting-scholar opportunities and attract graduate students to a faculty. Some were more esoteric or individualized. For example, Friedman (2018) described his sabbatical as "the gift that keeps on giving" (p. 656), wherein the academic networks and collaborations continued for decades post his sabbatical. Gallagher (2018) reflected on general academic development: "[T]the time away enables exposure to new ideas, to new contexts and to new people. Some of the relationships made on my journey developed into friendships that will endure and new collaborations that will reap rewards for the international field of ethics and care [Gallagher's discipline]" (p. 953).

Some articulated specific benefits to the institution and to students. Friedman (2018) indicated there was an institutional advantage, where returning sabbaticant clinicians would "bring back new skills to enrich those [working with them]" (p. 658). Bai and Miller (1999) observed that, upon return, sabbaticants felt intellectually renewed and more enthusiastic about working with their students. They stated "faculty 'felt a sense of rejuvenation and reward,'" felt "up-to-date," and felt as though "their professional life had been substantially enriched." Curiously, the "lowest rated benefit" was that faculty felt "caught up on their research and writing schedule" (p. 1).

This section highlighted the academic purposes and benefits of sabbaticals or research and scholarship leaves as pertains to the day-to-day life of an academic. The following section distinguishes administrative leaves from academic sabbaticals.

Administrative Leave Versus Sabbaticals

Some literature included references to administrative leaves, and these were frequently conflated with sabbaticals. As we explored this subsection of sabbaticals, we found some administrative leaves had purposes quite different from academic sabbaticals. There were references to administrative leaves being employed for academic misconduct or suspected malfeasance (Spectrum News 1, 2017; Upshaw, 2019; WAAY-TV 31 News, 2019). In these cases, the administrator was placed on paid or unpaid leave while an investigation would be conducted. If the administrator was exonerated, then the leave was lifted and the individual returned to their duties. In cases where the charges were upheld, legal action ensued and the individual was either disciplined or had their employment terminated.

Other references to administrative leave related to leaders who were returning to the professoriate ranks upon completion of a leadership term (Blum, 2007; Else, 2015; Harley, 2005; June, 2018; Sale, 2013; Wildman, 2012). The purpose for these administrative leaves was described as a period to re-engage with teaching, and to provide the requisite time to "jump-start" a leader's research agenda "after a lengthy hiatus" (June, 2018, p. 2; Sale, 2013). Sale indicated that administration was frequently "'the kiss of death' for scholarship" (Sale, 2013, n.p.). Therefore, this transition time was important for leaders to ponder if a change in research direction was needed, to identify a research agenda, and to link up with their colleagues through conferences and professional meetings. He also suggested time to reconnect with new research methodologies and technologies, and to explore what funding opportunities were available.

For some re-engaging with their research agenda was a reality check, especially related to how difficult it was to obtain research grants within the contemporary research landscape (June, 2018). Both Sale (2013) and June (2018) iterated the need for leaders to reacquaint themselves with "teaching and grading." June recommended leaders observe expert peers' teaching and step-up to take the harder classes, such as large undergraduate classes, to gain credibility among their colleagues. Sale recommended leaders engage with colleagues during their leaves to discuss teaching innovations, course design, become familiar with the new teaching technologies, and gain insights about how to handle contemporary issues in the classroom (e.g., students' mobile-phone use and accessibility services, etc.).

A common perspective was the need to decompress and overcome burnout (Else, 2015). Blum (2007) discussed the benefits of the release from constant emails. She also noted the associated health benefits from uninterrupted sleep and felt more relaxed while on administrative leave. Harley (2005) mused that administrative leaves were an important pause for reflecting on what was important in the leader's life and "the organization's culture, to think creatively about growth opportunities and innovation" (p. 78). Reflection was also mentioned by June (2018), "Former administrators . . . must adjust to a work life with fewer perks, less power, and different expectations from colleagues" (p. 2). Sale (2013) went further and expressed that reflection time afforded a refocusing on "returning now to the light side: that role we envisioned as we exited graduate training and took our first position" (n.p.).

Overall, administrative leaves were discussed in terms of time for reorientation to academic life, reintegration into teaching and service, and to rekindle a research agenda. More subtle themes emerged regarding the psychological adjustment from a leader mindset to a collegial one, which entailed adjusting to the shift from "power and authority" to that of "collegiality, collaboration, service, and student-centredness."

Psychosocial Benefits of Sabbaticals

The most important and interesting point for us was the overt acknowledgement of the legitimacy of psychosocial outcomes of sabbaticals, even though these may only have a secondary benefit to the institution and on productivity outcomes.

These psychosocial influences (see figure 1.2) hold benefits to the individual and potentially to the culture of the institution. For example, authors described the gift of time to spend with loved ones, say elderly parents or children (Friedman, 2018; Marshall, 2014; Smith, 2020; Smith et al., 2016), thereby *enriching family relationships*. Others cited the importance of time to care for one's *mental and physical well-being,* which included more restful sleep and more exercise

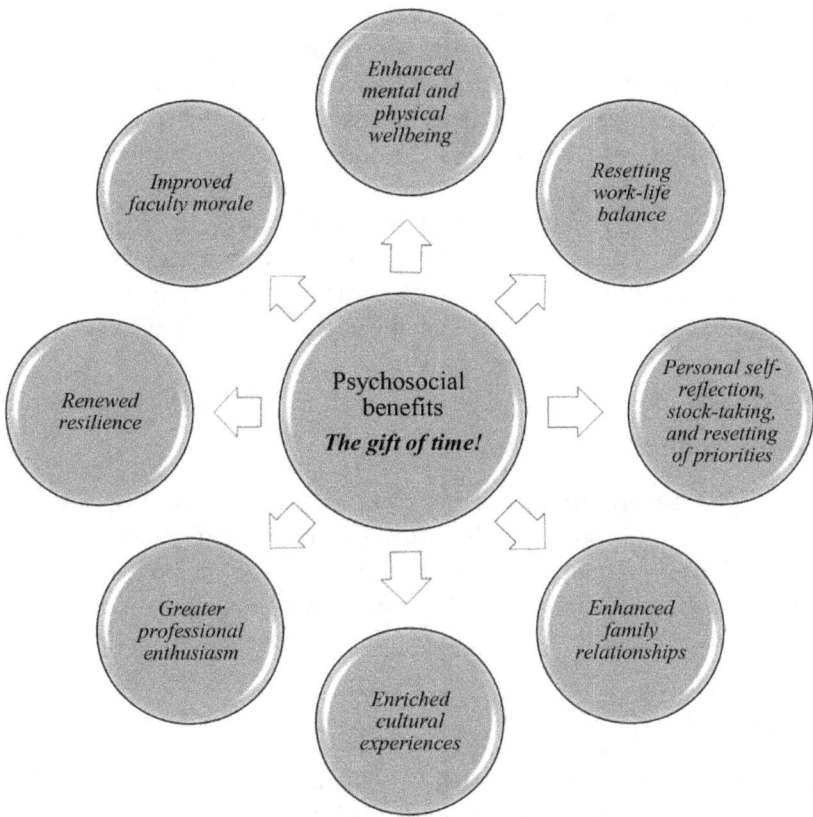

Figure 1.2. *Psychosocial benefits of sabbaticals.*

(Benshoff & Spruill, 2002; Blum, 2007; Davidson et al., 2010; Gilbert et al., 2007; Parkes & Langford, 2008; Smith, 2020; Swenty et al., 2011). Lakkoju (2020) cited sabbaticals as a strategy to address issues with family relationships and *work-life balance*. Within this psychosocial aspect, authors discussed reducing stress and burnout recovery (Benshoff & Spruill, 2002; Blum, 2007; Gilbert et al., 2007). Gallagher (2018), Kraus (2018), Marshall (2014), and Smith (2020) highlighted the value of *personal self-reflection, stock-taking,* and *resetting priorities,* both professional and private. Many also cited advantages in terms of *enriching cultural experiences* and the broadening of perspectives as a result of travel and living elsewhere (Friedman, 2018; Gallagher, 2018). Else (2015) and Lakkoju (2020) discussed *greater professional enthusiasm and renewed resilience* as benefits of sabbaticals. Benshoff and Spruill (2002) noted that sabbaticals can improve *faculty morale*. All these non-academic benefits were overtly linked to taking a break from the hectic pace of academic life and seemingly never-ending responsibilities. The advantages of taking time out from frenetic academic routines was hardly surprising given the research about the negative impacts of faculty workloads (Davidson et al., 2010; Sabagh et al., 2018). What was encouraging was the overt acknowledgement of the legitimacy of these non-academic or performance outcomes and the recognition of the importance of individual well-being and its impact on an institution's culture.

Problems and Conundrums

There were several problems and conundrums surrounding sabbaticals that emerged from the literature (see figure 1.3). These included political issues, concerns with a lack of policy transparency and/or academic empowerment, gender issues and/or service responsibilities, financial implications, and graduate supervision.

Political

One key problem with sabbaticals is the political dimension. Miller and colleagues (Bai & Miller, 1999; Miller & Bai, 2006; Miller et al., 2012) noted that sabbaticals were not without controversy. As early

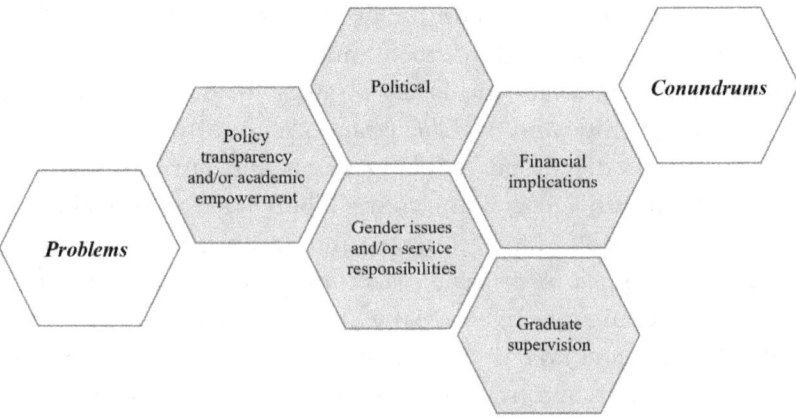

Figure 1.3. *Problems and conundrums.*

as the 1960s, the sentiment that "when a man gets paid, he ought to work" (*Industrial Relations News*, 1963, p. 50) was presented with an underlying notion that sabbaticals were paid vacations which damaged productivity. Gilbert et al. (2007) identified that in the early 2000s the US government wanted to eradicate or dramatically modify academic sabbaticals. Happily, these moves did not result in wholesale change. Others noted that in business and government the opinion has been proffered that sabbaticals are a "perk" of academia, with the subtext that it is undeserved and simply extended paid vacation. For example, Spencer and Kent (2007) reported that

> the picture given of university sabbaticals is somewhat hedonistic. Perhaps as a result of such exposure, one American commentator argued that academics found themselves in the position of countering the belief that sabbaticals are extended vacation, "perks" available only to a group that also benefits from job security and pleasant working conditions unavailable to professionals outside the academy. (pp. 651–652)

Sima (2000) encountered negative arguments about sabbaticals, though she suggested that sabbaticals were crucial in academe because the press of work was such that time to remain current in a field is rare. Therefore, released time is essential to ensure currency, new networks, and to develop new programs, curriculum, or be exposed to different approaches to teaching. Given that Sima's report was published twenty years ago, her argument related to workload has become more poignant due to the intensification of workload as noted by Parkes and Langford (2008), and most recently by Lakkoju (2020), who examined issues of work-life balance and the pressures of expanding workloads in engineering faculties.

Miller and his colleagues (Miller & Bai, 2006; Miller et al., 2012) warned that many institutions have loose accountability mechanisms for reporting sabbatical outcomes and/or sharing with others the knowledge and skills acquired. They cautioned that university leaders should tighten accountability to ensure that outside stakeholders cannot use lackadaisical reporting as evidence to remove sabbaticals.

Smith et al. (2016) posited a direct linkage between political views of sabbaticals and the entrenchment of the "neoliberal" or corporatization of universities in the New Zealand higher-education sector. They identified that with the importance of university competitiveness, which is frequently linked to research performance, the importance of sabbaticals—and who is able to access them—has become an important issue.

An interesting aspect to this political dimension was that in later literature we encountered a resurgence of interest in the desirability of sabbaticals across other sectors. For example, Altmann and Kröll's (2017) research examined linkages between recent work-life balance policies across Germany aligned with sabbaticals in private and public companies. They explored the relationship between supportive leadership and employees' desire to take a sabbatical. It should be noted though that the sabbaticals in their study were leave time designed to overcome burnout and to increase time spent with families, unlike academic sabbaticals, which have different accountabilities and purposes. Similarly, Long (1973) addressed the importance of sabbaticals for lawyers practising law. Leung et al. (2020) discussed the value of sabbaticals for health-system pharmacists. Therefore, the original purpose of sabbaticals as a leave for rest and rejuvenation or work-life rebalancing has surged across sectors other than higher education.

Lack of Policy Transparency and/or Academic Empowerment

One important conundrum was that many faculty members are unaware of their institution's policies and, thus, do not avail themselves of sabbatical leaves (Friedman, 2018). Else (2015) noted that some universities lacked transparency surrounding their policy framework on sabbaticals, which may explain why some academics may be unaware of the provisions. Smith et al. (2016) identified problems where "the application process was too bureaucratic or lacked transparency; gate-keepers behaved unfairly or were nepotistic and the criteria were unrealistic or corrupt" (p. 599). Drawing upon Mamiseishvili and Miller's (2010) research, Smith et al. indicated another transparency concern—that is, the dynamics of privilege and inequality, wherein sabbaticals were granted as a reward for attracting external research funds rather than as academic development.

A common theme among the science and medical papers read was that some feared taking a sabbatical as they perceived time away would "jeopardize" their career, would slow the grant writing and publishing momentum, and would result in a relative loss of power given their absence from faculty (Straus & Sackett, 2015). Another problematic view was that academics who took a sabbatical were "unsuccessful academics who were looking for a new job," "goofing-off," or "burnt-out" (p. 174), stigmas which discouraged some from taking sabbaticals.

Another contention about the timing of a sabbatical was whether to take it prior to, or after attaining, tenure. Pre-tenure faculty are frequently nervous about taking a sabbatical prior to attaining tenure; however, others advised that sabbatical time for writing and publication would only enhance a candidate's tenure portfolio (Hedges, 1999; Straus & Sackett, 2015).

Gender Issues and/or Service Responsibilities

Smith et al. (2016) reported gender issues related to sabbatical leaves. They highlighted that the proportion of males who achieved tenure, who were then qualified for a sabbatical, was disproportionately higher to that of their female counterparts. Consequently, many more female academics were unable to access the sabbatical benefits due to their contractual terms: "Women tended to take fewer, shorter sabbaticals" (p. 600). However, there were a number of key factors that influenced female academics' sabbatical behaviours and perceptions.

Some female academics in New Zealand reported unfair treatment when seeking approval for sabbaticals in comparison to their male colleagues. Smith et al. found "more women (28%, n=41) than men (12%, n=23) attributed negative influences to the HoD [head of department]" (p. 595). Participants reported capriciousness by department heads, a lack of transparency for non-approval of the sabbatical application, or indicated insufficient "Performance-Based Research Fund" outcomes—a reference to a higher-education funding process in in New Zealand—specified in their leave applications (p. 595). Another tension women reported was inaccurate information related to the application process. For example, one respondent reported her colleague had been allowed to take a sabbatical to complete a PhD. She was not granted leave when forwarding a similar request. This promoted the view that sabbaticals were "administered unfairly," with some granted leave while others were denied under "equivalent circumstances" (p. 599).

Spencer and Kent (2007) indicated academic women take on more pastoral work in the faculties, which "may 'mark' them as not serious about research or scholarship." These pastoral-care activities leave them with no time for research, even if they are "patently" committed to their research activities (p. 662). Indeed, Smith et al. (2016) stated:

> Sabbaticals are ... widely considered to facilitate career progression. It has the potential to act as a pathway to get the academic underclass into better-paid, secure positions with rewards and esteem. So, the very system that relies on an underclass to perform instrumental, but less prestigious academic labour, also ensures that those who undertake it (significantly, mostly women) remain second-class citizens of the university. (p. 600)

Considering these gender issues, it is surprising and disturbing that in our contemporary university settings, where gender should no longer be a negative factor, it remains a discriminatory influence.

Sabbaticals and Financial Implications

There have been concerns reported regarding the financial implications of sabbaticals. Carraher et al. (2014) noted that "with reductions in government funding, many universities are reducing the number and compensation rates of sabbaticals . . . thus limiting faculty members' opportunities to engage in a sabbatical" (p. 296). This explains why the qualification periods and compensation rates varied significantly across different institutions (Gilbert et al., 2007). The linkage between sabbaticals and expense in the literature encompassed several different dimensions. For example, there were costs to the institution in covering released faculty members, as well as for the academic, depending on what type of sabbatical experience they organize. Many authors noted the additional financial cost of travel or engaging in overseas collaborations, particularly if they travelled with their family (Smith, 2020; Smith et al., 2016; Stelfox et al., 2015). The desirability of travel and experiencing other cultures were highlights for many, but some felt time spent at home in a "staybatical" (Smith, 2020, p. 1; Marshall, 2014) or a "mini-sabbatical" of shorter duration (Gibb, 2011; Pillinger et al., 2019; Wilson, 2016) was more desirable and/or viable. This was particularly pertinent when academics had to organize the redistribution of their workload to colleagues, and in some areas of extreme specialization, finding replacement faculty may not have been possible (Smith et al., 2016). Smith et al. (2016) also noted the increased logistical complications when travelling and moving to an overseas research site, which involved finding accommodation, settling children into different schools, accessing childcare, and so on. The other key factor in choosing mini sabbaticals was linked to reducing costs in time away from their department, accommodation costs, and the loss of income for partners to leave their work to accompany the sabbaticant (Smith, 2020).

Another financial dimension was addressed in Miller and Pikowsky's (2010) paper on the tax implications of sabbaticals. Their extensive paper outlined some of the allowable and non-allowable expenses within the US tax code and advised accountants (and interested sabbaticants) of potential pitfalls within the law. This is less of an issue for Canadian academics, but for academics in countries where work-related expenses are considered legitimate deductions on their income tax, this paper highlighted the importance of drawing upon the expertise of an accountant who understands the tax implications for sabbatical expenses to ensure strict compliance with the law, as no one wants trouble with tax authorities.

Graduate Supervision

The commitments of teaching were frequently identified as a key aspect of academic life and, in some references, a contribution to pressure, high workloads, and burnout (Carraher et al., 2014; Gilbert et al., 2007; Lakkoju, 2020). Eisenberg (2010), Burton (2010), Carraher et al. (2014), and Sima (2000) all noted that academics may encounter difficulties in being released from the ties of graduate-student supervision. This was particularly difficult for those in the sciences who held responsibilities for supervising laboratories (Eisenberg, 2010). Carraher et al. (2014) linked the press of students to the reduction of funding to universities and the increasing demand to service full-fee programs, which help to financially sustain universities (Marginson, 2013). Alongside this advantage to the university is a disadvantage to academics who have large student-related workloads (Hornibrook, 2012). It should be noted that in discussions about quality teaching and learning in the literature, large undergraduate classes are frequently noted as problematic (Prosser, 2010; Prosser et al., 2008). This is chiefly due to the difficulties in establishing positive and close relationships with so many students, the pressure of establishing and grading authentic assessment tasks, and, in some institutions, the administrative load for coordinating a team of tutors (Glazer, 2014; Yang et al., 2018) to ensure quality teaching across classes in the same course (Metzger, 2015; Rawle et al., 2018; Rideout, 2018). However, finding a substitute instructor for an undergraduate course-based class is significantly easier, even though there remains a financial implication, than finding doctoral-supervision cover for a sabbaticant. Indeed, handing over coursework teaching is much less complicated than handing graduate students into the care of a colleague for a six- or twelve-month period.

We know that good supervision involves establishing positive, caring, and trusting relationships; however, these relationships may be damaged if supervisors pass their graduate students over to others in their faculty who may or may not provide effective and caring supervision (Delany, 2009; Halbert, 2015). The other concern surrounding supervision is the rise of graduate-supervision loads for many in the academy. Increased supervisory loads can mean faculty members may not be able to take a sabbatical free of supervision responsibilities, and supervisory ties may influence the effectiveness of the sabbatical. If a supervisor maintains their supervision loads, then this can deleteriously impact the time for sabbatical activities. As Burton (2010) wittily mused about his lack of sabbatical progress, "about seven of my doctoral advisees had unwittingly 'conspired' to begin making major progress toward completion of their dissertations at the same time. This required me to schedule 4 to 8 hours each week to read drafts of dissertation chapters" (p. 1). Therefore, good supervisors frequently experience genuine concern about letting their students down by transferring their supervision because of a sabbatical; but they also want to enjoy dedicated time for their own research or teaching activities away from the demands of their graduate students. This, therefore, presents a conundrum.

Conclusion

Even though the concept of the academic sabbatical was born in 1880 as a strategy to attract and retain pre-eminent scholars, the purposes of sabbaticals have morphed over time from a period of rejuvenation and rest to one of increased productivity. This was noted in the shift in nomenclature from "sabbatical," with its underlying philosophy of "rest," to that of "research and scholarship leave," which has the explicit expectation of greater research productivity and/or teaching innovation. One interesting point from undertaking this literature review was the enhanced relevance that this "gift of time" has for the twenty-first-century academic. Academics day-to-day realities of navigating the ever-increasing expectations for greater research productivity and teaching and learning quality, as well as the larger administrative loads due to reduced funding and higher accountability, have heightened the importance of the academic sabbatical.

The academic purposes and benefits spanned intellectual and academic rejuvenation, increased research productivity, the reduction of stress and burnout, advancements in teaching and curriculum development, collaboration and collegial networking, skill development, the completion of graduate studies, and as a reward for long and loyal service or leadership. There was also a range of psychosocial outcomes—enhanced mental and physical well-being; the resetting of work-life balance; personal reflection, stock-taking, and resetting of priorities; enhanced family relationships; and enrichment from exposure to new cultural experiences. The psychosocial advantages to both the individual and the institution encompassed greater professional enthusiasm, renewed resilience, and improved faculty morale.

A dark side of sabbaticals encompassed a political dimension, lack of policy transparency and academic empowerment, gender issues, financial implications, and the conundrum of graduate supervision. These problematic dimensions highlighted the importance of leaders promoting fairness, equity, transparency, and academic empowerment.

Our final point was to advocate for the retention of the academic sabbatical as a means to promote quality research and teaching, but more importantly, to ensure the maintenance of a healthy, balanced, and resilient academy. The sabbatical truly is a valuable "gift of time"!

References

Altmann, S., & Kröll, C. (2018). Understanding employees' intention to take sabbaticals. *Personnel Review, 47*(4), 882–899. https://doi.org/10.1108/pr-01-2017-0021

Bai, K., & Miller, M. T. (1998). *Sabbatical as a form of faculty renewal in the community college: Green pastures or fallow fields?* ERIC. https://files.eric.ed.gov/fulltext/ED417778.pdf

Bai, K., & Miller, M. T. (1999). *An overview of the sabbatical leave in higher education: A synopsis of the literature base*. ERIC. https://files.eric.ed.gov/fulltext/ED430471.pdf

Benshoff, J. M., & Spruill, D. A. (2002). Sabbaticals for counselor educators: Purposes, benefits, and outcomes. *Counselor Education and Supervision, 42*(2), 131–144. https://doi.org/10.1002/j.1556-6978.2002.tb01805.x

Blum, S. (2007). Sleep and the sabbatical. *The Chronicle of Higher Education, 53*(25), 1–2.

Burton, L. D. (2010). Sabbatical. *Journal of Research on Christian Education, 19*(1), 1–6. https://doi.org/10.1080/10656211003641106

Carraher, S. M., Crocitto, M. M., & Sullivan, S. (2014). A kaleidoscope career perspective on faculty sabbaticals. *Career Development International, 19*(3), 295–313. https://doi.org/10.1108/CDI-04-2013-0051

Davidson, O. B., Eden, D., Westman, M., Cohen-Charash, Y., Hammer, L. B., Kluger, A. N., Krausz, M., Maslach, C., O'Driscoll, M., Perrewé, P. L., Quick, J. C., Rosenblatt, Z., & Spector, P. E. (2010). Sabbatical leave: Who gains and how much? *Journal of Applied Psychology, 95*(5), 953–964. https://doi.org/10.1037/a0020068

Delany, D. (2009). *A review of the literature on effective PhD supervision*. https://www.tcd.ie/CAPSL/assets/pdf/Academic%20Practice%20Resources/Effective_Supervision_Literature_Review.pdf

Easteal, P., & Westmarland, N. (2010). The virtual sabbatical: A pioneering case study. *Innovative Higher Education, 35*(5), 297–311. https://doi.org/10.1007/s10755-010-9153-9

Eisenberg, M. J. (2010). *The physician scientist's career guide*. Springer US. https://doi.org/10.1007/978-1-60327-908-6_5

Else, H. (2015, April 16). Recharge, refocus, relax. *Times Higher Education*, 42–49.

Friedman, S. L. (2018). A sabbatical: The gift that keeps on giving. *Cellular and Molecular Gastroenterology and Hepatology, 5*(4), 656–658.

Gallagher, A. (2018). The value of a sabbatical: Four countries, three conferences and two homecomings. *Nursing Ethics, 25*(8), 953–954. https://doi.org/10.1177/0969733018811260

Gibb, B. C. (2011). The two-week sabbatical. *Nature Chemistry, 3*(7), 495–496. https://doi.org/10.1038/nchem.1080

Gilbert, G., Day, B., Murillo, A., Patton, J., Sibley-Smith, A., & Smith, B. (2007). *Sabbaticals: Benefitting faculty, the institution, and students*. The Academic Senate for California Community Colleges. ERIC. https://files.eric.ed.gov/fulltext/ED510576.pdf

Glazer, N. (2014). Formative plus summative assessment in large undergraduate courses: Why both? *International Journal of Teaching & Learning in Higher Education, 26*(2), 276–286.

Halbert, K. (2015). Students' perceptions of a "quality" advisory relationship. *Quality in Higher Education, 21*(1), 26–37. https://doi.org/10.1080/13538322.2015.1049439

Harley, D. A. (2005). Sabbaticals for rehabilitation administrators: Advantages disadvantages, and implications. *Journal of Rehabilitation Administration, 29*(2), 71–81.

Hedges, J. R. (1999). Sabbaticals: What's the big deal?! *Academic Emergency Medicine, 6*(9), 877–879. https://doi.org/10.1111/j.1553-2712.1999.tb01233.x

Hornibrook, S. (2012). Policy implementation and academic workload planning in the managerial university: Understanding unintended consequences. *Journal of Higher Education Policy & Management, 34*(1), 29–38. https://doi.org/10.1080/1360080X.2012.642329

Industrial Relations News. (1963). The pros and cons of executive sabbaticals. *Management Review, 52*(10), 47.

June, A. W. (2018). Ex-administrators reveal the secret that eased their return to the faculty. *The Chronicle of Higher Education* (September 7).

Konrad, A. G. (1983). Faculty development practices in Canadian universities. *Canadian Journal of Higher Education, 13*(2), 1–13.

Kraus, P. L. (2018). A primer on librarians' sabbaticals: A case study of a six-month sabbatical at home and abroad. *Journal of Religious & Theological Information, 17*(4), 121–127. https://doi.org/10.1080/10477845.2018.1446700

Lakkoju, S. (2020). Work–life satisfaction in academia: Myth or reality? *Decision, 47*(2), 153–176. https://doi.org/10.1007/s40622-020-00243-9

Leung, J. G., Barreto, E. F., Nelson, S., Hassett, L. C., & Cunningham, J. L. (2020). The professional sabbatical: A systematic review and considerations for the health-system pharmacist. *Research in Social and Administrative Pharmacy, 16*(12), 1632–1644. https://doi.org/10.1016/j.sapharm.2020.02.011

Long, T., G. (1973). Sabbatical leaves from a jealous mistress. *American Bar Association Journal, 59*(7), 749–752.

Maranville, S. (2014). Becoming a scholar: Everything I needed to know I learned on sabbatical. *Higher Learning Research Communications, 4*(1), 4–14.

Marginson, S. (2013). The impossibility of capitalist markets in higher education. *Journal of Education Policy, 28*(3), 353–370. https://doi.org/10.1080/02680939.2012.747109

Marker, D. G. (1983). Faculty leaves. *New Directions for Higher Education,* (41), 37–46. https://doi.org/10.1002/he.36919834105

Marshall, S. M. (2014). Sabbatical reflections from an academic mother. *Women in Higher Education, 21*(12), 33–34. https://doi.org/10.1002/whe.10407

Metzger, K. J. (2015). Collaborative teaching practices in undergraduate active learning classrooms: A report of faculty team teaching models and student reflections from two biology courses. *Bioscene, 41*(1), 3–9.

Miller, M. T. (2002). *Creation and validation of a sabbatical assessment instrument*. ERIC. https://eric.ed.gov/contentdelivery/servlet/ERICServlet?accno=ED462892

Miller, M. T., & Bai, K. (2006). Sabbatical leave programs as form of faculty development. *Academic Leadership: The Online Journal, 4*(1), n.p.

Miller, M. T., Bai, K., & Newman, R. E. (2012). A critical examination of sabbatical application policies: Implications for academic leaders. *College Quarterly, 15*(2), n.p. http://collegequarterly.ca/2012-vol15-num02-spring/miller.html

Miller, J. A., & Pikowsky, R. (2010). Taxation and the sabbatical: Doctrine, planning, and policy. *The Tax Lawyer, 63*(3), 375–410.

Parkes, L. P., & Langford, P. H. (2008). Work-life balance or work-life alignment? A test of the importance of work-life balance for employee engagement and intention to stay in organisations. *Journal of Management and Organization, 14*(3), 267–284.

Pillinger, M. H., Lemon, S. C., Zand, M. S., Foster, P. J., Merchant, J. S., Kimberly, R., Allison, J., Cronstein, B. N., Galeano, C., Holden-Wiltse, J., Trayhan, M., White, R. J., Davin, A., & Saag, K. G. (2019). Come from away: Best practices in mini-sabbaticals for the development of young investigators: A white paper by the SEQUIN (mini-Sabbatical Evaluation and Quality ImprovemeNt) Group. *Journal of Clinical and Translational Science, 3*(1), 37–44. https://doi.org/10.1017/cts.2019.369

Prosser, M. (2010). Faculty research and teaching approaches: Exploring the relationship. In J. Christensen Hughes & J. Mighty (Eds.), *Taking stock. Research on teaching and learning in higher education* (pp. 129–137). McGill-Queen's University Press.

Prosser, M., Martin, E., Trigwell, K., Ramsden, P., & Middleton, H. (2008). University academics' experience of research and its relationship to their experience of teaching. *Instructional Science: An International Journal of the Learning Sciences, 36*(1), 3–16. https://doi.org/10.1016/j.learninstruc.2007.01.004

Rawle, F., Thuna, M., Zhao, T., & Kaler, M. (2018). Audio feedback: Student and teaching assistant perspectives on an alternative mode of feedback for written assignments. *The Canadian Journal for the Scholarship of Teaching and Learning, 9*(2), 1–17. https://doi.org/10.5206/cjsotl-rcacea.2018.2.2

Rideout, C. A. (2018). Students' choices and achievement in large undergraduate classes using a novel flexible assessment approach. *Assessment & Evaluation in Higher Education, 43*(1), 68–78. https://doi.org/10.1080/02602938.2017.1294144

Sabagh, Z., Hall, N. C., & Saroyan, A. (2018). Antecedents, correlates and consequences of faculty burnout. *Educational Research, 60*(2), 131–156. https://doi.org/10.1080/00131881.2018.1461573

Sale, P. (2013). Leaving the dark side for the light: Twelve strategies for effective transition from academic administrator to faculty member. *Administrative Issues Journal, 3*(2). https://doi.org/10.5929/2013.3.2.5

Sima, C. M. (2000). The role and benefits of the sabbatical leave in faculty development and satisfaction. *New Directions for Institutional Research, 2000*(105), 67–75. https://doi.org/10.1002/ir.10506

Smith, D. R. (2020). Is sabbatical a dirty word? *EMBO reports, 21*(7), e50886. https://doi.org/10.15252/embr.202050886

Smith, D., Spronken-Smith, R., Stringer, R., & Wilson, C. A. (2016). Gender, academic careers and the sabbatical: A New Zealand case study. *Higher Education Research and Development, 35*(3), 589–603. https://doi.org/10.1080/07294360.2015.1107880

Spectrum News 1 (2017). *U of R professor accused of sexual misconduct placed on administrative leave.* https://spectrumlocalnews.com/nc/triangle-sandhills/top-stories/2017/09/19/u-of-r-professor-accused-of-sexual-misconduct-taking-leave-of-absence

Spencer, M., Clay, H., Hearne, G., & James, P. (2012). A comparative examination of the use of academic sabbaticals. *International Journal of Management Education, 10*(3), 147–154. https://doi.org/10.1016/j.ijme.2012.06.003

Spencer, M., & Kent, P. (2007). Perpetuating difference? Law school sabbaticals in the era of performativity. *Legal Studies, 27*(4), 649–677. https://doi.org/10.1111/j.1748-121X.2007.00064.x

Stelfox, H. T., Straus, S. E., & Sackett, D. L. (2015). Clinician-trialist rounds: 27. Sabbaticals. Part 2: I'm taking a sabbatical! How should I prepare for it? *Clinical Trials, 12*(3), 287–290. https://doi.org/10.1177/1740774514567970

Straus, S. E., & Sackett, D. L. (2015). Clinician-trialist rounds: 26. Sabbaticals. Part 1: Should I take a sabbatical? *Clinical Trials, 12*(2), 174–176. https://doi.org/10.1177/1740774514562917

Swenty, C. F., Schaar, G. L., Phillips, L. A., Embree, J. L., McCool, I. A., & Shirey, M. R. (2011). Nursing sabbatical in the acute care setting: What is the evidence? *Nursing Forum, 46*(3), 195–204. https://doi.org/10.1111/j.1744-6198.2011.00225.x

Upshaw, M. (2019). *Delphi confirms superintendent placed on paid administrative leave while they investigate financial issues.* Wlfi.com. https://www.wlfi.com/content/news/Delphi-confirms-superintendent-placed-on-paid-administrative-leave-while-they-investigate-financial-issues-558394961.html

WAAY-TV 31 News. (2019). *High school baseball coach on administrative leave* [Video]. https://www.youtube.com/watch?v=KH1KW_kKBJg&ab_channel=WAAY-TV31News

Wildman, K. (2012). *Staff sabbaticals: An examination of sabbatical purposes and benefits for higher education administrators* [Doctoral dissertation]. University of Iowa.

Wilson, A. K. (2016). Mini-sabbaticals: Routes to reenergize chairs and their departments. *The Department Chair, 26*(4), 13–14. https://doi.org/10.1002/dch.30076

Wyman, M. (1973). Tenure, tenure procedures and sabbatical leave. *Queen's Quarterly, 80*(1), 12.

Yang, N., Ghislandi, P., & Dellantonio, S. (2018). Online collaboration in a large university class supports quality teaching. *Educational Technology Research & Development, 66*(3), 671–691. https://doi.org/10.1007/s11423-017-9564-8

Yarmohammadian, M., Davidson, P., & Yeh, C. (2018). Sabbatical as a part of the academic excellence journey: A narrative qualitative study. *Journal of Education and Health Promotion, 7*, 119.

Appendix: Methodologies within the Literature

Methodology	Authors
Survey (15)	Altmann & Kröll (2017) Bai & Miller (1998) Benshoff & Spruill (2002) Davidson et al. (2010) Gilbert et al. (2007) Hedges (1999) Konrad (1983) Lakkoju (2020) Marker (1983) Miller & Bai (2006) Parkes & Langford (2008) Sabagh et al. (2018) Smith et al. (2016) Spencer & Kent (2007) Spencer et al. (2012)
Autoethnographic (9)	Blum (2007) Burton (2010) Easteal & Westmarland (2010; reported as action research) Friedman (2018) Gallagher (2018) Gibb (2011) Maranville (2014) Marshall (2012) Smith (2020)
Opinion/Advice (6)	Eisenberg (2010) June (2018) Long (1973) Sale (2013) Wilson (2016) Wyman (1973)
Literature review (5)	Carraher et al. (2014) (with theoretical modelling) Harley (2005) Leung et al. (2020) Sima (2000) Swenty et al. (2011)

Methodology	Authors
Narratives (3) (more than one voice)	Bai & Miller (1999) Else (2015) Yarmohammadian et al. (2018)
Case study (3)	Kraus (2018) Stelfox et al. (2015) Straus & Sackett (2015)
Mixed methods (1)	Wildman (2012)
Policy analysis (2)	Miller et al. (2012) Pillinger et al. (2019)
Methodological (1)	Miller (2002)
Legal (1)	Miller & Pikowsky (2010)
Unclear (methodology not stated) (4)	Industrial Relations News (1963) Clip Syndicate (2017) Clip Syndicate (2019a) Clip Syndicate (2019b)

SECTION 1

The First Sabbatical Experience

Perhaps the simplest model of a sabbatical begins with the notion that one continues doing what one had been doing but the ratio of teaching, service, and research changes. The institution and faculty office remain accessible, while the focus is on research, which is underway. In this mode, one might arrange travel for conferences, vacations, collaboration opportunities, or simply to work in a different environment for a change of pace—but it is not necessary to achieve goals beyond the regular academic role.

This section begins with a short chapter by María del Carmen Rodríguez de France. She identifies the serendipitous timing, in 2015, of the Truth and Reconciliation Commission of Canada's final report and her sabbatical. Carmen's position as an Indigenous academic and scholar saw sabbatical time invested in realizing changes suggested in the report because of her deep understanding of the issues. That responsiveness may have caused some questioning of whether it was *research*, even though the commission called for the dissemination of such understanding. It is a provocative chapter, where the academic role clearly fits well with meeting a societal need but the alignment of internal processes of the ivory tower may be at odds with the addressment of those needs.

The second chapter, by Susan Elliott-Johns, is oriented inwardly. She looks at the juncture of professional identity with personal well-being and the prospect of retirement on the horizon. Within this chapter, we find evidence of a busy academic wrestling to carve out personal space. Travel for conferences includes time to enjoy the opportunities on a personal front as well. While this sounds like a synergetic merging of travel for work and vacation time, the frenetic pace and high degree of professionalism speak to the challenge of balancing work and life.

Third is the chapter by Victoria Handford, who, despite planning and approval of plans, had to make unanticipated changes because of the pandemic and the health issues of a loved one. To say her six-month sabbatical went sideways might be the simplest way to capture the challenges she faced. Yet in her chapter there is an unusual change of pace from her academic focus on educational leadership. It does not sound restful, nor would one describe it as supporting the well-being that one might expect during a sabbatical, but it definitely is a change from her usual tripartite role. This chapter is the first that raises the issue that supervisions and administrative roles do not simply disappear.

The final chapter in this section, by Tim Sibbald, examines the sabbatical from the perspective of the passage of time. Within his chapter we find different projects and agendas are braided in a manner that is only feasible because of the flexibility of time afforded by the sabbatical. He shows an unusual work-life balance that is not uniform, suggestive instead of the ebb and flow of workload within the context of academic work.

Together the chapters in this section give the flavour of sabbaticals that are essentially a continuation of research and scholarly activities. They point to issues within the academy and challenge various components of academic work, but despite commonalities of the sabbatical structure and academic work, they are notable for the variety of approaches and activities that take place.

Note: Among the authors in this section, Carmen, Tim, and Victoria have contributed to two earlier books about academic experiences during the tenure-track stage, and around the time of tenure, allowing the interested reader to connect these chapters to their longitudinal history.

CHAPTER 2

Not All That Shines Is Gold: What I Learned during My Sabbatical Year

María del Carmen Rodríguez de France

An important time in the calendar at many universities or colleges is that of reading break, which happens halfway through an academic term. The mid-term week of non-scheduled classes constitutes breathing space for students and instructors alike. However, some do not seem to be sure of the purpose of the break, and year after year people continue to ask (sometimes in humorous ways) if the break is *from* reading (assuming that everyone has spent much time reading theses, papers, and assigned course materials) or if the break is *for* reading (supposing that few have engaged in reading to then). Either way, the break is a welcomed time to recharge and look forward to the end of the term.

Another important time within the calendar (in terms of career) is that of the academic leave, known as a sabbatical due to the biblical reference, which states the need for the land to have a year's rest after the sixth year of productivity. At the arrival of the seventh year, "fallow land is plowed, tilled, the weeds kept down, but no crops raised" (Eells & Hollis, 1962, p. 5). Different researchers offer different accounts of how academic leaves were established in the US, and where they began. According to Lewis B. Cooper (1932), Harvard was the first institution to create a statement of a sabbatical plan, in the nineteenth century, followed by Wellesley, Brown, Columbia, and Cornell. Crosby (1962) reports that the idea of academic leave dates back to 1907, when a Trustees of Columbia University report noted that "[t]he practice now prevalent in Colleges and Universities of this country of granting periodical leaves of absence to their professors was established not in the interests of the professors themselves but for the good of university education" (cited in Crosby, 1962, p. 253). The sabbatical time was seen as a reprieve from other duties related to teaching and scholarship, as well as an intellectual and practical necessity.

Contrary to popular belief outside of academia, a sabbatical is not a vacation or a time to relax. In fact, over time, the idea of what a sabbatical is has changed, and each person uses the available time in different and unique ways: Some individuals travel to engage in cross-cultural research, others dedicate the time to pull together years of research and turn it into a book, others might explore new pedagogical approaches, and some may decide to engage in activities that might enhance and/or support skill development such as learning to use new platforms or technologies for teaching and learning.

While it is true that the idea of not having to tend to one's regular academic responsibilities is appealing, it is also true that some of those responsibilities remain, such as continued support for one's graduate students, unless one requests a colleague to do such work. This can be advantageous for the person on leave, but it might create instability for the students as they have to work with a new person, an "acting" supervisor, for the duration of the leave—whether six or twelve months. When applying for a sabbatical, one needs to remain mindful of the privileges and responsibilities this leave grants. In this chapter, I will share some of the experiences I had while on academic leave, as well as some of what I learned while being away from the office—not away from the work.

A Picture Is Worth a Thousand Words

As a person who started her teaching career at age seventeen, my life has been devoted to service and supporting learning whenever I can. Aside from my job within a university, I also work as a consultant and as facilitator of professional-development opportunities for educators. This passion for everything that spells teaching and learning kept me busy during my academic leave. Yes, I engaged in research as was expected. Yes, I enjoyed having time for physical activity. Yes, I enjoyed reading novels and works of fiction that had less to do with being a teacher (or so I thought). I soon realized they had everything to do with being an educator. Perhaps, out of all the activities in which I engaged, establishing a book club in my local library to introduce patrons to the works of Indigenous writers, poets, and novelists was the highlight of my sabbatical year. Conversing about social issues, history, humour, tradition, values, and other Indigenous perspectives allowed me to remain current in regard to publications, authors, and present events. Most importantly, however, was the opportunity to share some of what has been shared with me and entrusted to me by way of relationships with the Elders in the communities where I am fortunate to collaborate, and by way of the students and other community members who have taught me and reminded me of my responsibility to witness and share. This was one important way in which I was heeding the calls to action from the Truth and Reconciliation Commission (Canada, 2015), as an educator, as a community member, and as a parent. The interest that the report garnered was such that what started as a small gathering of interested people soon turned to be a gathering of people concerned with creating their own path toward reconciliation and contributing to creating a shared future. Stories, poems, and fiction were the doors through which we learned some of the true histories of this country; histories that had remained untold until now. In sharing these stories, and in doing this work wholeheartedly and with responsibility, I was sharing the belief of the Haudenosaunee and other First Nations that say that the work that one does has an impact on the next seven generations.[1]

The timing for doing all this could not have been better. The final report of the Truth and Reconciliation Commission was published in June of 2015, and the need for heeding the calls to action of the report was not only required, it was indispensable. This translated into the need to develop curriculum, facilitate workshops, and create resources and materials that would support teachers, public servants, and citizens in every walk of life. Requests poured in from institutions, organizations, and individuals wanting to advance their knowledge in regard to Indigenous people and culture, and thus begin to fulfill their responsibility as citizens of this place. While I was supporting all these organizations and colleagues, I realized my 365 days of leave were almost gone, my calendar was running out of pages. But I also realized that I was starting to paint a clearer portrait of myself as an Indigenous scholar.

Nothing Ventured, Nothing Gained

In putting pen to paper or rather fingers to keyboard, I was able to see my "productivity" and what I had accomplished in 12 months. To some, this variety of activities might seem scattered and not focused on an area of expertise (as is the expectation in academia). However, the picture I painted of myself as a scholar, as a researcher, as a community member (beyond the university), and as an educator, fulfilled *my* own expectations. As a former international student, as an immigrant to Canada, and as a grateful inhabitant on the lands of the W̱SÁNEĆ Nation, and the Lekwungen- and SENĆOŦEN-speaking people, I feel a continued responsibility to give back to the communities that have offered me so much, and that have welcomed me with open arms and open hearts. In doing all this work, I might have disrupted the more conventional notion of needing to formally engage in research while on academic leave. However, I could not help asking myself, What is research, anyway? Opaskwayak scholar Shawn Wilson (2008) says that Indigenous research is the ceremony of maintaining accountability to the relationships one establishes with community to support and advance Indigenous ways of knowing and being. I was content and at peace in having become accountable to my relations, and to have advanced some of my knowledge about Indigenous ontologies and ways of living in the world.

While the original idea of having a year to "rest" might have been the thought behind the principles originally established at Harvard in the 1880s, Boening's research (1996) showed that faculty "take advantage of sabbatical leaves not only to further explore their subject matter in their own discipline, but to learn how to be better teachers as well" (p. 9). Further, Miller and Kang (1998) reported from their research that upon return from academic leave, faculty felt "intellectually renewed in knowledge in their fields of study, teaching methods, and viewed themselves as better teachers who were eager to work with their students" (p. 10). I know I share those feelings.

I realize now that the number seven (as in sabbath or sabbatical) was forever present in much of what I did: I acted as consultant for seven different companies or institutions locally and nationally. I delivered seven keynote presentations, and facilitated seven workshops for international cohorts from China, Japan, Mexico, and Panama. I offered workshops for in-service teachers at seven different locations in British Columbia. I worked on seven book chapters (and co-edited a book), and I developed curriculum in collaboration with seven different local organizations, including the Art Gallery of Greater Victoria.

After my leave, I was excited to go back to my office, to meet with students, to converse with colleagues, to start some meetings looking out the window, witnessing the wisdom and rhythm of nature as the leaves on the maple tree changed at autumn. Leaves continue to change, and the Earth follows its rhythms. I am reflecting on past moments at the time of a pandemic when life at the university takes on a different rhythm and pace. I am three years away from my next academic leave but I am taking this change of pace as graciously as I can, being grateful for having the opportunity to take this time within the original posit of a sabbatical, which was a time to rest. This is my quasi-sabbatical time to rejuvenate, to grow in personal and professional ways, and most importantly, to unlearn and relearn.

Endnote

1   For further reference to this foresighted principle, see https://www.haudenosauneeconfederacy.com/values/

References

Boening, C. H. (1996). *Who gets a sabbatical? A ten-year study of sabbatical application patterns at the University of Alabama, 1986–1996* [Unpublished doctoral dissertation]. University of Alabama.

Canada. (2015). *Truth and Reconciliation Commission of Canada*. Queen's Printer. See https://nctr.ca/about/history-of-the-trc/trc-website/

Cooper, L. B. (1932). *Sabbatical leave for college teacher*. Gaylord.

Crosby, W. (1962). The origin and early history of sabbatical leave. *AAUP Bulletin, 48*(3), 253–256.

Eells, W. C., & Hollis, E. V. (1962). *Sabbatical leave in American higher education*. U.S. Government Printing Office.

Miller, M. T., & Kang, B. (1998). A case study of post-sabbatical assessment measures. *Journal of Staff Programs & Organizational Development, 15*(1), 11–17.

Wilson, S. (2008). *Research is ceremony: Indigenous research methods*. Fernwood Publishing.

CHAPTER 3

The Voyage Continues: Navigating Discovery between Two Sabbaticals

Susan Elliott-Johns

> *Identity and Integrity are not the granite from which fictional heroes are hewn. They are subtle dimensions of the complex, demanding, and life-long process of self-discovery.*
>
> Palmer (1998)

The timely opportunity to write a chapter revisiting lived experience during my first twelve-month sabbatical (July 1, 2013–June 30, 2014) comes when I am looking forward to a second, and probably final, sabbatical (July 1, 2020–June 30, 2021). Both sabbaticals were awarded by administrative decision and represent key landmarks on my voyage of discovery as a teacher and researcher. A professor of education for the past fifteen years, and before that a teacher, consultant, and school leader, I intend to retire from full-time university teaching in June 2021. This was factored into my written plan when submitted to my dean. After sabbatical I anticipate continuing to supervise graduate students, and to research and write.

This chapter presents reflections on experience of the sabbatical as a voyage of discovery, 2013–2014, and reflexively extends beyond that year to briefly consider where I find myself today—that is, looking ahead to a sabbatical of a very different nature in 2020–2021. Reflection is understood as a way of allowing ourselves to step back from experiences and assist the development of critical-thinking skills and understanding through close analysis of that experience. That said, "reflection is *after* and *individual* whereas reflexivity is *ongoing* and *relational*" (Lyle, 2017, p. vii). I also regard reflectivity and reflexivity as moving along a continuum, with reflexivity occurring as a quite mature and somewhat rare form of reflection. I would also contend that by practising reflexivity, "we become *responsible* and *accountable* for our choices, our actions, and our contributions to a relational system" (Oliver, 2004, p. 127). Furthermore, Lyle states (2017, p. vii):

> By its very design, then, reflexivity disrupts normalized assumptions about how we come to knowledge and presents essential questions about our capacities as artists/researchers/teachers to account for an ever-evolving understanding of our experiences. This understanding resides in a humanizing pedagogy and has as its goal facilitation of re/humanization and appreciation of perspective diversity.

Exploring Professional Identity

Consistent with Palmer's (1998) conceptualization of identity, I have also come to a recognition of identity as an evolving nexus—all that comprises the mystery of "self" and a constantly moving intersection of the inner and outer forces that make me who I am—personally as well as professionally. Some of my very earliest insights into *who I am* were shared with my audience when I was a guest speaker at the Australian Reading Association Conference, in Melbourne, in 1993.

> Now, in Infant School, two years before starting Primary School, we did "work" all morning and, after lunch, took a nap in the afternoon on little cots set out all over the classroom. That is, some of us took a nap! An active child, I well recall the strange feeling of lying there, peering around the hushed, darkened room and wondering why? Why did I have to lie there (wide awake) when the very last thing I felt like doing was sleeping? All those books, puzzles and games, friends to talk with and they wanted me to sleep?! Keeping still was not my forte and, I guess, I must have been even more restless than I recall because, very shortly, I was being sent to the Headmistress to read aloud to her. Something I rapidly discovered I'd much rather do than take a nap. (Elliott-Johns, 1993)

While my memories of reading to the headmistress were most likely the result of finding a way to mitigate my disruptive behaviour and enable others to nap, even if I didn't, I was blissfully unaware of that at the time. Suffice to say, mitigating my own overactive behaviour became my responsibility as an adult and, in retrospect, I think it's probably fair to say I took this inner drive and curiosity into my work as a professional educator—manifested at times to the point of workaholism.

Always a practitioner first, even since moving to work in the academy, I have worked hard to cultivate what I consider to be an authentic *practitioner–scholar* perspective. That is, while I have a sound record of published scholarly work, I remain passionate about ensuring my research extends beyond academic shelves alone. I prefer that this work influences my own practice and the developing practice of teacher candidates I work with, as well as fellow teacher educators and other practitioners in school settings. A firm believer that teaching cannot be regarded as merely technique, I also concur with Palmer (1998) that the reduction of teaching to intellect alone results in a cold abstraction. Therefore, the intentional dissemination of my research to a wide variety of audiences—through books, journals, and media accessed by other practitioners—also demonstrates my unfailing support for a view that encompasses *research informing practice* and *practice informing research* (I have not always encountered appreciation of the connection between the two in academe. On the contrary, I have frequently witnessed a contrived separation of these and the need for further work in this domain).

The significant influences, over time, of inspirational, collegial, and generous relationships on my evolving identity and work as a practitioner—scholar are not lost on me—and, on reflection, these influences can easily be detected woven throughout my experience of sabbatical leave. To date, because of the influence of many significant voices in the immediate field and beyond, I continue to grow and learn, both as an educator and a human being. An explicit priority on clearly relational aspects of my life and work is also evident in terms of their countless contributions to an ability to sustain energy, motivation, and inquiry, thus enhancing and enriching my life's work as an educator for over forty years.

Conceptualizing Sabbatical

My first sabbatical was approved for 2012–2013. I deferred it for a year as I wanted to teach in my university's PhD program in the summer of 2013, a decision that resulted in teaching, doctoral supervision, and committee participation throughout the next phase of my career. Deferment was therefore a timely decision that supported alignment of doctoral engagement with the synergy I see between research and practice.

The call for chapters for this book described the purpose of a sabbatical as "giving an employee a chance to step back from their role at work and focus on personal enrichment and professional development." Working from that understanding, I primarily explore my experience in 2013–2014, which was an opportunity to work without regular teaching responsibilities in the BEd program or service responsibilities to the university. In this way, explorations of the nuances of identity and integrity in my life and work—an ongoing voyage of discovery in and of itself—are shared. I mention this as a novel scenario for someone whose career trajectory developed largely in public-school systems, where I had never considered a leave of this nature as an option. Suffice to say, the opportunity to step back and take a year's paid leave to conduct research and write, after which I'd return to my tenured academic position, was regarded as a privilege. In retrospect, (a) what did I *plan* to do? and (b) what were the outcomes of work accomplished?

The original call for this collection caught my attention as having a rare focus (i.e., a brief search of the literature indicates little appears to have been written on this topic), also due to the inclusion of the following gentle reminder from the editors to prospective authors:

> We appreciate that sabbaticals often entail some rest, vacation, and frolicking with family. These activities, while wonderful, are not the focus of the book. We encourage you to focus on the academic benefits of the sabbatical. You may also wish to acknowledge the flextime, and the ability to navigate family (particularly if they live far away, you have young children, aging parents, etc.), however, we wish to respect that sabbatical is first and foremost an academic endeavour. While there are many auxiliary benefits, they are not the reason for sabbatical.

The editors' comments reflected my own experience with some renditions of (what often seemed to me) disproportionate sabbatical time spent on many of those "auxiliary benefits." In retrospect, and as I review a list of publications connected to my sabbatical, I was laser-focused on the academic benefits inherent in an earned sabbatical. Evidently that was the case as the sabbatical report submitted to the dean in September comprised of four pages and an addendum summarizing ten additional scholarly activities completed during my sabbatical (i.e., not originally listed in my sabbatical plan—one of which was the faculty-facilitator role included in the narrative reflections here).

The twelve months of the sabbatical were indeed spent compiling a productive publication record, presentations at national and international conferences, participation in an international practicum, and program design and course development (including work on a proposed BEd in adult education, one that, unfortunately, was never offered because of internal university politics and a lack of funding). As previously mentioned, the nature of sabbatical leave was quite novel in my career to date, and *personal enrichment* also translated to the kind of work that was difficult to accommodate when teaching full time at the faculty. While I would not have regular classes that year, I anticipated working on my research and writing. In other words, it was going to be a different kind of busy, and most certainly not a vacation.

Working in collaborative partnerships with like-minded others, I have always embraced opportunities to grow and learn as both an educator and a human being. This was how I envisaged the sabbatical as a voyage of ongoing discovery; the access to focused time to continue work on my evolving identity as an educator and ongoing contributions to the field of knowledge and practice. In this regard, the wisdom of David Booth and Bill Moore (2003) still resonates for me, speaking to the embodiment of who I am today as both teacher and researcher.

> As teacher, you come to your classroom carrying a backpack of poems but, in truth, you are the words you read. Your children take in the teacher and the teaching as one – a single, complete event. Your life is your poem: your experiences illuminate your present classroom moments. The children discover your parents, your teachers, your poetry past, revealed in your choice of words, your manner of reading to them, your attitude towards them, your eyes as you read them. You are the poem. (p. 7)

I believe how we teach is intimately connected with our personal histories, knowledge, experience, commitments—the habits and attitudes of our lifetimes. These are nuanced by ongoing professional learning through programs of education, professional-development opportunities, and efforts to integrate key elements of our professionalism with who we are. We teach, and research, according to who we are. If we accept that *how we teach* depends very much on our own personal history, knowledge, experience and commitments—the habits and attitudes developed over a lifetime—I would argue it follows that how (and why) we conduct and share our research would also contribute to decisions around how (and why) we elect to allocate time during a sabbatical.

What Was Planned for the Sabbatical?

> *To accomplish great things, we must not only act, but also dream; not only plan, but also believe.*
>
> Anatole France

When applying for sabbatical at my university it is customary to provide a sabbatical plan to the dean. I saw this as capturing what I hoped to accomplish during the year if the leave was granted. Equally, the sabbatical report, due following completion of the sabbatical, is supposed to bear some resemblance to the work planned. Essentially, at the heart of my sabbatical plan was the intent to further pursue and develop my research program and writing for scholarly publication that I had successfully established and sustained since arriving at Nipissing University seven years earlier—the focus being on the self-study of teacher-education practices (S-STEP) and literacy-teacher education for contemporary classrooms.

Beyond further development of my research and writing for publication, the sabbatical was to facilitate the expansion of options for future teaching assignments. Furthermore, the leave would enhance my ability to work with my increasing network of national and international partners in teacher-education research and practice; specifically, partnerships forged at recent scholarly conferences and resulting from work as a member of the executive for both the Canadian Association for Teacher Education (CATE) and the International Study Association for Teachers and Teaching (ISATT).

That said, with specific reference to research *and* teaching, I planned to work on several related goals during the sabbatical year. These included the publication of a co-edited text that was underway (*Perspectives on Transitions in Schooling and Instructional Practice*, 2013) and the completion of a text for which a proposal had just been accepted by a publisher (see Elliott-Johns, 2015). As a result of papers being accepted in 2013, and in order to present findings from my research and writing in process, my plan for sabbatical also included attending and presenting papers at two international conferences and one national conference.

To my mind, the opportunity to research and reconceptualize courses taught, and thus to (potentially) also expand my teaching repertoire in the future, was inherent in a sabbatical leave. For example, the pre-service teacher (BEd) program includes language arts (for junior/intermediate division; i.e., Grades 4–10). I had been responsible for teaching this language-arts course since I joined Nipissing University and felt it would benefit from further revisions, specifically in terms of purpose, content, and anticipated learning outcomes. It had been tweaked and revised for currency numerous times as a 72-hour course, a 60-hour course, and then as a 36-hour course. A focus on key components for contemporary classrooms was essential. Simultaneously, I was assisting with the design and development of a BEd in an adult-education program, specifically researching and presenting detailed course descriptions for stage-two submission to the university's senate. (Unfortunately, while this innovative program did receive stage-three approval, it was never offered because of internal university politics and lack of funding.) As previously mentioned, it was my intent to become more involved in teaching and supervising students in the newly minted doctoral program at my university, so I planned a great deal of critical reading in educational theory to support such work on my return from sabbatical.

Discovery: What Was Accomplished as a Result of the Sabbatical?

Over and above evidence of my productivity, what is not explicitly conveyed are the more intangible effects of considerable time spent thinking, planning, and writing during that year; for example, the benefit of delicious days available for further contemplation around

Palmer's (1998) "trifecta" of intellectual, emotional, and spiritual nourishment richly afforded by the sabbatical.

To elaborate, intellectually I invariably immerse myself in projects (whether research, teaching, or service) with energy and enthusiasm, and, as a colleague once wrote to me, tend to exhibit "never-ending positivity and astonishing work ethic" (P. Fisher, personal communication, September 7, 2016). Time here was a luxury and spent, literally, *devouring* books, articles, and multimedia to contextualize projects planned. Without the need to balance a regular teaching schedule, the novelty and sheer joy of this time to read, write, and think was truly a unique experience—one that I relished, soaking up the experience like a sponge! Books, papers, links to video clips, journal entries, sketches, musical interludes, meaningful quotations, and even satirical cartoons were noted and recorded as catalysts for further reflection—often as inclusions in my personal journal.

Revisiting this time has, in turn, taken me back emotionally to a major life decision, also as part of the sabbatical, to experiment with the scheme of moving to live full time in the lakeside cottage we had then owned for two years and had recently finished renovating. The purchase of this exquisite retreat had been partially driven by an increasingly acute realization that I needed to make more of a concerted effort to spend less time immersed in work-related activities and to unplug from the computer more frequently!

The weekends and holidays we had begun to spend at the cottage, where there was, purposively, no internet connection, signaled a gradual, but very tangible, process of my accepting the need to consciously devote more time to family, friends, and interests beyond my work—actually, to my*self*. I can attest to this presenting a complex untangling of ways of being when one is sufficiently privileged to have work that is as enjoyable and enriching as I find teaching and learning to be. Very soon after we began spending time at the lake on a regular basis, I also began to take up (or *re*-take up) nourishment for the soul I had not even missed before but was definitely missing from my workaholic lifestyle. For example, reading favourite genres for pleasure and relaxation (novels, biographies, poetry, even magazines), all of which had been subsumed under mountains of research-related reading and preparation for teaching classes; assisting with interior-decorating choices as the renovations became home improvements; gardening—there is something primal about getting one's hands dirty moving piles of earth, spending time digging and planting, seeding, and waiting for the transformation of perennial spaces; the other image etched into my mind from this time are the countless hours just spent watching the water—infinitely calming and rejuvenating for the mind, body, and spirit. Later, five years after selling the property, I still get a lump in my throat when I see pictures of that cottage and its idyllic setting. Those are the times I can still hear the wind rustling the trees, the waves gently lapping on the shore, smell the fragrance of my garden, and experience the shadow move across the deck as the magnificent bald eagle glides overhead and out over the lake, headed toward its nest on the opposite shore. In a scholarly sense, the significance of that place and time is still sometimes difficult to explain. But, as Lyle (2020) also suggests, "I wonder if we struggle because we are conditioned to negate the emotive and the spiritual" (p. 4), and she goes on to say: "Both Parker Palmer (1998) and David Gruenwald (2003) remind me that we are shaped by the particular places we inhabit and how we are shaped is, in large part, contingent upon the quality of attention we give those places and ourselves in relation to them" (Lyle, 2020, p. 10).

Increased recognition of the spiritual as a result of sabbatical cannot be underestimated. To paraphrase Palmer (1998), my guide in many things connected with explorations of self-knowledge and the need to attend to the voice of the teacher within, spiritual here refers to the diverse ways in which we ourselves are in tune with our heart's longing to truly connect with the largeness of life—beyond ourselves—"a longing that animates love and work, especially the work called teaching" (p. 2). At the beginning of the sabbatical, particularly in the serene setting of trees and lake, I became acutely aware that I needed to be paying more attention to listening to the teacher within, my inner teacher, and to be actively seeking solitude, silence, reading, and thinking deeply (meditating on the world of things), communing with nature, and really listening—or "talking to myself." Palmer reminds us: "We need to find every possible way to listen to that voice and take its counsel seriously, not only for the sake of our work, but for the sake of our health (p. 12). Sabbatical as retreat (literally, considering the cottage location too) enabled me to take a deep breath inward and to work on rebuilding my capacity for connectedness. For example, re-energizing intellect, emotion, and spirit where they converged in my personal and professional self, and making much needed adjustments to what was becoming routine and fragmented. As an integral part of an ongoing voyage of discovery, sabbatical allowed the time and an activation of my internal compass, to steer my ship back on a spiritually rejuvenating course, and toward fostering more wholeness in praxis. "Integrity requires that I discern what is integral to my selfhood, what fits and what does not. . . . By choosing integrity, I become more whole, but wholeness does not mean perfection. It means becoming more real by acknowledging the whole of who I am" (Palmer, 1998, p. 6).

For the purposes of this chapter, I have elected to highlight four significant experiences through the lens of sabbatical as a voyage of self-discovery, and to explore each of these in terms of: How did the granting of a sabbatical extend and enhance the work involved in each? What was accomplished? How did the overall experience contribute to my ongoing learning as a practitioner–scholar? The four experiences explored are (1) initiation of an edited book project (subsequently completed and published); (2) presentation of papers at international, national, and provincial conferences; (3) ongoing work as an active member of the broader scholarly community, as a peer reviewer, and membership on various editorial/advisory boards; and (4) the role of faculty facilitator with an international practicum in Italy.

Leadership for Change (2015): An Edited Book
Prior to the year my sabbatical was taken, I was engaged in a number of compelling discussions with colleagues across the country as we examined understandings of components, purposes, and effectiveness of teacher-education programs in Canada in the shifting contexts of teacher-education reform (Falkenberg, 2015). This was also the period just before, in my home province of Ontario, when teacher education evolved to a four-semester program (Elliott-Johns & Richardson, 2017; Kitchen & Petrarca, 2017; Ng-A-Fook et al., 2017). Even then (six years ago, at the time of writing), technological developments, financial constraints, and shifting demographics, along with a range of other factors, were increasingly contributing to climates of acute uncertainty. Bringing about positive change (e.g., by governments, university leaders, and other stakeholders) appeared increasingly complex and challenging. While educational change, including *teacher*-education change, is, undoubtedly, political, multi-faceted, and uncertain, in my experience it also takes time and skilled leadership. As I continued to read and reflect deeply

on contemporary issues related to teacher education (social, political, and economic), I began to question why we were not hearing the voices of deans of education in the national conversation? And what *would* we hear from deans of education invited to share their perspectives on leadership for change in contemporary teacher education? The result was the hatching of my project that led to the publication of *Leadership for Change in Teacher Education: Voices of Canadian Deans of Education* (Elliott-Johns, 2015), the central purpose of the book being to compile a collection of brief, engaging, provocative essays to disseminate ideas and perspectives on leadership for change in contemporary teacher education from deans of education across Canada.

The project was launched in February of the sabbatical with the acceptance of the book proposal by Sense Publishers (now Brill), after which I contacted more than seventeen deans of education in faculties of education across Canada, with fourteen agreeing to participate. Contributors were made up of relatively new as well as more experienced deans. The project was formulated by requesting participants share reflections on guiding questions related to five broad themes of interest and, more specifically, in relation to their own situated leadership for contemporary teacher education. Five guiding questions were offered for consideration:

- What critical issues, research, and current ways of thinking about teaching, learning and pedagogy for teacher education inform your leadership of a faculty of education?
- What are the most important external/internal conditions and inherent tensions encountered in your work?
- What insights can you share about the ways contemporary thinking about teacher education and change are reflected in pre-service programs at your current location?
- What important changes, transitions, or transformations are you experiencing in leadership for teacher education?
- What is your vision for teacher education, going forward?

The result was an illuminating collage of voices on a topic that continues to have a limited profile in the literature. In the foreword, Claire Kosnik (Ontario Institute for Studies in Education/University of Toronto), summarized the project this way:

> Leadership is demanding anyway but is made ever more so in our increasingly politicized context. The criticisms of teacher education programs abound and it is often the Deans who are the "face" of the institution. They are required to respond to seemingly never-ending demands. Ironically, Deans of Education as individuals are often overlooked in the rush to improve education, implement mandates, shore up sagging finances, attend to the concerns of stakeholders, and on and on. Susan Elliott-Johns recognized this void in the literature which led to her compiling and editing *Leadership for Change in Teacher Education: Voices of Canadian Deans of Education*. This is a laudable goal which she fulfilled admirably by presenting a unique text that provides insider's stories of the work of Deans of Education. This collection of essays highlights the work of 14 highly committed individuals all of whom are working in demanding situations. Giving them a voice deepens our understanding of the complexity of leading a school of education and adds another piece of the "puzzle" of teacher education. (Kosnik, 2015)

In addition to the insights and positive feedback in Dr. Kosnik's foreword, I think recognition of the significance of the work was best captured in the review below from Professor Fern Snart, then dean of education at the University of Alberta. Her words resonated deeply for me as having achieved the goals of the project, thus making all the work involved in inviting, editing, and compiling the resulting collection of work from leaders of teacher education across the country more than worthwhile.

> *Leadership for Change* was a catalyst to immersing myself in this book, promising as it does the "Voices of Canadian Deans of Education." A member of the Association of Canadian Deans of Education (ACDE) for over a decade, I have been honoured to join these voices around many conference tables and other informal sessions. The promise of important insights these voices can share is fulfilled within every one of the compelling chapters. The book reminds us of the diverse geographical, political, and theoretical contexts that enhance understandings of multiple perspectives on leadership and the complex educational challenges inherent in contemporary teacher education. A deep commitment to public education and a profound work ethic towards

stellar, relevant teacher education resonates across the work of these deans of education. This thought-provoking book makes a valuable contribution to the literature on reconceptualising leadership for teacher education.

How did the granting of a sabbatical extend and enhance this work? First and foremost, the extensive time involved in communicating with contributors was made available, which supported my work on reading and responding with suggested edits and revisions as the authors worked with me on their contributions. (I must say, it often felt like an exercise in skill, diplomacy, and courage, acting as editor for these well-known deans from faculties across Canada.) Accolades for the work from the Association of Canadian Deans of Education, which launched the book with a reception following an invited symposium at a Canadian Society for Studies in Education (CSSE) conference, were another significant outcome of the project, and their recognition for this academic achievement truly made the sabbatical feel like a gift that kept on giving.

The book was a labour of love on a combination of topics I remain passionate about, leadership for teacher education, and is still one of the publications of which I am most proud. However, and I stress again, it is highly unlikely the book would have been completed without the deep contemplation afforded by the sabbatical focal time, which led to the recognition of the need for this work.

Publication of Papers Presented at International, National, and Provincial Conferences

While selected as a significant experience, I acknowledge that attending and presenting papers as part of a sabbatical is a common occurrence. I highlight what was accomplished here because, in turn, these conference presentations led directly to considerable productivity during this period. The single and collaborative presentations made at five international conferences, two national conferences, and a provincial conference contributed to the publication of seven refereed and four professional publications during the sabbatical year. Furthermore, as a scholarly member of the self-study community, I both initiated and guest co-edited a special issue of the *Studying Teacher Education* journal (vol. 9, no. 2). The special issue had a guest editorial and nine research articles on the theme of exploring the transformative nature of self-study of teacher-education practices.

The granting of a sabbatical clearly extended and enhanced this work simply by making the necessary time available, not only to initiate but to also complete a great deal of writing—as well as coordinating publication of the work of others (Elliott-Johns & Tidwell, 2013). A recurring challenge for me when teaching full-time has always been redirecting focus and energies to finishing pieces of writing. While it is always good advice to have various pieces at different stages of completion, I often found it difficult to be in serious writing mode while also in serious teaching mode. The lack of distraction/multi-tasking during sabbatical was therefore extremely beneficial to me, personally and professionally—facilitating both collaborative writing and subsequent publication because of conference participation, for example. Over the course of my sabbatical, my motivation remained high and additional articles submitted for publication were under review as my sabbatical was completed, and were subsequently accepted for publication.

Ongoing Contributions to the Scholarly Community (Peer Review/Editing)

Since becoming a member of my current faculty in 2006, I have found contributing to peer-review processes and assisting with the work of other scholars both informative and helpful in the development of my own writing. A long-term member of three international review boards, *LEARNing Landscapes* (https://www.learninglandscapes.ca), *Journal of Adolescent & Adult Literacy* (International Reading Association), and *Voices from the Middle* (National Council of Teachers of English), I was also a regular reviewer of conference proposals for several professional associations (including American Educational Research Association (AERA), Canadian Society for Studies in Education (CSSE), and related special interest groups Canadian Association for Teacher Education (CATE), and Self-Study of Teacher Education Practices (S-STEP). As with all commitments we make in our work, the nature of these activities could also usurp a great deal of time, but I believe anything worth doing is worth doing well.

In short, therefore, the granting of a sabbatical contributed to my abilities to not only continue with this learning work but afforded time to extend and enhance interactions with the scholarly community in a couple of other ways too. For example, in March of the sabbatical year I was appointed an associate editor with the journal *Teachers and Teaching Theory and Practice* (ISATT) and formally joined the international advisory board of *Studying Teacher Education*. Prior to and beyond the sabbatical, the networks forged because of these activities have been a continuous source of scholarly learning, research partnerships, inspiration, and collegial support, here in Canada and around the world. Essentially, I consider my engagement with the scholarly community goes beyond service. Rather, my commitment to service as professional learning moves it firmly into the intersection of research and service.

Faculty Facilitator, International Practicum

A direct result of the sabbatical, a decision was taken to travel to Italy in May of the sabbatical year and spend three weeks in Sulmona as a faculty facilitator, accompanying a group of thirty-eight teacher candidates (all fifth-year concurrent-education students close to graduating from both their undergraduate and BEd programs at Nipissing University). The other two faculty facilitators with the international practicum were colleagues, but I did not know any of the teacher candidates before leaving as they attended classes at Nipissing's Brantford Campus. I had previously declined such invitations because the international practicums on my campus were generally scheduled February–March, and since I routinely did not teach during the winter semesters, it was closely guarded as precious research/writing time. The granting of a sabbatical made it possible for me to give serious consideration to this venture, and three weeks in Italy in May, without jeopardizing my time for writing for publication (after all, I had a whole year!). It also presented an exciting opportunity to travel, support, and work with a dynamic group of young people who were poised on the brink of setting out on a short-term adventure of their own—international teaching—just before making longer-term life decisions about their respective futures as teachers. Suffice to say, I was in.

As a unique component of the sabbatical experience, the trip to Italy contributed to enriching and enhancing both my personal and professional experience from the outset. We flew from Toronto to Venice, which was in itself an interesting experience, as many of the twenty-something-year-olds we were accompanying had not travelled outside of the country before, and certainly had not taken an eight-hour transatlantic flight. (The departure scene at the airport reminded me of so many school trips taken, with doting parents waving goodbye to their Grade 8 sons and daughters as we left for two- or three-day trips to Ottawa or Québec City. The parents of these young adults were just as anxious—and there were a few tears shed among the joyful smiles and last-minute hugs and advice.) Once on the "other side," navigating through the terminal to security and beyond, we became teachers again as our knowledge and experience reassured and assisted our travelling companions, who had questions even before we were sitting on the plane. This, however, also enabled the immediate forging of trust and rapport as I began to build relationships with all these young people with whom I'd be spending the next three weeks. Informally, confidence was boosted when individuals' anxieties were quietly assuaged by activating "assumed" knowledge and experience in the situation. I found myself noting how easily we are able to slip into the relational as teachers in new surroundings—a learning experience in itself—but one we're not always aware of unless we step out of our familiar routines. A teaching context in Italy drew out my inner teacher every bit as much as a teaching context in Ontario and past experiences teaching in the United Kingdom and, within Canada, in Quebec, Nunavut, and Prince Edward Island. But that's a whole other story!

It was also a bonus to be a member of the faculty team of three colleagues I knew well and with whom I had been looking forward to spending this time. Most probably as a result of my own considerable experience as a world traveller, as well as being a well-seasoned member of the teaching profession, I rapidly felt much at ease with the whole group and, subsequently, sat back to enjoy the flight to Venice.

Before the drive to Sulmona, two days after arriving in Italy, we spent a day touring Venice and soaking up the sights and sounds of Venetian culture in the sunshine. Many gondola trips were taken that day by excited teacher candidates. As we shopped, my colleagues and I would catch glimpses of them disappearing under bridges and out the other side again, grinning up at us like Cheshire cats. It must be said, the professional calibre and personality bandwidth of the teacher candidates on the trip were immediately evident to me, and this is also something I know made the experience incredibly rich and enjoyable. We were sharing time with young adults whose goals were twofold: to engage fully in a valuable professional learning experience—and to enjoy everything else the opportunity offered. (While I have heard this is not *always* the case for everyone who accompanies these international practicum excursions, my colleagues and I certainly lucked in with this group.) In turn, this positionality made a huge difference to how we, as faculty, were able to relate authentically to the group as a whole and to work effectively with individuals—in essence, as colleagues.

Our three weeks spent in Sulmona, a beautiful little city in the province of L'Aquila, Abruzzo region, steeped in medieval history, found us 163 kilometres directly east of Rome—and the aqueducts, squares, awe-inspiring architecture, and ancient cobblestone streets were indeed a daily reminder we were visitors to another time and place. Immersion in the Italian language and culture were, of course, also central to the experience (even while the language of the practicum was English). Living and working somewhere, albeit briefly, rather than being there entirely as a tourist is a rather special way to experience different places, people, institutions, and lifestyles. Technically, my role was to be a practicum advisor to students who would be teaching English and other subjects (in English) in Italy. Working in pairs, teaching teams, teacher candidates were assigned to classes in a range of elementary and high schools throughout the small town of Sulmona. The time in Sulmona included visiting classrooms to consult daily, more frequently if necessary, and toward the end of the placement I would observe a specific lesson, at a mutually agreed upon time, and provide a formal report on their teaching.

My time in Italy, facilitated by the sabbatical, encompasses so many rich and enduring recollections that go beyond the scope of this chapter. But the one vivid memory of Sulmona is the sheer novelty of being able to *walk* to all the schools in town where the teacher candidates were teaching. This made it possible to drink in and really absorb the sights and sounds of our location, so much more so than hopping into a vehicle and driving everywhere. It also required planning ahead in order to arrive places on time and not in a state of disarray; most days were very hot and sunny, 27–30 degrees Celsius. No complaints, though! I vividly recall the delights of sampling the parks en route to supervision, of peering in shop windows and planning to return in the evening (post-siesta, when stores opened again); climbing the stiff gradients of narrow cobble streets with ancient buildings on each side, and everywhere I walked in town enjoying a panoramic view of the magnificent mountains surrounding Sulmona. Those magnificent, brooding mountains, still snow-capped in May, remain etched on my heart as a reminder of that place in time, and the need for humility. Compared to those mountain ranges, we play only a very small part in the scheme of things, but I'm also reminded of Baldwin et al. (2013), that "place matters because it encourages new ways of questioning and being in the world" (p. 2).

I can clearly identify those daily walks in bright sunshine as a significant aspect of personal/professional growth for me as, while a part of my responsibilities there, walking offered the time to step back, reflect, and SLOW DOWN—to meditate with even more critical consciousness than usual. Being removed from the familiar—even my responsibilities were different too—contributed to a greater sense of the growth and, as I now see, signalling my deepening interest in reflexivity and the beginnings of a subtle shift away from reflection alone.

In summary, I share the following reflections on how the sabbatical extended and enhanced this work in terms of the most rewarding and most challenging aspects of the learning experience undertaken in Italy. The opportunity to travel abroad with a fascinating group of young people, and to share their experience, was incredibly rewarding. In addition to the time spent living and working in Sulmona with the teacher candidates, associate teachers, and other educators. We also experienced the culture by travelling to L'Aquila, the archaeological site at Pompeii, the Amalfi Coast (Sorrento), Florence, and Rome. Seeing stunning vistas visited through their eyes was enormously rewarding, as well as further satisfying my own thirst for seeing and doing as learning, thus embellishing the landscape of my own career as a professional learner.

Interestingly, one evening several the teacher candidates shared how they really enjoyed spending time with the three of us and found our indirect modelling of enthusiasm for ongoing personal and professional growth inspirational. They acknowledged that we were not at all jaded by being in the later stages of our careers. (By which I think they were too polite to say, "so old.") Nevertheless, I guess we were seen as being authentic in truly "teaching who we are," and, to me, that was a huge reward in and of itself.

The most challenging aspect of this adventure was my acute awareness of language as barrier while in Italy. I had a very limited, and quickly learned, Italian vocabulary, but I sometimes found it frustrating because there was *so* much rich dialogue I would have loved to engage in—about history, customs, experiences, the educational system, politics, cuisine—and I could not. So many of the Italians we worked with had good English (which helped), and we also had a fluent, Italian-speaking colleague with us, but it's not the same thing as fluently engaging in conversations oneself. *Next* time I visit, I hope to have acquired at least a working knowledge of Italian.

The Reflexive Turn: Looking Back, Moving Forward

> *Why do you go away? So that you can come back. So that you can see the place where you came from with new eyes and extra colours. And the people there you see differently too. Coming back to where you started is not the same as never leaving.*
>
> Terry Pratchett (2012, p. 332)

Flexible schedules and more autonomy have allowed me to organize my life and work at the faculty, compared with my former life and work in a busy school, where I worked to resolve minute-to-minute crises generated by students, teachers, and other school-community members. However, flexible schedules and increased autonomy also facilitate crossing too many boundaries between personal and professional space, and the struggle to keep a work-life balance becomes a significant challenge. This has been my experience; I hold no one but myself responsible. A critical downside of loving one's work is that it can stealthily burrow itself into the very fabric of daily life, almost to the point of being unrecognizable as "work." The need to be cognizant and selective of personal and professional boundary crossings is vital if one is to nourish the soul through critical consciousness and a balanced approach to intellectual, emotional, and spiritual growth. This self-work continues.

Non Satis Scire (To Know Is Not Enough), is a touchstone I consider integral to the fostering of wholeness in praxis. My interpretation of the phrase regards knowledge as an organic process subject to continual revision and growth. More specifically, for me, it evokes positionality: how we move through the world with our knowledge, understanding, passion, and empathy; how we work to make a difference in the lives of others; and how we continue to learn (about) ourselves. I also firmly believe that "[g]ood teaching cannot be reduced to technique; good teaching comes from the identity and integrity of the teacher" (Palmer, 2018, p. 2). As I hope these reflections on my sabbatical experiences and continual voyage of personal and professional discovery serve to demonstrate, the granting of sabbatical only extended and enhanced these deeply held convictions and my ability to *live* them as fundamental to my teaching and research contexts.

For example, being and becoming more intentional about how I spend my time working has been one of the most beneficial aspects taken forward from the sabbatical. Deeply held values, beliefs, and convictions inherent to my research and practice were mobilized throughout my sabbatical journey, but the time to reflect also led to a much-needed shift in outlook. The proactive pressing of a reset button was the result of authentically turning a reflexive lens squarely on myself and my work habits, and closely examining the exhausting lifestyle I had created. Recognition soon followed that I should not (could not?), realistically, maintain the pace I had set for myself prior to my sabbatical. Changes in health, lifestyle, and work habits remain a priority, but I'm still a work in progress. My punishing work ethic and inner drive to be successful in my work have not entirely retreated, but I now nurture and value the understanding that I must keep my finger on that reset button.

In the six years since the sabbatical, I have remained an active member of my university community, albeit having physically distanced myself long before the COVID-19 pandemic, and I no longer live in close proximity to campus. Acknowledging sage advice from Sibbald and Handford (2017), that "physical, emotional, and mental health need to be involved in the list of priorities and that work-life balance requires effort" (p. 266), I can viscerally relate to their point: "The mental aspect is fundamentally challenging because academics, generally, work with a mental capacity that can't simply be turned off" (p. 266). The priority has been on creating work-life balance and the cultivation of praxis in the context of an ethic of care (Noddings, 2012)—care for my students *and* myself—including a move away from detrimental patterns of working too hard and making wiser professional choices. Palmer's explication (1998) of the importance of resolving internal and external forces that jeopardize our abilities to live an undivided life speak volumes for me as I continue to wrestle with the role of my own identity, integrity, and personal Möbius strip moving forward. This has meant purposefully abandoning fragmentation and concerns with who others might think I *ought* to be in the world rather than an understanding of who I choose to be in the world. To reiterate, as Pratchett (2012, p. 332) so eloquently put it: "Coming back to where you started is not the same as never leaving."

At the time of writing, radical changes beyond our control have taken place in a very short time due to the impact of the COVID-19 pandemic on our society and ways of life, including restrictions on our ability to travel locally and overseas. With a second sabbatical on the horizon, the plans I had made to travel and present at conferences in New Zealand (cancelled) and in Bari, Italy (ISATT conference, postponed by a year), are no longer viable. However, my work will continue on a co-edited book project that is currently in process, and I will capitalize on the opportunity to "shelter in place" and focus on deep reading and on some other writing projects. To quote Richardson and Adams St. Pierre (2018), "I am not certain how others will document their becoming, but I have chosen structures that suit my disposition, theoretical orientation, and writing life." (p. 826). (In the sabbatical ahead, notwithstanding pandemic parameters, maybe, just maybe, I'll try enjoying some of those "auxiliary benefits" too.)

At this stage in my career as an educator, with the next major transition after sabbatical most likely being retirement from full-time employment (and the hoops of tenure and promotion no longer of concern), I have the privilege of writing more for my own purposes (Lyle, 2019; Elliott-Johns, 2010; Peseta, 2009) and toward greater knowing, understanding, and acceptance of an undivided self.

> To be whole is to be part;
> true voyage is return. – Laia Asieo Odo
> Ursula K. Le Guin (1974, p. 95)

References

Baldwin, L., Block, T., Cooke, L., Crawford, I., Kim, N., Ratsoy, G., & Waldichuk, T. (2013). Affective teaching: The place of place in interdisciplinary teaching. *Transformative Dialogues: Teaching and Learning Journal*, 6(3), 1–20.

Booth, D., & Moore, B. (2003). *Poems please! Sharing poetry with children* (2nd ed.). Pembroke Publishers.

Elliott-Johns, S. E. (1993). *Reading aloud allowed* [Keynote Address]. Australian Reading Association Conference, Melbourne, Australia.

Elliott-Johns, S. E. (2010). Reflections of a Teacher Educator on the Process of Making a Case for Tenure. *Kansas English, 94*(1), 39–51.

Elliott-Johns, S. E. (2015). (Ed.). *Leadership for change in teacher education: Voices of Canadian Deans of Education*. Sense Publishers.

Elliott-Johns, S. E., & Richardson, C. (2017). The first year of implementation: The enhanced teacher education program at the Schulich School of Education (Nipissing University). In D. Petrarca & J. Kitchen (Eds.), *Initial teacher education in Ontario: The first year of four-semester teacher education programs* (pp. 127–154). Canadian Association for Teacher Education. http://cate-acfe.ca/polygraph-book-series/

Elliott-Johns, S. E., & Tidwell, D. L. (Eds.). (2013). Different voices, many journeys: Explorations of the transformative nature of the self-study of teacher education practices. *Studying Teacher Education: A journal of self-study of teacher education practice, 9*(2), 91–95.

Falkenberg, T. (2015). (Ed.). *Handbook of Canadian initial teacher education*. Canadian Association for Teacher Education (CATE)/Association Canadienne de formation d'enseignement ACFE).

Kosnik, C. (2015). Foreword. In S. E. Elliott-Johns (Ed.), *Leadership for change in teacher education: Voices of Canadian Deans of Education* (pp. vii–viii). Sense Publishers.

Le Guin, Ursula K. (1974). *The Dispossessed*. HarperCollins.

Lyle, E. (2017). *Of books, barns, and boardrooms: Exploring praxis through reflexive inquiry*. Sense Publishers.

Lyle, E. (2019). Engaging self-study to untangle issues of identity. In E. Lyle (Ed.), *Fostering a relational pedagogy: Self-study as transformative practice* (pp. 1–9). Brill.

Lyle, E. (2020). Identity landscapes. In E. Lyle (Ed.), *Contemplating how the places we dwell, dwell in us* (pp. 1–13). Brill.

Kitchen, J., & Petrarca, D. (2017). (Eds). *Initial teacher education in Ontario: The first year of four-semester teacher education programs*. Canadian Association for Teacher Education. http://cate-acfe.ca/polygraph-book-series/

Ng-A-Fook, N., Kane, R., Crowe, T., Karagiozis, N., & Schira-Hagerman, M. (2017). The first year of implementation: Reconceptualizing teacher education at the University of Ottawa (pp. 217–242). In D. Petrarca & J. Kitchen (Eds.), *Initial teacher education in Ontario: The first year of four-semester teacher education programs*. Canadian Association for Teacher Education. http://cate-acfe.ca/polygraph-book-series/

Noddings, N. (2012). The caring relation in teaching. *Oxford Review of Education, 38*(6), 771–781.

Oliver, C. (2004). Reflexive inquiry and the strange loop tool. *Journal of Systemic Consultation and Management, 15*(2), 127–140.

Palmer, P. (1998). *The courage to teach*. Jossey-Bass.

Palmer, P. (2018). The heart of a teacher: Identity and integrity in teaching. http://www.couragerenewal.org/PDFs/Parker-Palmer_The-Heart-of-a-Teacher.pdf

Peseta, T. (2009). *For whom do we write? The place and practice of writing in developing the scholarship of teaching and learning*. Paper presented at the Plenary Address at International Society for the Scholarship of Teaching and Learning Conference, La Trobe University, Australia.

Pratchett, T. (2012). *A hat full of sky*. Corgi.

Richardson, L., & Adams St. Pierre, E. (2018). Writing: A method of inquiry. In N. K. Denzin & Y. S. Lincoln (Eds.), *Handbook of qualitative research* (5th ed. pp. 818–838). Sage.

Sibbald, T. M., & Handford, V. (Eds.). (2017). *The academic gateway: Understanding the journey to tenure*. University of Ottawa Press.

CHAPTER 4

The Sabbatical Voyage: A Triptych of Renewal, Reflection, and Research

Victoria (Tory) Handford

I am an art lover. Galleries of any sort hold great appeal. Beyond the creations on display, I enjoy considering how the art is framed. Art lovers see this "zone for art" as an art itself. The frame is frequently chosen by the curator rather than the artist, rendering framing a "show within a show." I have used the metaphor of frame and triptych for this chapter. A triptych is an artistic trilogy, where three panels of art hang side by side and are related to each other, even as they are separate. The frame, as a metaphor, I had anticipated would highlight the joys of time away, exploration, energy creation through new contacts and travels, and a certain *je ne sais quoi* arising from the absence of office disturbances. It is not what happened; my sabbatical experience was framed by global and personal events outside of my control. This reality in no way resembled the frame as metaphor I had imagined.

The Frame: Pandemic, Injustice, Climate Change

I finished this chapter at the beginning of August of 2020, a scant six weeks post-sabbatical, affording me little time for deep reflection prior to writing. Additional time and deeper reflection will reveal how the profound events of sabbatical influence future hopes and aspirations. Perhaps future events will lighten the frame, but as it stands over 29,000,000 people have contracted the coronavirus globally and, at the time of writing, almost 930,000 have lost their lives. We are experiencing multiple days in a row of the largest single-day increases in infection rates. The end of the first and the beginning of further waves in the northern hemisphere is upon us, spurred on by those who are unable to heed advisories or inform their actions by reading and listening to research-informed sources. Others are choosing to participate in unrelated, huge, and necessary public protests despite World Health Organization guidelines against gatherings. This is not a scenario conductive to minimizing the pandemic. It is not, to reference Winston Churchill, our finest hour.

The negative impacts to my sabbatical productivity caused by the pandemic, by global outrage regarding the murder of George Floyd and the issues of systemic discrimination, and by climate disaster now in clear evidence in the Arctic are inestimable. The world is unhealthy. If only Leonard Cohen had been right in the 1990s, that "democracy is coming." My assessment of available evidence suggests Cohen, not known for his upbeat or sunny portrayal of life, was overly optimistic in this writing.

When I turn away from the news, it feels like I am somehow denying the reality of global and local intolerance and indifference, and no longer empathizing with the pain of others. Yet, not turning away from all this is also crippling. Reverence for informed intelligence and the good of democratic processes, perhaps never real, is now blatantly scorned by many. The duplicity of leadership—global, national, local—is laid bare. It is both hypnotizing and painful for me to watch the ramp up to the 2020 US presidential election.

Resistance to global and individual threats is a component sequence of my DNA. My mother, a teacher and the only working mother in my neighbourhood, set a strong example. She raised me to resist oppression in a variety of forms, as it was understood in the 1960s and by this quite unconventional woman. She was a founding member of the Voice of Women, long before nuclear disarmament and the women's movement were acceptable topics of conversation in polite company. She attended the 1963 March on Washington, following which an influential uncle visited us from the United States. We were not quite "average" enough to be a political non-issue for the above reasons. Given his status within the scientific and defence communities and the Cold War political environment, the visit was deemed risky. The RCMP paid us a visit just to be sure there were not security interests in play. Though the incident was resolved—of course there were no security concerns—this experience left a permanent mark on my identity. I still wonder what possible threat my mother posed and what the government was so concerned about. It seems independence of thought is and was closely "observed." More important than the indelible mark this and other elements of my socially conscious family left on my identity, resistance in modern times seems useless, possibly even dangerous—again. I guess this is how the powers that be want us to view resistance. It seems I have been marching since birth, with little progress made.

For me, the evident oppression of women continues, much as society likes to claim progress. While I am relieved to see global protests and cries for humanity in relation to dignity and equality, I am skeptical of this amounting to more than opportunities for further oppression. Figure 4.1 shows me (with the sign) participating with a small but mighty, mostly female, group of students asking for women to be included, directly, in the American constitution. The forty years since these efforts, and subsequent efforts, have not resulted in change to the document. We have been crying out for a very long time, with few results.

There have been countless other battles for justice worthy of attention and effort. I try to balance this despair with thoughts about Lincoln's first inaugural address and calls for hope that our "better angels" will prevail, but I struggle to feel optimistic.[1] We are in danger of succumbing to the conquering of our better angels. The strong potential for collapse of compassion leaves me struggling to speak at all.

Amid all this, writing a chapter on sabbaticals feels trivial. It has been dark, darker, darker still—again, Leonard Cohen surfaces, truer to form (Cohen, 2016). I did not want it darker.

This is the frame surrounding my sabbatical voyage. If you can identify with the frame, you will know how challenging it has been to muster the optimism required to put words on the page at this time. It is also tiring for you, dear reader, to stick with the reading. Thank you for your efforts to continue—with this chapter, with your important work. It is more than tough slogging, for all of us, but this is my frame. The triptych that follows will describe the three separate but related images of voyage during sabbatical that mattered to me.

Figure 4.1. *Many of us participated in ERA Yes student activism for the Equal Rights Amendment, 1982.*
Source: *Florida Flambeau*, courtesy of Florida State University Libraries, Special Collections and Archives.

The Voyage of Renewal

My sabbatical lasted six months. At my university, there is to be a zero effect on budget when a sabbatical is granted. This means academics who are not on sabbatical perform numerous formerly shared tasks while a colleague is away, with the expectation that this is reciprocated when it is their turn for a sabbatical. In my case, I have significant course release to serve as coordinator of our graduate programs in education, and I taught in the fall semester prior to my sabbatical, so my teaching requirements were completed. Our chair filled in as coordinator while I was gone. Next year, when he is on sabbatical for six months, I will be both coordinator of graduate programs and chair of the School of Education. This arrangement is demanding, but this is how we do these things. It required investing time pre-sabbatical helping the chair learn many details of our large graduate program. All in, there was too much to do to take a vacation pre-sabbatical.

Additionally, my progression from tenure-track assistant professor to tenure and associate professor was demanding, as it is for everyone. I understand most people begin sabbatical with exhaustion as the presenting condition. Some time is "lost" in the first few weeks just recovering from the journey. Recovery time is costly as demonstrating productivity is necessary, and recovery amounts to lost time. The following summarizes my perception of the six sabbatical months.

January
January flew by, seeing pieces of work completed, other work begun, and some work removed from the list as not worthy of time. This first month was about organizing expectations: publication deadlines, conference deadlines, the needs of co-authors and their time constraints, and the realities of tiredness. Exercise was a priority; I continued to work out using a gym regimen I had begun in October, an annual process of fall preparation for the downhill ski season. Positive results both in the gym and on the slopes were noted. Great.

February
By February I had a clear, reliable work routine. I was surprised all this research was waiting beyond the sabbatical gateway! Writing was taking shape and a large scoping review of literature was visibly making progress. Chapters, conference proceedings, applications for presentations at conferences, active research, and articles were all beginning to flow. There was no pause in the exercise. This was new: typically, by February gym trips are a thing of the past, but I was still at it.

In mid-February, my husband experienced two serious health events, just as the COVID-19 pandemic was gaining strength. Everything stopped as we managed specialists, tests, family concerns, and our own anxieties. While others might not have yet begun to understand the magnitude of the coming global change, I was highly aware that my husband, with his lengthy list of risk factors, was vulnerable in ways beyond his health events. I cancelled plans to attend conferences where I was presenting in April, May, and June and moved office equipment from my campus office to home. The gym routine and skiing stopped, but exercise continued through goal-oriented outdoor walking. By the end of the month, I had cancelled all conference registrations and presentations scheduled to the end of August.

March–May
March, April, and May involved many medical appointments for my husband, and ceasing all face-to-face interactions. My husband and I maintained a significant walking routine that frequently topped 40 kilometres a week, and we ensured our diet was optimal. I settled back into focused work, but my focus was shorter, and distraction was a significant issue. I missed a deadline for a book chapter I am co-authoring, though smaller and simpler pieces of writing were successful. This is an example of doing what can be managed, although not an example of doing the important or the urgent. Perhaps that is all that could be expected.

June
The COVID-19 pandemic started to seem manageable in British Columbia. Masks, grocery delivery, stable routines, and a refusal to look in mirrors all helped. I could go to a garden centre at non-busy hours, and I did venture into one or two stores during seniors' hours. My son defended his doctoral dissertation on a virtual platform (Zoom). Things were different, but my own dissertation defence, years ago, included details I had not anticipated. His was not only virtual, but the external examiner had to leave mid-defence because a forest fire was roaring down the hill and he needed to gather belongings and evacuate his home. Wow! Global warming also weighing in. We celebrated his successful completion of the PhD in philosophy as the incredible achievement it is. Walking continued, but a tiredness that just would not let up crept in.

The Black Lives Matter movement surged in the wake of the horror of the murder of George Floyd in Minnesota. This combined with global protests and fears of what these large gatherings would mean in terms of the pandemic. Personally, it meant I just could not keep trying to be productive. When the Milne Ice Shelf in the Tuvaijuittuq marine protected area near Ellesmere Island, in Nunavut, was set adrift, it felt like the world was finally completely coming apart from the weight of so many injustices. I called an American friend from our years in graduate school in the United States. She and I had participated in many protests, back in the day. None of the protests appeared to have made any difference, but they did help us learn to articulate our thoughts. The lengthy conversation we had was just as intense as our relationship had been in our youth, I remembered. This further suppressed any lingering sense of optimism.

Summary
A renewal voyage occurred. It may be somewhat like emerging from a cinema having seen a horror film. Renewal may not be the first word that comes to mind, but the change of pace still reaps positive rewards.

The Voyage of Reflection

Part of the value of a sabbatical is the time to consider possibilities, and I was able to create time for this. I looked beyond my main research agenda and reflected on the roles of gateways in our lives, in education, and in the academy itself.

Gateway as Professional Growth
One gateway for me is that of Tim Sibbald, the co-editor of this book as well as two other books and several academic-journal articles, who has been very much part of a voyage that has resulted in professional growth. My JK–12 education career was spent on the teacher-to-principal journey, culminating in provincial work both at the Ministry of Education and at the Ontario College of Teachers (OCT), the largest self-regulatory body in Canada. It was at the OCT where I first met Tim. Little did I know in the OCT days that Tim would be a gateway to academic maturity for me.

    Tim and I left our JK–12 careers and began as assistant professors at approximately the same time. Our shared experience gradually turned from a sole focus on JK–12 education to that of life in the academy. We talked for many hours, eventually determining we should write about this experience. As anyone who regularly writes with a colleague knows, the relationship evolves over laughter, frustration, glimmers of hope, and publications. Moments of annoyance give way to the much more enduring satisfaction and pride in shared accomplishments—on the page and with each other. The books turned out to be a gateway for us; one that led to an understanding of the process of publishing, of collaboration, and of growth as academics. Thanks for the voyage of discovery Tim! We are not yet done!

Gateway as Professional Delineation
It was also at the OCT that I developed a sharp focus on professionalism. School leaders think about these issues frequently. Regulatory-body employees consider them constantly. So, as I was thinking about gateways, or simply gates, I reflected on issues of professionalism and the application of expectations for professionals. As a further step, I did some light research into the legal context of schoolhouse gates.

Back in the olden days, schools frequently had fenced, gated yards, through which people would enter and exit school property. Education law relates to these markers, making it important for educators, students, parents, and the public at large to consider what is the same, and what is different, depending on which side of the schoolhouse gate an individual is on.

In Canada, as in the United States, the courts may intervene in issues of competing rights. The courts determine which right will prevail, and why, in some circumstances. In the context of public education, the Canadian Charter of Rights and Freedoms has made parents, students, and teachers more aware of their rights. The Charter has also led to the judicialization (Mackay et al., 2013) of education in Canada. We work and live in the education legal framework created by the Charter. Do parents, students, and teachers check their rights at the schoolhouse gate? The answer is, "it depends."

The US Supreme Court case of *Tinker v. Des Moines Independent Community District School* is the source of the phrase that students do not "shed their constitutional rights to freedom of speech or expression at the schoolhouse gate" (*Tinker*, 1969). This phrase has been cited repeatedly in both American and Canadian education-law arguments and decisions since *Tinker*.

The *Tinker* case is as follows. Mary Beth Tinker and a group of friends decided to wear black armbands to school to protest the war in Vietnam. They were suspended and told they could not return to school wearing armbands. The students wore black clothing for the remainder of the school year, but they did not wear armbands. They also sued, believing the restrictions were encroaching on their First Amendment rights. A component of the *Tinker* decision involved the limits on student rights at school, and whether certain actions by students created a "substantial and material disruption," which would mean there was justification for limits on First Amendment rights while at school. Black armbands were not such a disruption, but limits on freedom of speech, in certain circumstances, did exist.

Efforts to identify the gates limits and appropriate application have continued for fifty years. In Canada, as in the US, the results have been mixed. In the case of the *British Columbia Teachers' Federation v. British Columbia Public School Employers' Association* (2014), a teacher wore a black armband to protest the administration of an annual test, known as the Foundation Skills Assessment, to Grade 4 students. In doing so, she also engaged in discussion with the students, which caused the students to cheer and be disruptive. In this case, the arbitrator determined that teachers have a right to freedom of expression under section 2(b) of the Canadian Charter of Rights and Freedoms but are not to engage students in protest. That it was disruptive to the school was an important component of that decision. There is freedom of expression, but this case provides a sense of a limit.

In the case of *Cromer and British Columbia Teachers' Federation* (1986), a parent, who was also a teacher, attended a public parent meeting at her children's school, where input into a new sex-education curriculum was invited. The parent made several personal comments, which were offensive to the teacher conducting the meeting. The teacher, when she discovered the parent commenting was also a teacher, charged the parent with unprofessional conduct for violating the BC Teachers' Federation code of ethics. The federation found the complaint had merit and could proceed. However, the parent applied for a judicial review to the Supreme Court of British Columbia in which she argued her freedom-of-expression rights had been violated. Eventually it ended up at the BC Court of Appeal, which said the following:

> I do not think people are free to choose which hat they will wear on what occasion. Mrs. Cromer does not always speak as a teacher, nor does she always speak as a parent. But she always speaks as Mrs. Cromer. The perception of her by her audience will depend on their knowledge of her training, her skills, her experience, and her occupation, among other things. The impact of what she says will depend on the content of what she says and the occasion on which she says it. (*Cromer and BC Teachers' Federation*, 1986).

The court found that, because Mrs. Cromer's comments were personal criticisms or attacks on the teacher counsellor and not addressed to the subject matter of the meeting, her speech was not protected by section 2(b) of the Canadian Charter of Rights and Freedoms. She was therefore bound by the code of ethics at the time she made the statements about the teacher counsellor and was dealt with accordingly. In short, professional responsibility is not restricted to in-role events. Professional responsibility extends to one's other identities as well. In some circumstances, it extends to life.

In *Lutes (Litigation Guardian of) v. Prairie View School Division No. 74* (1992), secondary students at Milestone School, in Milestone, Saskatchewan, were told they could not sing a popular rap song titled "Let's Talk About Sex." Because the school is in a rural town to which most students were bussed, some would go downtown during lunch break. One day, while the students were downtown, one Grade 9 student, Lutes, noticed one of the staff members on a street corner. Followed by his friends, Lutes approached the teacher and sang said song. When Lutes returned to the school, his behaviour in town was addressed by the administration. He was given noon-hour detentions for a month for singing the song in front of and embarrassing the staff member. Lutes's parents sought an injunction to stop the detention, arguing that the student's right to freedom of expression under the Charter had been violated. The judge did not grant the injunction ending the detention, but he did find the student's freedom of expression had been violated. He said that if the student had been disciplined for his behaviour and not for singing the song, there would have been no Charter violation.

Two Supreme Court of Canada decisions related to religious rights in schools (*Chamberlain v. Surrey School District No. 36*, 2002; *Multani v. Commission scolaire Marguerite-Bourgeoys*, 2006) reinforce the importance of the Charter of Rights and Freedoms. The Chamberlain case addressed issues of religious values, same-sex relationships, and books in schools. Chamberlain wanted to use books in his primary classroom that included images and stories of same-sex parents raising children. Banning books was not allowed. The enduring quote from this case is: "Tolerance is always age-appropriate, children cannot learn unless they are exposed to views that differ from those they are taught at home." The schoolhouse gate needs to be open to a variety of possibilities.

In the *Multani* case, the issue was the wearing of a kirpan (a metal dagger worn by many Sikhs that symbolizes virtue and honour, and is always to be worn). In a time of zero-tolerance for "weapons" in schools, this kirpan became an issue. It was determined that the kirpan was not worn for violent purposes, had never led to a violent incident at a school, and that the kirpan represented a religious symbol for the student. Freedom of religion was upheld.

In both Canada and the United States, students and faculty do not leave their constitutional or Charter rights at the schoolhouse gate. Most citizens and courts consider it important for democracy that the values present in the Charter are learned and mostly practised in mandatory public education. Rights permeate and are practised on both sides of the gates. Some restrictions apply. Education is a legal environment that has a special status, and schools are different entities when it comes to rights under the Charter. They are viewed by the courts as places where order and discipline must prevail, and the authority to ensure the learning environment is intact is a significant consideration when adjudicating issues. Courts have determined that rights are limited in the school context if the order of the school is disrupted. Which laws permeate the gates, and which laws are susceptible to limits because of the gates, is a matter of judgment, which depends in part on circumstances. The gates themselves, however, matter.

Gateway as Limen
I have never forgotten the speaker's address at my doctoral convocation, which focused on university gates. I have thought about this address each time I step on and off my university's campus.

Over the years, I have searched the convocation website for that address, but it was not posted. I contacted the convocation office and received no response. I googled information on university gates, which never revealed significant details. Then, early in my sabbatical I searched the university website and came up with three possible academics who might have delivered this address. When I wrote Professor Ron Bartlett, he was kind enough to write back, send me the convocation address, and interact with me about the topic. This informal research would never have occurred had I not been on sabbatical.

Professor Bartlett's address focused on the characteristics of university gates, and why they might exist. He noted that at many universities, including my doctoral alma mater, the University of Toronto, the gates cannot be closed. He speculated about why an institution would create these uncloseable gates and suggested there had to be some reason to mark when one is on a university campus and when one is not. The gates may signify more than a property demarcation. Perhaps, he wondered, it was related to the purposes of the university itself.

For Dr. Bartlett, university gates serve as a limen. A liminal point is the moment when something different, some change, can be perceived. The opposite, subliminal, is something that is present, but not consciously perceived. This element of liminality or just-noticeable difference (JND) is an important component of the Weber–Fechner law, and often relates to field of vision, sound, or other components of human perception. With university gates, what is the JND they are signaling, as either warning or invitation?

First, university gates do signal territory. There are legal issues related to these gates as well. They are also important, although not precisely the same, for universities. For instance, students are adults, the duty of care on the part of faculty is vastly different from professionals in the public-school system.

The intellectual work is more focused. Students gain deeper content mastery and think about that content more critically. Learning is on a field of study ideally related to their interests, rather than exposure to broad, general knowledge. Many students learn invaluable lessons about living with others. They are adults. Responsibility changes to include much higher levels of personal responsibility.

Other skills such as learning to challenge, learning to tolerate, understanding multiple perspectives, and generating thoughts that are informed by understanding of the larger body of knowledge are some of the core purposes of a university education. "You are wider, you now contain multitudes, at least indirectly" (Bartlett, 2011). The work of life formed us prior to university; the work of life reforms us with this added dimension retreating into university life invited. Students enter and then cross back through the gate changed. When I work with graduate students, I often tell them, "if you leave here with exactly the same thoughts as when you arrived, then the educational experience has not been valuable for you."

There is a limen for faculty as well. Faculty spend years learning, teaching, establishing careers of research, and creating academic and community value. Tenure and promotion requirements virtually always incorporate elements of participation in and contribution to society. Research and research funding frequently relate to current societal need. Faculty "crossover" to the university environment but disseminate the findings often well beyond the university gates. In the end, the goal is to better society. Freedom to pursue research and academic goals is recognized as not always related to immediate benefit. It is hoped the results will ultimately benefit society. The limen is there. There is a JND between being on or in a university and its campus and being in the community. Within the campus there is freedom to research, with a responsibility to cross that information over society via teaching, discovering, publishing, presenting, and so on.

So, what is the JND my sabbatical has made for me? Right now, with very little reflection time, my time outside the gate of the university has resulted in some renewal of purpose, and some acceptance of the limits I face in relation to purposes.

The Research Voyage

The primary purpose for a tripartite sabbatical is to engage in a focused research agenda, with time to generate real progress. For me, this included three primary themes:

- complete *Beyond the Academic Gateway* (Sibbald & Handford, 2020) and make headway on this book on sabbaticals,
- make progress on another book about strong school districts and their leaders, and
- continue strengthening connections between my university and the school districts.

Research has been difficult. People are experiencing online-meeting fatigue, which limits collaborations with fellow researchers. My data gathering also stalled once universities and school districts moved to emergency remote communications. Attention for everyone has been a struggle to sustain, in general. The writing itself has not come as easily as I had hoped; each thought has taken a frustrating amount of time to crystallize and to preserve on the page. Despite these challenges, I have been productive, and I have been concerned that others will minimize the challenges I experienced as a result.

I set a higher benchmark for myself than was achieved, and that is what I measure myself against.

The challenges I have faced are not completely unique to my sabbatical. There is research showing a drop in publishing for women, particularly as first authors, since the beginning of the pandemic (Andersen et al., 2020; Gabster et al., 2020). Additionally, there is "emerging data that show that the psychological impacts of COVID-19 are more pronounced among women in the general population" (Madsen et al., 2020). The research cited identifies the dual demands of life for many women (work, caregiving), which may have resulted in reduced work productivity during COVID-19, as demands, combined with societal anxiety, became overwhelming.

Beyond the Academic Gateway (Sibbald & Handford, 2020). This was nearly drafted when my sabbatical began; however, the many steps to be taken including peer review and resubmission are time consuming. Work generated by the editorial suggestions from the University of Ottawa Press, checking and rechecking iterations of proofs, and then the index, semi-final galleys, and final galleys takes time. In our case, a book release and conference presentations were all cancelled due to the pandemic, but the many steps related to physical production of the book were all completed. It was wonderful to have the time to focus on this and I am proud to say that the book, again co-edited with Tim, is better than our first (Sibbald & Handford, 2017). The contributing authors, who were the same, wrote more confidently and with clearer purpose, while we have grown as editors.

Strong Districts. My research made gains, but it was slow and painful work. I completed the scoping review of literature we needed (2005–2020), which resulted in ninety-three article summaries, tabled by theme. At the end of this process what I found was an inability to write the chapter I needed to contribute, and it is still waiting for attention. This work matters; it is core work for a faculty member who teaches leadership. I know the material, so it is curious to me that this project is the one I have struggled with the most. A scoping review is tiring work. Many hundreds of articles are rejected. The few that need to be included are frequently dense reads that take hours to distill to the critical pieces of information that are relevant. I have set up some unrealistic thoughts in relation to this project that revolve around wading back into this material, which would mean clearing everything else from the task list, because once I'm in it I will be in it for weeks. I probably need to re-examine this thinking. Alternatively, it may be that leadership itself has become problematic material for me. When I consider the frame for this triptych it is possible that my perception of failures of leadership around the world leaves me wondering where in the world I will find the optimism to write about this topic.

University and School District Connections. These are important to my roles in the university. Focus on this was part of the sabbatical plan. The relationships build future opportunities, but the geographic location itself increases the need for connection.

The interior of British Columbia, where I live, is unique in that there are three mid-sized cities of approximately 85,000 to 150,000 people and hundreds of small towns and villages. In general, this part of the province and of the country might be called flyover. Politicians do not typically invest time or money visiting the interior, possibly because at least half of the population of BC resides in the lower mainland. The voice of the interior is not rural, urban, or suburban, and due to the geography of the province it is a region that is somewhat difficult to reach. The region is bounded on all sides by significant mountain ranges and rivers. Winter travel often finds a rockslide closing one highway, an avalanche barring another, and significant snowfall affecting one or more passes, thus eliminating any routes of travel. As a result, and despite the lower cost of living compared with the Lower Mainland and Vancouver Island, recruitment of qualified educators beyond the three cities is problematic. Even in the major interior cities there can be talent shortages, particularly in specialty areas.

I deliberately began writing a chapter for a book with two local practitioners to create clear evidence that I value and hear them, to share the value of research in relation to their voices, and to ensure the amplification of their voices. The chapter was accepted and is in the publication process. When an opportunity to write a short article about school and district leadership, and what learning had occurred to date in navigating the pandemic, we collaborated again. We expanded the team to include a group in another province, in a small city, but in a French-language school district within an English-speaking province. The writing was much faster, and the purposes of the conversation ahead of the writing were clear to those who had co-authored the first piece with me. Long-term benefits may accrue from this, including sites for future research and greater engagement between Thompson Rivers University and the school district. The individuals I worked with will soon be published writers, whose leadership practices are worth writing about. This may lead to a sense of efficacy, and consideration of research in practice that I hope grows. Even better, the voices, talent, and achievements of those working in the interior of BC will continue being heard long into the future and shine a spotlight to attract even brighter talent.

Several other writing and research issues received a portion of time during the sabbatical. Work on research related to our graduate student success centre was completed, albeit with fewer surveys and interviews than we anticipated. An article is waiting for me to write in relation to this. I continued working with multiple thesis students, with one article co-authored by a former student I had supervised being submitted to a journal. I completed an invited essay for a colleague's book. I wrote a flap-jacket review for another colleague's book. It sounds productive, but I had hoped for more.

Did my research voyage matter? While I did not achieve everything I had hoped, I did make very real gains in several areas. My writing has improved, and I have had time to edit and re-edit my work. Yes, this voyage mattered, and was one where discovery occurred.

Academics typically present their research at international conferences during their sabbatical. International conference presentations are important as they help one gain a global perspective on issues related to their field, meet colleagues at universities in distant areas, and consider joint research initiatives that span international borders. When applying for the rank of full professor, there is a need to demonstrate presence and value on the international stage. Given time, a sabbatical is the most reasonable opportunity to pursue such travel. For me and indeed for most others, this opportunity, which encompasses so many aspects of the next five years of research, vanished during the pandemic (Madsen et al., 2020). It is very likely going to influence promotion.

Back in the Harbour Again

I have listened to colleagues talk about the intense work at the onset of the pandemic, particularly in March and April as adjustments were being made to expectations of students, support staff, and faculty. Adjusted expectations for those on sabbatical may have dealt with the moment, but there is no evidence of considerations of the long-term expectations for promotion. Sabbatical comes along every several years. It is a moment in time that must create future opportunities.

I have returned but I seem to be lacking that liminal lighter step that sabbatical almost always creates, that sense of purpose that reflection often clarifies, the pride of achievement in relation to research goals, and the sense of renewal that comes from change.

Perhaps others fared better during the pandemic. However, being on sabbatical with no face-to-face interaction and constant global threats in every imaginable dimension of life has led to deep reflections about future directions. It is evident from this chapter that I continued with academic publishing, but it remains significantly challenging to generate forward-looking research in turbulent times.

The metaphorical frame is very dark. Inside, however, there is a triptych that retains some significant threads of optimism. Perhaps this is personal resilience trying to shine through. As I look back, I realize that while never enough is accomplished, gains that sabbatical invited, particularly in relation to writing, occurred.

I was discussing limens and liminality with a colleague the other day. It was interesting to observe myself as this crept into my conversation—there is, in fact, a just-noticeable difference that is a result of the time to reflect on gateways! This thought will be with me for some time, finding its way into other writing and thinking. This morning, as I talked with a student about thesis topics, I realized I was glad to be part of encouraging the student's thinking. Surely, this is also renewal.

I have had the voyage of discovery that is sabbatical. I have been asked about my time away, how it was. The assumption that all goes on as normal for those on sabbatical is fallacious but irrelevant to those who think they alone experienced rapid changes in expectations. The very nature of both pandemic and sabbatical determines that sabbatical in the time of COVID-19 is not a shared experience.

Will the way forward include optimistic progress involving growth intellectually, professionally, and personally? We often rely on our pasts to predict components of our futures. The future, however, is less predictable now. In the world of 2020, everything is suspended until further notice. Stay tuned.

Endnote

1   This famous phrase, "the better angels of our nature," was used by President Abraham Lincoln in his first inaugural address, in 1861. It is thought that he was familiar with Shakespeare's play *Othello*, one of the earlier uses of the phrase.

References

Andersen, J. P., Nielsen, M. W., Simone, N. L., Lewiss, R. E., & Jagsi, R. (2020). *COVID-19 medical papers have fewer women first authors than expected.* eLife (June 15), 1–7. https://doi.org/https://doi.org/10.7554/eLife.58807

Bartlett, R. (2011). Convocation address [Unpublished]. University of Toronto.

British Columbia Teachers' Federation v. British Columbia Public School Employers' Association. Supreme Court of Canada. 2014. 2014 SCC 70. 3 SCR 492.

Chamberlain v. Surrey School District No. 36. 2002. 2002 SCC 86. 4 SCR 710.

Cohen, L. (2016). *You want it darker.* Columbia Records.

Cromer and British Columbia Teachers' Federation. 1986 CanLII 143 (BC CA). https://canlii.ca/t/1p6ph

Gabster, B. P., van Daalen, K., Dhatt, R., & Barry, M. (2020). Challenges for the female academic during the COVID-19 pandemic. *The Lancet, 395*(10242), 1968–1970.

Lutes (Litigation Guardian of) v. Prairie View School Division No. 74. 1992. S.J. No 198 Saskatchewan Court of Queen's Bench. 101 Sask. R. 232.

MacKay, A. W., Sutherland, L., & Pochini, K. D. (2013). *Teachers and the law: Diverse roles and new challenges* (3rd ed.). Emond Publishing.

Madsen, T. E., Dobiesz, V., Das, D., Sethuraman, K., Agrawal, P., Zeidan, A., Goldbert, E., Safdar, B., & Lall, M. (2020). Unique risks and solutions for equitable advancement during the Covid-19 pandemic: Early experience from frontline physicians in academic medicine. *NEJM Catalyst: Innovations in care delivery.* Massachusetts Medical Society.

Multani v. Commission scolaire Marguerite-Bourgeoys. 2006. 2006 SCC 6. 1 SCR 256.

Sibbald, T. M., & Handford, V. (Eds.). (2017). *The academic gateway: Understanding the journey to tenure.* University of Ottawa Press.

Sibbald, T. M., & Handford, V. (Eds.). (2020). *Beyond the academic gateway: Looking back on the tenure-track journey.* University of Ottawa Press.

Tinker v. Des Moines Independent Community School District. 1969. 393 U.S. 503 (1969).

CHAPTER 5

(Re)Discovering Academia through a Sabbatical

Timothy Sibbald

In my fifth year in academia I earned tenure. It was a long, stressful journey, and much of the sixth year was spent reflecting on the process. I did reduce my workload where it was convenient to do so, but much remained unchanged. So, when the opportunity for a sabbatical arose, I had no hesitation and opted for a full-year sabbatical at 85 percent pay. To earn a leave required submitting a plan for the sabbatical that had to be approved, but that was all. There was no peer review or competition; it was a matter for the dean to render a decision about approval.

What that sabbatical proved to be is multi-faceted and sheds light on the core values of the academy. I take a self-study approach to analyzing my sabbatical year. However, where qualitative research methods use tools like the constant comparative method, I take a different approach and look at time usage within the context of achieving both the formal outcomes that were in my plan and a hidden agenda. It is the interplay of what I said I would do along with various unspoken truths that reveals the importance of the sabbatical.

Methodology: Time as a Variable

The year before I went on sabbatical I was at a conference in Regina and saw a film by Brian Stockton (2015) called *The Sabbatical*. It was about a fictional sabbatical that showed a struggling professor whose research slowed to a snail's pace. However, by the end of the film, due to unforeseen circumstances, the result was the achievement of the sabbatical objectives. The film resonated with the audience and was a fitting event close to the beginning of my own sabbatical. However, the major notion I took from it was the way time seemed to become non-linear in the fictional world of the lead character. I recognized a grain of truth but it was toward the end of my sabbatical year that I recognized the importance of this notion.

Methodologically, it is unusual to consider time the focal detail of a study. The reason for doing so is necessity. The thematic components of my sabbatical are clear—there is no way to alter the interpretation of a three-week holiday with no email. What is unclear is that the distribution of time between tasks is of primary importance. Ås (1978) writes: "Activities are segments of time" (p. 126), and identifies an activity as being composed of a fundamental unit, the "act." Within the sabbatical, the orchestration of acts associated with different objectives is the focus of this chapter.

To achieve the desired result, a grounded-theory approach to the usage of time was pursued. The strands of activity are analyzed in terms of thematic uses of time that were significant to the year. It was understood from the outset of this analysis that this is not simply a matter of time proportioning. It entails time on tasks, along with task switching, and the way usage of time was chosen. Consider, for example, approaches to studying during a course where some people may take a steady approach of routinely studying in roughly equal amounts of time, while others may cram before tests and exams. It is that usage of time in the context of a sabbatical with known strands of activity that is examined and is revealing about the nature of a sabbatical.

Themes: The Primary Players

The formal application for sabbatical mentioned four specific objectives: (1) to finish a book pertaining to higher education, (2) to pursue two key directions specific to mathematics-education research, (3) to continue work on a course support (that will ultimately become a book), and (4) to use a synthesis research method (also called meta-research). These were not new objectives but were intended to advance progress that had been slow. The objective was to accelerate progress and realize the understandings I had.

For the first item, the book proposal had been accepted for a book. It was the follow up to an earlier book. The first book had looked at tenure-track experiences, and the second book was to be edited during the sabbatical (along with co-editor Dr. Victoria [Tory] Handford). The focus of the second book was experiences around tenure decisions within faculties of education (Sibbald & Handford, 2020). During the period between the two books, Tory and I had discussed at length how to model tenure-track experiences. I had been an advocate of self-determination and intrinsic motivation being key attributes. Later, as the second book progressed, this idea was tempered as it did not generalize to the extent anticipated.

The research for one of the key directions in math education had been done and written in a pair of technical reports. The objective was to finally get around to writing an academic paper regarding it, a personal struggle because it required detailing an unorthodox methodology as well as the results of the methodology. An earlier experience publishing on the same topic had proved peer review can be difficult when both the method and consequences are examined. The other key direction in math education arose from a book I had edited and pointed to a need for thought on the philosophical underpinnings, pragmatic teaching considerations, and rehabilitative approaches to numeracy. This was somewhat open ended because two attempts to acquire funding had failed, and it seemed there was little appetite for a point of view that might challenge the status quo.

The course support was a draft document that would support my classes. The document was in excess of a hundred single-spaced pages. The goal was to add to this in a manner that might become a book proposal. The challenge being that there is little consensus about how to teach mathematics education. I knew this having seen two other book proposals and having had a proposal I had written undergo peer review. All three were rejected because of differences of opinion between the academics.

Using the synthesis method had been a goal for a long time. It was a method I had read about during my graduate studies, and I believed that it could be interpreted as a bridge between a literature review and research methodology. I had in mind that it would fit with objectives that entailed considerable literature review, such as the math-education resource that needed numerous links to the research literature, and examining aspects of higher education such as sabbaticals. There was, of course, a literature review in preparation of this volume, but the literature was not amenable to a synthesis analysis.

A Hidden Agenda

The primary players were the formal details of the sabbatical plan. What lurked behind the formal plan was the intention to find an improved work-life balance. I realized this was compromised by the amount of time that graduate studies had taken over the years. Then the extensive dedication to ensuring that the tenure deliberation was successful had encroached on the many responsibilities of daily life. In short, work had received a lot of attention and, given that there are only so many hours in the day, that means something had been receiving less attention.

There was more to it, however. Prior to pursuing graduate studies in education, I had sought out graduate programs in mathematics. At the time I found three master's-level programs that, in principle, I could pursue, though there were serious issues with each. In addition, I interpreted the state of graduate studies, particularly doctoral programs, as requiring that students be available between 10 a.m. and 2 p.m. some weekdays. This was in direct competition with my full-time job and was therefore not a credible option.

At the university in which I taught, there was a clause in the collective agreement that allowed me to take courses with tuition fees waived. I recognized an opportunity to both pursue graduate studies and realize a long-standing goal, but also to conduct research in the value of higher education in mathematics for teachers of mathematics. The goal would see earning a master's degree in mathematics, with much of it occurring during the sabbatical, but also recognizing that this degree had been deemed to be without value in academia because I had been hired on the basis of a terminal doctorate degree.

I saw the pursuit of the graduate degree as an opportunity that was time critical and that would have to fit with my sabbatical for it to be achievable. On the home front, this needed to come from the academic allocation of time, but that would see the sabbatical plan shortchanged in terms of time. I saw that as a challenge, but not insurmountable because I could achieve quite a bit in a compressed amount of time when motivated. That is, if I put my mind to it, I could operate efficiently and achieve the requirements of the sabbatical in less than 85 percent of the time required by the contract, or by working late into the night when my spouse would not be cognizant of what went into balancing work and life. I could, in effect, attain personal goals on two fronts.

A third hidden agenda was a desire for particular travel that was only an option in the off-season, which usually conflicted with the schedule of classes. This entailed two trips of approximately three weeks, one being in the fall semester and the other the winter semester. In both cases, the work-life balance was enacted through a refusal to take a computer or access email while gone. It was a period for recuperating and thought that would break from the routine.

Literature Review

The allocation of time, particularly when there is considerable time available, has received little attention in the literature. Often it is viewed through a managerial lens, both as time management and how tasks are sequenced or scheduled to achieve necessary outcomes in a timely fashion. An example is Jones and Howley (2009), who use allocation of time as a proxy of the level of attention superintendents give to various aspects of their roles. Simultaneously, usage of time can be interpreted across many contexts because the constituent elements of personal agency interact with time in ways that are largely independent of context. Consider, for example, that being "late" holds meaning regardless of what one is late for, and that often the context is simply a value-laden addition (late for a wedding vs. late for your wedding). For this reason, a broad search of literature was used to determine what interpretations of time have been used.

Jia et al. (2018) examined study habits. They distinguish analytic decision makers as using a value agenda and working to achieve the highest value items first, even when they have time to achieve all the work they set out to do. This contrasts with intuitive decision makers, who tend to be impulsive and impatient, with responses emphasizing speed rather than accuracy. The results are indicative of executive functions contributing to realizing value that is available through selectivity of activities.

Sebastian et al. (2018) identify contextual variables as well as distinctions between different time scales (time of day, day of week, season) relevant to the work of school principals. The context of the time usage is a busy role that is tied to the overall organizational structure of time.

Brotherson and Goldstein (1992) identify time as a critical constraint within the scope of providing care within a family. In particular, they identify the number of tasks, coordination between people, and flexibility in scheduling as key considerations. "Issues of time were interwoven with those of other family resources, such as families' physical environment, family structure and allocation of responsibilities, and personal abilities" (p. 522).

Ås (1978) provides hierarchal categories for distinguishing different usages of time. In order of importance, they are necessary time, contracted time, committed time, and free time. Necessary time entails time needed to meet physiological requirements, such as eating (and associated time), sleeping, and bathing. Contracted time is paid work time and associated activities such as commuting. Committed time includes activities that are unpaid and consequences of prior choices, such as home maintenance. Finally, with the lowest priority is free time, which is defined as not fitting the other categories.

Theoretically, the notion of cognitive flexibility (Scott, 1962) is the parent concept of cognitive shifting and task switching. Both of these are relevant, with cognitive shifting being suited to changes within academic work where the primary task is thinking, but the focal topic of the thought process is changed. Task switching is suited to changes that entail a change in physical activity, for example, if one is working on a piece of writing and stops in order to make dinner. The concept of cognitive flexibility encapsulates these types of changes, while allowing refinement between tasks that are strictly cognitive and those that have a change of physical activity.

Another concept that is well known in computer science is the notion of "time slicing" (Gerber & Hong, 1997). This refers to a process by which a microprocessor can be active with more than one task. In simple terms, time is divided up between the tasks, with regular task-switches, so that all tasks receive a share of the available time. The process of slicing time naturally allows prioritization of tasks and time slices may differ in size.

The literature review draws on several disparate views of usage of time. All have merit within particular contexts. Furthermore, they all resonate in one way or another with my own experiences with time through the sabbatical year.

The Sabbatical Year

In my case, the formal sabbatical year ran from July 1 to June 30. However, this is misleading in as much as courses in my faculty finish in late April and I am not involved in any summer classes. Therefore, my perception of the sabbatical, and the period I choose to examine, is from late April to late August of the following year.

The earliest stage of the sabbatical was dominated by prior commitments to the period of conferences, which emphasizes May. It is a routine period that focuses on presenting at different venues for the purpose of disseminating work that has been done. In the case of the sabbatical year, it ran the way it normally does and, in that sense, is not worthy of mention, except that it was contrasted by the sense of beginning my sabbatical and questioning why I was working as much as I was. This began a process of questioning the allocation of my time, in general terms, between different academic tasks. I did not change the conference pace I have routinely maintained but began applying executive-function thinking to the sabbatical process.

I recall being very happy-go-lucky about my time when it came to the final conference I had scheduled, essentially absorbing what I saw without feeling I had any rush to act on it. Alternatively, perhaps I thought that I had a significant amount of time to consider what I heard. In either case, there was a feeling that the pressure was off and much of my time was invested in thinking about the hidden agenda of my sabbatical.

Theme 1: The Slowdown

The earliest stage of the sabbatical, and just prior to ramping up to return to classes from the sabbatical, can be characterized as a slowdown. On entering the sabbatical, the conferences I had committed to were over and the next scheduled class was over a year away. The process of slowing down led me to avoid the university. This may sound odd, but some roles, such as health and safety inspections, continue year-round and I wanted to avoid being called on simply because I was on hand.

To alter my own mindset, I allowed some intuitive decision making (Jia et al., 2018) and considered what I should have done around the house to improve my own circumstance in a direct manner. My workshop, for example, had moved when I joined academia, but it had never regained its proper functionality. To address this my intuition led to significant upgrades in terms of organization and availability of electrical outlets. I was not, however, fully removed from academia because I do not slowdown well and continued with a low level of academic activity through June.

I had also chosen to continue my role as the editor of a teacher-oriented publication. It represented well-placed professional development in my career; in particular, copy-editing is often hidden from authors, denying them the opportunity to fine-tune their polishing skills. The editorial role requires three weeks of significant attention while an issue is being prepared. This only happens four times a year (July, October, January, and April), so while there was a slowdown, July raised my activity level.

Toward the end of the sabbatical, the slowdown was essentially taking advantage of the final opportunity and changing gears. It was a time to begin contemplating how I might alter my teaching, and a time for getting projects that had been in high gear for the sabbatical to slow to a pace manageable when teaching and service re-entered my role.

Theme 2: Fewer Tasks

From July to September, it took an active effort to balance academic activities with various home/life tasks. A key consumer of academic effort was a pair of courses toward the master's degree in mathematics. My educational research moved along slowly because it was squeezed between coursework and family priorities. The family aspect involved travelling to visit our children and extended family in various parts of the province. In one case, we helped with selecting a home as one of the children and their spouse were moving 400 kilometres closer to home for their work.

The period had analytical decision making (Jia et al., 2018), with values separating courses and family from sabbatical research that could have a lower priority. The number of tasks was relatively small and consistent with Brotherson and Goldstein (1992), coordinated between family members and scheduling. Additionally, the tasks that were being focused on where distinct, with two courses focused on substantially different areas of mathematics with different instructors, and various home repairs and visits with children being quite distinct as well.

The fewer-tasks period also occurred in the weeks leading up to Christmas, and again in March and July of the second year. The distinctive aspects of December and March was that family visits were at a minimum. Those periods had fewer tasks, but the tasks focused on my sabbatical research, particularly preparation of a book in December and other writing in March. In those seasons, home repairs slowed. There was a bathroom renovation in December, but it was done quite slowly, with periodic shopping trips and pauses of days between rounds of activity. Similarly, another renovation project began in March and continued through July at a steady but slow pace. In both cases, the time allocated to the renovation would be a larger or smaller part of the day, according to the other demands I had.

Theme 3: Rising Action

In October, and again in January, there were periods of rising action. We had three week-long trips in November and February that I intended to be genuine downtime. I decided I was not going to take a computer and was not going to check my email. The primary academic task on both trips entailed a lengthy math book that was used in the final course for my master's degree in the fall and continued as a guide for my thesis work that I was thinking about on the February trip.

The rising action saw changes in the pace of work on particular tasks and task switching to coordinate with my spouse. It was akin to the busyness of principals (Sebastian et al., 2018), whereas the intensity of activity increased and the temporal focus moved from the day of the week to the tasks of the day. I lengthened the day to get more done, knowing that I would catch up on rest during each trip.

The rising action preceded the trips and saw academic work intensify as the trips neared. Projects needed to be left at a suitable point to be picked up after the trip. Work around the house tailed off as preparation for the trips picked up. It was an intense period of increasing action until the denouement of leaving for each trip.

Theme 4: Free Time

Ås (1978) defines free time by it not being contracted, committed, or necessary time. That was the experience of travelling because we did not prepare meals, and the itinerary was set (by my spouse). The contracted aspect of my life was put on hold and the committed part focused on travel with my spouse. It could be argued that taking a math book was committed time, but when one is pursuing an area of genuine interest, as they should for a thesis, it is not committed time in the sense of an obligation that was unforeseen. Instead, it was a conscious choice to achieve a particular goal.

There is little to say about the free time. I did contemplate my lot in life and various aspects of the work-life balance I had experienced over the previous few years. In some ways, I was trying to make sense of the tenure-track experience, and what tenure meant. I mulled over why those structures exist and whether there are realistic alternatives.

It is also notable that while I had four hundred emails on return, I rapidly reduced that to about forty that required significant attention. Of those forty, I addressed all but three within a day. This put the "importance" of email in perspective and helped contextualize my work-life balance. This is larger than just the emails, as I recalled at the tail end of the second trip, fully seven weeks into the second semester, thinking that I hadn't even thought about the occurrence of the new semester. To me that was surprising but spoke to becoming rested. A colleague did not have the same reaction and forewarned me that sabbaticals teach you just how replaceable you are. That was not a concern I experienced.

Theme 5: Frenetic Task Switching

April brought a period like no other in the year. Various efforts had reached accomplishments and led to new opportunities. However, the new opportunities required substantial efforts. Just as finishing the course work for the master's degree wrapped up and the thesis was the one item left, it became a time-consuming focal task. It was, in fact, a very slow task, slower than I had anticipated.

While the usual tasks continued and began to require more time, several unforeseen tasks arose and a stage with too many tasks emerged. There were days where I would work on a task until it got challenging and would then simply change tasks. The notion was that doing something else would allow time to mull over the challenge. However, the juggling act with too many balls was not sustainable and ultimately the challenges piled up and had to be resolved.

The surprising aspect was how varied the challenges were: Determining the details of the duoethnography methodology. How to fix a puncture through the wall of a dishwasher? What happens when two monohedral tilings are overlaid to create a new tiling? Needing to identify a flaw in the process of making some picture frames that was leading to them not being quite rectangular?

The issue subsided as challenges got addressed. It seemed to be an episodic experience that was driven by a cascade of unexpected tasks in addition to planned tasks. However, it was likely exacerbated by being about the house through the day and the availability of time—"I had all day and didn't get that done!" Yet, in any role requiring regular hours this would not be a valid point of view.

Discussion

The five thematic structures of time usage account for the entire year. While I have presented them largely in chronological order, they occurred at different stages through the year. Each had a definitive feel and was distinct from the other periods. I do not suggest that other usages of time could not arise; in fact, I am quite certain, especially in talking about future sabbaticals, that other structures can occur. That suggests that this may be viewed as a call for attention to a point of view that I find quite informative about the sabbatical, because it is not grounded in the details but has structural significance.

The slowdown is characteristic of major shifts of direction. It arose at the beginning of the sabbatical, when I had to acclimatize to the new structure, and it arose in the summer ahead of returning to ramp up for fall classes. It is the proverbial calm before the storm. I suspect there is a degree of intention driving it within the context of one being able to slowdown.

The few-tasks period is the personal sweet spot, when I can achieve the most. It is an equilibrium that emerges when frenetic periods calm down or because of selectively initiating tasks after a slowdown. It is measured and allows variations in time allocation to correspond to the progress one is making. However, it does not stall because there are only a few tasks and the cognitive load does not hinder progressing. So, unlike the frenetic period, variations in time allocation are not unwieldy, rather they are a tool for enhancing effectiveness.

Rising action is typical ahead of deadlines. What made it unusual with the sabbatical was that it was life events, not work deadlines, which drove the rising action. The distinction meant that it was an internal locus of control driving the rising action rather than an externally imposed obligation. One could argue that the distinction lies in having control over how one responds to missing a self-imposed deadline, where one might not be able to influence the consequences otherwise.

Free time was not in abundance, but it did get carved out. I found work-life balance to be somewhat contradictory. What if I pursued a doctorate and designed my research program around activities that I find interesting? In this scenario, the conflict is an internal challenge of understanding how the work I am doing dovetails with life. I found myself asking why I find meaning in what I am doing but asking this without hesitation that I do. That led me to wonder what retirement, which is a long way off, will look like, and whether my current fervor for what I am doing will have run its course by then.

Frenetic task switching was a depressing period of the sabbatical. Luckily, it only arose once and was episodic. It was a lesson in taking a measured approach to what one chooses to engage with. There will always be uncontrollable activities that arise but controlling what one can ensures that there is time in the day to address the unforeseen items that arise. It was a period that had implications for the service aspect of my role beyond the sabbatical. There are service roles that require significant commitments, and the frenetic task-switching period was indicative of needing to be measured in considering the extent of time commitments.

Conclusion

The sabbatical is unlike any other experience I have had in my working life. I achieved a lot, though much of the end product seems to be an internal balance within the role. The plan I had was realized but there is much more that goes on with a sabbatical. In preparing the literature review for this book (which was done in conjunction with this chapter being written) I wondered about the implications for my own teaching and productivity.

The short answer is that my sabbatical had nothing directly to do with my teaching except to allow me to come back to it with fresh eyes and enthusiasm. I am sure I will revamp my classes, and that will take time, but that may well be seen as a decline in teaching scores. I anticipate next year will see my classes being refreshed and part of the reason is an infusion of ideas from my research, but it is also due to conversing with the instructors who took over during my absence.

Productivity is a devilish concept that is ill-defined in academia. I will come off the sabbatical more focused on a few projects that are time consuming. That will likely reduce my general "output" but shows a maturation through the sabbatical toward achieving a sustained effort to specific projects. My sense is that the sabbatical has allowed me to address a wide range of interests so that I have recognized particular activities that have significant potential to flourish. However, by flourish I mean all around growth in my research, support of student opportunities, sustainable long-term knowledge generation, and a philosophically based sense that they are projects where there will be a long-term definitive benefit that goes beyond my personal need for tenure and the like.

References

Ås, D. (1978). Studies of time-use: Problems and prospects. *Acta Sociologica, 21*(2), 125–141.

Brotherson, M. J., & Goldstein, B. L. (1992). Time as a resource and constraint for parents of young children with disabilities: Implications for early intervention services. *Topics in Early Childhood Special Education, 12*(4), 508–527.

Gerber, R., & Hong, S. (1997). Slicing real-time programs for enhanced schedulability. *ACM Transactions on Programming Languages & Systems, 19*(3), 525–555.

Jia, X., Li, W., Cao, L., Li, P., Shi, M., Wang, J., Cao, W., & Li, X. (2018). Effect of individual thinking styles on item selection during study time allocation. *International Journal of Psychology, 53*(2), 83–91.

Jones, K., & Howley, A. (2009). Contextual influences on superintendents' time usage. *Education Policy Analysis Archives, 17*(23), 1–24.

Scott, W. A. (1962). Cognitive complexity and cognitive flexibility. *Sociometry, 25*(4), 405–414.

Sebastian, J., Camburn, E. M., & Spillane, J. P. (2018). Portraits of principal practice: Time allocation and school principal work. *Educational Administration Quarterly, 54*(1), 47–84.

Sibbald, T., & Handford, V. (2020). A substantive model of Canadian tenure-track experiences. *International Journal of Humanities and Education, 6*(14), 455–469.

Stockton, B. (Director). (2015). *The sabbatical*. [Film]. Autumn Productions.

SECTION 2

First Sabbaticals with Significant Travel

The first section highlights that a sabbatical can be a continuation of a program of research without an unusual increase in travel. While that is the case, there can be benefits to travel. The flexibility of time provided by the sabbatical facilitates realizing opportunities at a distance. The authors in this section have used travel as part of their sabbatical for various reasons that, in all cases, includes academic enrichment.

The section begins with Anahit Armenakyan writing about using travel as a means of reconnecting with her family and roots in Armenia. Throughout her chapter there is a richness of teaching, conferences, and research ideas that arise. She engages culturally, and a fusion of academic engagement, personal learning, and the circumstances results. The aspect of fusion is necessary since the scope of what she achieves academically could not be done solely on a professional expense allowance. While some academics wrestle with balancing work and life, the chapter highlights a productive balancing act that works in an interesting way.

Pei-Ying Lin travelled to Taiwan and engaged in a research laboratory that was relevant to her overall area of research. The travel allowed her to reconnect with her Taiwanese culture and family, while using research tools that were not available at her home institution. The experience clearly fused the learning of novel research methods with a lived experience. She speaks of reconnecting with the culture of her childhood. Yet she describes the overall experience as uneven.

The final chapter in this section, written by Lee Anne Block, explores place-based learning. Travel allowed for place-based learning in a very different location. The contextual aspects evolve and the experience, along with the learning arising from it, came home. Lee Anne then engaged that knowledge in a place-making effort contributing to her own community. This chapter, unlike the two others in the section, is very much about the transference of expertise.

The chapters collectively highlight the benefits of travel during a sabbatical. It is clear the authors were successful and had benefits beyond the usual academic objectives. Yet, all three chapters are distinct; again, highlighting the richness of texture that sabbaticals yield.

Note: Among the authors in this section, Lee Anne has contributed to two earlier books about academic experiences during the tenure-track stage and around the time of tenure, allowing the interested reader to connect her chapter to her longitudinal history.

CHAPTER 6

Life on the Two Sides of the Pond

Anahit Armenakyan

"I'll do that during my sabbatical!" I was having a Scarlett O'Hara moment time and again in my pre-sabbatical years.[1] That *that* was quite broad: a project with one colleague, a paper with another, a grant application . . . . The list kept getting longer and longer with each passing year. I do not think I am alone in this experience. Many in academia might say there is nothing strange in this thinking and wonder why I am making a point of it: we are all equally time-deprived and worry excessively about tenure, promotions, publications, performance reviews, teaching, and life that goes on outside of academia. Normally, I would agree, but writing this reflective chapter about my sabbatical journey in an attempt to understand my experiences has led me to believe there was something else there. But first, let me introduce myself. My name is Anahit Armenakyan, I am an immigrant from Armenia, and this is my sabbatical story.

I spend my everyday emotional life on two continents, North America and Eurasia, I guess, since Armenia, my motherland, is situated on the border of Europe and Asia, and there is no consensus on where it belongs. I find it ironic that I come from a country that is difficult to pin to any specific continent because I have difficulties understanding where I belong and what country (Canada vs. Armenia) I call *home*. When I came back from my sabbatical leave and was asked how it went and what I did, I heard myself telling the story of my journey using the phrase "back home" whenever I was talking about Armenia, yet I vividly recall thinking of Canada as *back home* when I was in Armenia. To further confuse the issue, I was quite selective during my sabbatical overseas travels on which country was *home*, quite an interesting phenomenon for a researcher who started her academic career with country-image and country-of-origin research (Heslop et al., 2010). As I kept reflecting on my sabbatical experience, I could not help but think how the years leading to it influenced my sabbatical plans and experiences. Putting on my researcher hat, I decided to narrate and capture possible interpretations of the nature of these experiences while trying to make sense of them. As I was thinking about the structure of this chapter, I tried to visualize my experiences and came up with a diagram that brings together the main themes around which this whole journey evolved (figure 6.1). There was a fluidity of theme and experiences so intertwined that it was impossible to draw clear borders between those personal, professional, and social experiences (Onorato & Turner, 2004) affecting my journey.

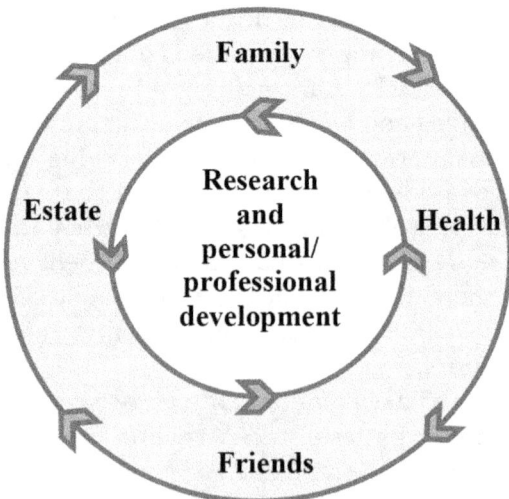

Figure 6.1. *Anahit's sabbatical.*

The Beginning

To choose is also to begin. —Author Unknown

Whenever I introduce a new concept to my students, I like finding its roots or historical meanings. In the same vein, I cannot speak about my sabbatical journey without reflecting on the experiences that led to it.

I never thought I would build my career in academia, though I had experience teaching in post-secondary institution long before I moved to Canada from Armenia. I taught computer science in the National Polytechnic University of Armenia. However, at that time I was not sure that this was the path for me. After a brief break from teaching, which led to a career switch from IT to business management and some in-field work experience, I realized that I missed being in the classroom: I loved challenging students and being challenged by them; I loved the interaction, and even that strange performance-like feeling. So, about fifteen years ago I applied for doctoral studies in Canada with the intention of building an academic career. I had already visited Canada before—while studying at the University of Pittsburgh, I drove to Montréal and Québec City as a birthday gift to myself and I felt strangely at *home* in this new country. I had no hesitation that Canada was my destiny, and, thus, I was not surprised when Carleton University accepted me into their doctoral program.

My plane landed in Toronto on a late December evening in 2005. Freezing rain and Christmas decorations in the airport welcomed me. The flight from Toronto to Ottawa was delayed, but a stranger—an immigrant himself, from Guyana—who sat next to me on the plane to Toronto arranged for his sister to come and pick me up so that I did not spend the night in the airport. I had a soft bed, a warm shower, and a wonderful family that took me in. In many ways it felt that they were Canada herself welcoming me. My whole trip from Yerevan (Armenia) to Ottawa (Canada) through Moscow, Frankfurt, and Toronto was full of kind people that stepped up and made my journey as pleasant as it could be. I took it all as a sign, being in Canada was meant for me. My goal was clear—I had to do whatever it took to become an academic in Canada.

In my first years of doctoral studies, I transitioned from being an international student to a Canadian citizen. I put in efforts to become fully integrated into Canadian society and yet I was still experiencing otherness (Badenhorst, 2017). Those years were full of struggles that are well known by any doctoral student, and particularly by any immigrant doctoral student. Questioning and doubting every single decision made, fighting with data analysis and thesis writing, balancing life and work—these are the daily battles for any doctoral student. There was another layer for me, though—I did not have the means or flexibility to go *home*—Armenia—and be with my parents, siblings, aunts and uncles, and cousins (have you seen *My Big Fat Greek Wedding*? Substitute Greek with Armenian and you will get the picture of a typical Armenian family!) At the end of the first year of my studies, I lost my uncle to a heart attack. We were very close. It hurt deeply that I could not attend his funeral and say my final goodbye. I did not realize how the lack of closure impacted me until two years later when I visited my family on the occasion of my first nephew being born. I took a month off my studies and hugged the newborn member of my family on his thirteenth day of life. It was an amazing experience, yet somewhere in the back of my mind an annoying thought was whispering that being so far away will rob me of playing an active part in his life, and in the lives of my other family members for that matter. The thought of becoming the *other* by those who were *mine* was unbearable. I decided that I would use every single opportunity to be with those who matter so much to me.

I had to find ways to be or feel closer to them; I showered them with gifts (Komter & Vollebergh, 1997), scheduled weekly meetings via Skype to keep in touch despite their reluctance to use a new technology at the time (Vroman et al., 2015), and looked for conferences that allowed detours to visit my family (Davidovitch & Eckhaus, 2018). When I shared my thoughts with Canadian friends, they did not understand the issue. "Why can they not just come to visit you?" Indeed, why can't they? That's where I had to remind my Canadian friends how privileged they are to have a passport that opens up many borders. I had to remind them that I am an immigrant from a country that is not a part of the Commonwealth. I am from a country whose citizens cannot just buy a ticket and join their families abroad whenever and wherever they want, unless they are granted permission to do so—a visa is required, which has to be applied for and paid for, with no guarantee that it will be granted. Besides, the cost of travel was too high for both my family's income and my student income. My dream was that once I graduated and found a position with stable income, I would be able to apply for my family members' visas and support their visits to Canada, or travel to visit them more often. I consider myself lucky—almost immediately after my thesis defense I became a full-time tenure-track assistant professor in the School of Business at Nipissing University. The first milestone was reached! I was full of optimism that everything from there would be smooth sailing. I had my stable income, I bought a house, I leased a car, and I arranged for my mother's visitor visa and had the pleasure of showing her Niagara Falls. I made a list of family members to visit me in Canada and developed a timetable for their visa applications. I had everything planned. Or so I thought.

My clear sailing ran into storms and excruciating winds. In the midst of the first ever Nipissing University Faculty Association strike, I received a late-night call from my brother. My aunt, who was like a mother to me, had suddenly passed away. I was devastated, I felt guilty for not inviting her to Canada first—after all, she was the one who would have been able to fully appreciate my achievements being herself the head of a geodesy department in her university. But how could I have foreseen her death: she was younger than my mother, she was healthier. I flew home to say my last good-bye to the person who supported and inspired me so much. I reached my little town in the south of Armenia, after more than twenty-five hours of travel, just half an hour before the funeral. I had my closure; I had my good-bye. She gave me so much while she was alive, but she gave me even more when she left: she gave another closure that I needed—as I shed tears for her, I felt I also finally said my goodbyes to my uncle. My aunt left something else for me, a reminder that one must cherish those one has, never taking them for granted; a reminder that life is short and every single moment counts; a reminder that plans can change in a second. As I returned to Canada a week after the funeral, I started putting together my application for tenure and promotion, and began thinking about my sabbatical—I wanted to be prepared for something that was still two years away even though I knew that things could change.

The Sabbatical

It does not matter how slowly you go, so long as you do not stop.
—*Confucius*

Nipissing University defines a sabbatical leave as "a leave from a tenured Member's normal responsibilities of teaching and service to focus on research and scholarship" (FASBU CA, 2015–2019, p. 92). By this definition, I was expected to increase my knowledge, further my research, stimulate intellectual interest, strengthen my contacts with the worldwide community of scholars, and, thus, enhance my contribution to the university on my return. When, on February 1, I received a letter from the dean granting my first twelve-month sabbatical, I was excited. It was the result of significant preparation, where I connected with colleagues in Canada and other countries for collaboration, applied for conferences, arranged with friends to host them in Armenia and for them to host me in Europe, and I started on visa paperwork for my family to join me in my travels. I was thrilled—the sabbatical was promising to be full of new places and cultures, while doing what I love and sharing those experiences with people I love. Everything was clear and simple. Or so I thought.

Although my sabbatical officially started on July 1, it felt like I started it when I landed in Vilnius on May 17. In only four days my first course of Integrated Marketing Communications in Vilnius University would start.[2] While this was a teaching experience, by all counts it was not normal. Not only was I entering a completely new cultural environment, I was also to experience a new teaching delivery approach—an intensive block teaching.[3] Not surprisingly, I was nervous. However, the friendly atmosphere in the marketing department in the Faculty of Economics and Business made the first hours very welcoming. As I entered the classroom full of mature students, I realized that they were as curious about me as I was about them. We spent the first half of the lecture time getting acquainted, and I quickly learned that I had a very mixed student body as the class was comprised of Lithuanian students, international students, and participants of the Erasmus Programme.[4] The challenges were similar to any other diverse class of students I had in Canada: I needed to find something that interested them all on an individual and a group level, and I also had to make sure that the long, 3.5-hour lectures at the end of their busy day were enjoyable as much as educational.

I discovered very early on that my Lithuanian students were very shy to speak up, so I used a few games to create a more relaxed atmosphere (jumping ahead, I used these game experiences to develop a conference paper closer to the end of my sabbatical). By the end of the second week, I had full-force in-class participation. The two weeks of daily lectures flew in a blink of an eye. To celebrate a successful end of the course and, coincidentally, my birthday, I decided to do something daring and challenging—a hot-air balloon ride over the city. I was always afraid of heights, yet somehow I was filled with a calm sense of pure joy as I was flying above the city that I was becoming fond of. As I was telling this story to the head of the marketing department in Vilnius University, he shared in his turn that students' feedback on the course was extremely positive and he would like me to come to Vilnius for the next year. I readily accepted the invitation as this was most definitely a fulfilling experience. Not only had I acquired an amazing experience teaching in a new cultural environment, and learned about the specifics of marketing and advertising in this Baltic country, but I also put a new teaching delivery method into my teaching toolbox. I like experimenting with different modes of teaching as it allows for a better understanding of the pros and cons of each, and so I considered my Lithuanian experience to be a useful and promising start to the sabbatical, and then headed to *home*—Armenia!

Health comes before making a livelihood. —*Yiddish proverb*

As I was making exciting plans for the rest of the sabbatical, my increasingly annoying breathing problems were getting worse. Sleepless nights and constant tiredness were becoming overwhelming and taking a toll. I have always had breathing problems because of a deviated septum, but they had worsened in the years leading to the sabbatical. Ignoring this was no longer an option and it was becoming clear that my grand plans for the sabbatical needed to include some smaller (or so I thought) but important adjustments. My family doctor in Canada informed me that these issues were considered non-life threatening and low priority in Ontario, which could mean an uncertain schedule for surgery and a long wait time (Fraser Institute, 2017). Such uncertainty was not an option for me as the required procedure also needed several weeks for recovery. Besides, while in many cases patients are allowed to go to work a few days after such surgery, given the public nature of my work—lecturing in front of students—I was uncomfortable with the idea of standing in front of students with a swollen, bruised face. While the procedure was considered straightforward, I was concerned about being alone, on my own. Who knows what kinds of complications there might be? Not surprisingly, I was waiting for my sabbatical to deal with this issue while I had time away from teaching and closer to my family.

Therefore, upon my arrival to Armenia from Lithuania, I arranged for a consultation with a doctor. The consultation and a few tests revealed that I would also need some facial plastic correction, which meant that the recovery time would eliminate any possibility of travel for at least two or three months. Initially, I thought that I would only need a couple of weeks for recovery, and, hence, I was planning to have the surgery in July, between two conferences I already planned for June (one in Armenia, one in Portugal) and a planned trip to Montréal in September to continue working on one of my research projects. However, with this new information, I had to revise my plans, and revise them drastically. The surgery had to be postponed until the end of November and, luckily, the sabbatical allowed for that flexibility. However, it meant that I had to renovate my Yerevan apartment: the heating system was broken. Winters in Yerevan could be severe even for someone who is used to -40 Celsius in North Bay, Ontario. This renovation was not something I had planned for—as I was hoping to spend the winter of that year with my parents in my hometown in the south of Armenia—and it was forcing major modifications to my plans.

Completely taken by the upcoming surgery and the necessity for renovation, I could not fully concentrate on my existing projects. I felt guilt for not paying due attention to my planned research and was also overwhelmed by the anxiety of the surgery and the disruptive nature of renovations. To cope with this stress, I did the only thing I knew would help—I put on my researcher's hat and dived into readings related to the upcoming procedure. I learned that my desire to be with family and my anxiety in such a situation are not unusual: family support was found to be particularly important for health and recovery among females living alone (Okkonen & Vanhanen, 2006). The more I read about the procedure, the more curious I became of the phenomenon of medical tourism. One day, during a breakfast meeting with a friend of mine—a young Canadian Armenian fellow who expatriated to Armenia—I learned that he is a founder of a medical-tourism firm and has clients who come to Armenia from Europe and North America for similar procedures. That was an unexpected and, frankly, exciting discovery. As we discussed his business and my surgery, we made plans to work on a case study that would present his digital concierge company—GetTreated.co—and the Armenian medical-tourism industry.[5] Jumping ahead, by the end of my sabbatical leave, I had our first draft ready and tested in the classroom by a Nipissing University colleague. The case study was positively accepted by the students and generated good discussions. It also had another benefit that I discovered later when I was back to my teaching duties in Canada. You see, being away for so long created a gap and many of the students whom I was teaching upon return did not know me, yet they linked my name to the case study they were exposed to a year earlier, which made the transition from the sabbatical to full-time duties smoother.

As I returned to Armenia from the June conference in Portugal, I immediately started the renovation works, which were required for post-surgery recovery stay in Yerevan. I was naive in my assumption that I would be able to work on research projects while the contractors were making changes in my tiny bachelor flat. The noise, the dust, and the summer heat were unbearable. This renovation was becoming excessively disruptive when an unexpected call from a university classmate and a close friend brought news of her visit to Yerevan, together with an invitation to stay with her. It was a welcome escape: while at her place, not only was I able to work on some of the research projects but I also spent some time with her and absorbed the offerings of my favourite city in the world. I knew there would not be another chance for a long stay for another seven or so years, so I took the opportunity to immerse myself into the cultural and culinary atmosphere of this vibrant city that I missed so much. By mid-September, about a week before my departure to Montréal, the renovations were sufficiently completed, which meant that I was prepared for the surgery scheduled for early December. Most importantly, I finished the draft case study on medical tourism, completed on-field data collection for my ongoing ecotourism in Armenia project, and conducted interviews for the Armenian part of a cross-cultural study (involving Canada, Armenia, Italy) on organic-produce purchase behaviour.

As I returned to Canada in the fall, I knew that I had to do as much as possible before the downtime imposed by the upcoming surgery. Those two months in Montréal were packed with networking and work on the research projects I had already lined up. Since I had accepted an invitation to give a talk at HEC Montréal—the graduate business school of the Université de Montréal—within the seminars organized by the Groupe de Recherche en Affaire Internationales in November, I decided to stay in Montréal, where I could continue my project on organic-produce purchase behaviour, this time interviewing Quebec residents. Simultaneously, I applied and secured funding for a project on youth sport participation within the context of the rapidly approaching 2018 Summer Youth Olympic Games. I also had a chance to participate in a conference organized by the Sport Canada Research Initiative, where I presented my earlier findings from the 2016 Winter Youth Olympic Games.

In late November, I returned to Yerevan for the surgery. The evening before the surgery I was comforted by my mother's and sister's support. As I took some photos of my face, I caught myself thinking that I am engaging in a classic divestment ritual I referred so many times while delivering lectures on consumer behaviour—I was preparing to part with something that had been part of me for over forty years, something that contributed to my identity and self-concept (Lastovicka & Fernandez, 2005). The surgery was a success and the recovery went well. The doctor was surprised that the bruises were completely gone in only two weeks, but I was still not allowed to travel. Those couple of months, as expected, were very slow in terms of research productivity because of the medications I was prescribed, but I took that time to explore a couple of online courses I was curious about. By the time the doctor cleared me for travel, I had completed an online course on First Nations principles of OCAP (ownership, control, access, and possession) offered by Algonquin College, in Ottawa; two online courses on artificial intelligence from Helsinki University; and a digital marketing course from the University of Illinois. I am convinced that the support I received from my family was the major factor of my fast recovery (Cardoso-Moreno & Tomás-Aragones, 2017); they were the reason I was able to do at least some professional work during that recovery time. They were the reason I felt strong enough to continue the sabbatical on my own and head to Università Politecnica delle Marche (Ancona, Italy) in April, where, in a position of visiting researcher, I supervised the Italian stage of data collection for the organic-produce project and delivered a guest lecture on service marketing within the context of medical tourism.

Family can make you or break you. —Armenian saying

Family is everything to me. Even though I have been independent since early adulthood, no matter where I go or what I do, the bonds with my parents, siblings, aunts/uncles, and cousins remain strong. We keep in touch, supporting and pushing each other. However, physical distance and markedly different cultural environments were slowly corroding our relationships. Studies in psychology and health have documented the impact of physical distance on frequency of contact, intimacy of relationships, and psychological well-being between grandparents and grandchildren (Taylor et al., 2005; Nesteruk & Marks, 2009; Liu et al., 2018), spouses (Copeland & Norell, 2002), and extended families (Segal & Marelich, 2011; Bevan & Sparks, 2011; Bevan et al., 2012). The findings show that physical distance contributes to social distance as family members grow apart while going through separate cultural experiences; additional relationship efforts are required to stay in touch.

With each visit to Armenia, I heard with increasing frequency phrases like "you have forgotten how things are done here" and "you are not in Canada." The growing disconnect was contributing to the increasing sense of otherness in my homeland and my family, while maintaining that identity was contributing to the same feeling of otherness in Canada (Badenhorst, 2017). I was given a "licence to leave" (Baldock, 2000, p. 209), with full family support to advance my career in Canada, yet I still felt guilt and frustration for being so far away. I thought I was not doing enough to be emotionally closer to my family as my years in Canada increased. I worried about the health of my aging parents and, living in the safety of Canada's stability, was apprehensive about the possibility of military escalation (that occurred after this chapter was submitted) on the border of our homeland.[6] Thus, I used the sabbatical leave as an opportunity to reconnect with my whole family. I knew that by the end of this academic leave I had to produce a report highlighting my academic achievements and research, so the question was: How could I dovetail family and research?

One benefit of academic life is that it allows for conference and research travel. Not surprisingly, similar to many of my colleagues, I chose conferences based on my research interests, but also based on the destination (Dann, 1997; Davidson, 2003; Davidovitch & Eckhaus, 2018). Usually, I would arrive to a conference host country a week earlier or extend the stay for another week to explore the destination as a tourist, which, I believe, adds to my understanding of place branding and tourism—among my research interests. The conference in Porto, Portugal, presented a perfect opportunity to take my parents and my sister with me (luckily, they were granted visas to enter Portugal). I have never travelled with them before, and I was anxious and thrilled at the same time. The flight was long; by the time we arrived, we were tired and hungry. As soon as we settled in our rental apartment, we went out for a bite. As we were dining, our waiter surprised us all with wishing bon appétit in perfect Armenian. We learned from him that Porto had a long history of Armenian connections and that there is even a little street called Armenia. We took that serendipitous moment as a sign that our trip would be wonderful. (Now that I am writing these memories, I cannot help but think that my whole sabbatical was full of similar signs that in one way or another connected me to one of my *homes*, Armenia and Canada.) That week before the conference was filled with moments that brought our family closer together, recreating connections and re-establishing supportive relationships (Durko & Petrick, 2016; Yoo et al., 2016). Together we went to the famous Livraria Lello bookstore, enjoyed amazing fado performances, visited museums and galleries, and tried Portuguese food and wine. But the most wonderful experience was watching World Cup 2018 football (soccer) games on the huge screens erected on the squares of Porto with my father: that kind of father-daughter quality time was precious.

On our last day in Porto, we saw a sudden increase in the number of people on the streets; they were walking everywhere and hitting each other and everyone else with big plastic hammers; this was supposed to bring good luck for the year to come. By pure coincidence we were in Porto during its annual São João festival. There was a lot of joy and happiness on the streets; people were making long tables in the neighborhoods, frying sardines and inviting passersby to enjoy them, as well as dancing and celebrating. Closer to midnight, lanterns and fireworks ornamented the sky. Such serendipitous moments cannot be planned and they brought a new level of experience to our family reunion (Shaw, 2010; Yoo et al., 2016). For the past fifteen years, I dreamt about sharing my travels with my family and it was amazing to experience these moments together. However, family vacations are indeed a double-edged sword (Chesworth, 2003). I needed some me time to prepare for the conference, but struggled while performing multiple duties as caregiver, negotiator, translator, daughter, and sister. I also made a note for future family travels to make sure to arrange for time for each member to be on their own (Yoo et al., 2016), and that meant that travels would have to be in countries where my family, fluent in Armenian and Russian languages, could navigate on their own.

Such an opportunity presented itself closer to the end of the sabbatical. During the conference in Porto, I had successfully pitched the idea of a special session in sport marketing to the organizers of the 2019 World Marketing Congress, in Edinburgh, and I had already accepted the invitation for a second round of teaching in Vilnius University. So, I gave my family two options for another family getaway: Scotland or Lithuania. While both destinations were very appealing and exciting, I was relieved when my father announced that their choice was the Baltic state. When I asked my mother why they chose Vilnius over Edinburgh, she confided that while she thoroughly enjoyed Portugal, at times she wished she could be on her own, and that is why they decided to join me in Lithuania for a week before the start of my second teaching session in Vilnius.[7] Just like in Portugal, we explored wonderful museums and castles, took a daytrip to Trakai, and, just like in Portugal, while walking along the Constitution Wall in the self-proclaimed Republic of Užupis, we stumbled upon an Armenian factor: there, on the wall, was an Armenian version of the Užupis constitution.[8] On our last days in Vilnius, we enjoyed an amazing performance of a young talented Armenian cellist, Narek Hakhverdyan, with the Lithuanian National Symphony Orchestra, and his out-of-program performance of a song by Komitas brought tears to our eyes.[9] Music has such a way of steering emotions—I could also see, while my family enjoyed their trip to Lithuania, they were ready to go home.

As wonderful as catching up was, I still had the feeling of guilt: my brother and his family were missed in those travels. Milardo (2009) points out that while there are many studies on contemporary families, the focus is usually on marriage and parenting, leaving aunts and uncles out of the scope. Yet my aunts and uncles played pivotal roles in my life, and I intended to do the same for my nephews. In some ways, the desire to be closer to my nephews was self-serving. I do not have children of my own and looked for ways to strengthen my relationships by engaging in different activities with them (Langer & Ribarich, 2007). While it was easy to be the holiday-fun, foreign aunt in their early years, and they were excited to talk to me on Skype, the closer they got to the teenage years, the more difficult it was to maintain the bond. So, amid my travels, work, renovation, and surgery during the sabbatical I made many trips to the town where my brother lives. A New Year's celebration was the first in almost twenty years when we had a family gathering with all eight of us being physically together—I could not wish for more!

Do not have 100 rubles, have 100 friends. —*Russian proverb*

Throughout my sabbatical journey, I was blessed with the support of my wonderful friends and colleagues: whether it was an escape from construction or a connection that led to a guest presentation or development of a case study! There is a word in Armenian for a network that reflects a person's social and professional connections and environment in its totality—*shrjapat* (/ʃrdʒɑˈpɑt/). The larger the *shrjapat*, the more social capital one has. *Shrjapat* is not something that could be easily defined. One person may belong to many *shrjapats*—familial, personal, professional, social—which might or might not overlap. These leaderless groups define who you are (Lourie & Davtyan, n.d.). The professional aspect is not dissimilar to networking, which is essential for developing research collaborations. In many ways, it could be translated to the expression "you are who you know and who you know defines who you are." This suits me well being an extrovert with a strong need for social connectedness and belongingness (Baumeister & Leary, 1995).

I have always appreciated the value of these *shrjapats*. As long as I can remember, I have liked meeting new people and establishing friendships or collaborations. In many ways, this desire for connectedness developed to compensate for being distant from my family in my early years of studies and continued as I moved to new cities, new countries, and new universities. I cannot recall any stage of my life when I did not tap into my *shrjapat*: family members, friends, colleagues, and acquaintances. They helped during my academic studies, they provided a shoulder to cry on from a broken heart or homesickness, they pointed out potential jobs, they assisted in navigating new cultural environments, they contributed to my well-being; the list is endless (Lee et al., 2008; Yoon et al., 2008; Hendrickson et al., 2011). These connections are not something I take for granted. There is a saying in Armenian: "One hand cannot clap alone," and in a hope to bring value to the table, I gladly invest in maintaining these relationships (Blieszner & Roberto, 2004). In many ways, my *shrjapat* shaped my individuality (Deutsch & Krauss, 1965) and, most definitely, it influenced my whole sabbatical leave.

The sabbatical introduced something I was always dreaming about: hosting friends and colleagues in my homeland. I already had friends visit me in Canada, which in many ways made me feel like an ambassador of Canada and helped me in reassuring myself that I am a full member of Canadian society (Griffin, 2015). However, my previous short visits to Armenia did not allow for the privilege of showing friends and colleagues the beauty of my homeland. So, when I made my sabbatical plans, I sent an invitation to my network of friends and colleagues to join me in Armenia.

One sunny summer day, when my renovations were close to the end, I received a call from a friend in Ottawa inquiring about the possibility of visiting Armenia. I was curious how she would feel in Armenia: being ethnically Armenian, she had never visited the country of her ancestors. I made a long list of places I wanted to take her. I wanted her to taste the real taste of apricots kissed by the Armenian sun and try *lavash*—traditional Armenian thin bread—baked in a *tonir* (also known as a tandoor). It was a rewarding experience: while seeing how she connected to the spirit of the land, I was reconnecting with it myself. Once again, the moments of unplanned discoveries elevated our experiences: while admiring the carvings of crosses and the architecture of the medieval monastery of Geghard,[10] we suddenly heard heavenly sounds of *sharakans*—Armenian chant liturgical songs—performed a cappella by a female quintet. When I was taking my friend to the airport, she announced that she is returning to Armenia next summer. The visit was a success! I felt an accomplishment in being an ambassador of Armenia and felt reassured that I have not lost touch, in all these years living abroad, with the land that brought me up.

Closer to the end of my sabbatical leave, when I was back to Armenia and working on the presentation for the upcoming Armenian Economic Association conference and data collection for the study of ethnocentrism and country image, I received another call. This time it was from a close Turkish friend who had been my roommate while studying in the University of Pittsburgh. If you know anything about Armenians and Armenian history, you know about the genocide of ethnic Armenians in the Ottoman Empire during the First World War. Despite all warnings coming from our respective circles about Turkish–Armenian friendship, we developed a close bond, finding lots of similarities and likings (Berg, 1984). Being a university professor herself, she had many conference travels, and I already had a chance to host her in Canada a few years earlier. Now that I was in Armenia and she was teaching in Turkish Cyprus, it seemed to be the perfect opportunity to host her in Armenia.

Very soon we both discovered that strained relationships between our countries, or should I say the lack of any diplomatic relationships between them, introduced some challenges.[11] Until her call, I did not realize how many place names in historic Armenia, and nowadays located in Turkey, we have in modern Armenia. Moreover, the two-headed Mount Ararat—the most sacred and identity-shaping national symbol of Armenia and Armenians—was overlooking the Ararat Valley and was visible from every single corner of the city as a painful reminder of the lost land and lives. I was lost and did not know how I could show her Armenia while sheltering her from possible unpleasant experiences that might offend her Turkishness, for she was also a patriot.[12] Because we were close to each other and always direct with each other (I believe that helped us navigate those dangerous waters before), I shared with her my fears and hesitations. To my surprise, she told me that the first place she wanted to visit was the Tsitsernakaberd (meaning swallow's fortress) Memorial Complex—the Armenian Genocide Museum and Memorial. In that very moment I realized that I had a lot to discover about my friend and learn from her.

It might sound surprising or strange, but this solemn place of commemoration of the victims of the genocide was, for me, also a place of recharge and meditation. Sitting next to the eternal flames, surrounded by twelve stabs representing the lost provinces of Armenia, somehow always brings peace to my mind, filling my soul with hope. Yet, I could never force myself to visit the museum that was located right next to the monument. I could not explain why I was so hesitant to visit it. After all, I had no similar hesitations when I visited the Holocaust Memorial Museum in Washington, DC, or the Museum of Occupations and Freedom Fights, in Vilnius, or the Jewish Ghetto in Warsaw; yet, somehow, something was keeping me away from the Armenian Genocide Museum. My Turkish friend was the reason I overcame my indescribable anxiety, and for that I am eternally grateful to her. On our last day, we raised glasses of delicious Armenian wine in the restaurant on the top of a high-rise building while enjoying the songs and dances of the fountain in the Republic Square. She confessed that she did not expect Yerevan to be such a vibrant city and that she would love to come again. It was a tremendous joy to hear those words, and it made me proud of who I am as a friend and as an Armenian.

My friends were truly helping me to rediscover myself and reconnect to my identity. Truly, this sabbatical was proving to be a journey that shed light on my life divided between two continents, two countries, and two *homes*, somehow bridging the two pieces of my divided identities into one complete piece.

Sabbatical Aftermath and Post-Sabbatical Shock

When things change inside you, things change around you.
—*Author Unknown*

In many ways, having the teaching course in Lithuania, along with conferences in Portugal and Armenia lined up in the beginning of the sabbatical, set the tone of the whole journey despite of the uncertainly introduced by unexpected adjustments along the way. Keeping that focus on research and professional development (while having my family close by and friends around me) was important. Nevertheless, if there was any one single feeling that accompanied me through my sabbatical journey, it was the feeling of guilt (Milambiling, 2016). No matter how much time I spent reconnecting with family and friends, it felt like it was not enough. No matter how much time I invested on my research and professional development, it also felt not enough.

Fortunately, I kept a record of my activities. I completed three grant applications (two were successful); delivered nine papers at seven conferences in Portugal, Armenia, Canada, and Scotland; successfully pitched and chaired a special conference session in Scotland; conducted twenty interviews in Armenia and Canada, as well as supervised the collection of ten more in Italy; collected online data for two projects on ethnocentric consumer behaviour and youth sport participation, and conducted field data collection for ecotourism; delivered two seminars in Canada and Lithuania and a guest lecture in Italy; developed and submitted for publication a case study on medical tourism; and peer-reviewed seven journal submissions for a number of leading marketing journals. On the professional-development front, I completed three online courses and audited two others, which were instrumental in the development of a new course on digital marketing that I was scheduled to deliver upon my return to Nipissing University. I also taught two sessions of a marketing course in Vilnius University, which prepared me to contribute first-hand insights to a discussion of the block teaching approach we were considering adopting in our School of Business. My experiences deepened my understanding of the topics that I was already involved in, but also opened new opportunities. I would not have imagined that my health issues would lead to researching medical tourism or that visiting and hosting friends would spark a curiosity in "visiting friends and relatives" research (Barnett et al. 2010), which I am currently exploring.

My academic activities are those as noted by Sima & Denton (1995) (i.e., conducting research, developing scholarship, learning new techniques and procedures), and while overall I was satisfied with my accomplishments, my lack of publication was generating a feeling of failure. I realized that, similar to so many of my colleagues, I was comparing myself to my peers using their sabbatical accomplishments as reference points (Kahneman, 1992), and that was not a healthy approach. The more appropriate approach would be to compare my activities against the Nipissing University's definition of the sabbatical: I increased my knowledge, furthered my research, stimulated intellectual interest, strengthened my contacts with international scholars, and enhanced my contribution to the university on my return. Most of all, I realized that all my travels, work, and connections with my family and *shrjapat*—friends and colleagues—affected me on a much deeper level than I expected. Every single interaction I had was filled with serendipitous moments that reinforced my understanding of who I am as an individual and as a professional, and where I stand in being and living on those two sides of the Atlantic ocean. My heart pounded with joy equally when I discovered "Niagara Falls," a stalagmite formation resembling cascading water, in the depths of magnificent Frasassi Caves of Genga, Italy, and when I heard the sounds of Armenian music at a street performance in Ancona, again in Italy. I felt accomplished being able to host and present both countries I call *home* to my friends who visited me in Yerevan and Montréal. Those were not accomplishments I could submit in my sabbatical report, but they are accomplishments in my assessment as they filled the void of connection and confusion of where I belong that I was experiencing in these years leading to the sabbatical.

Good (1959) defines the sabbatical as an opportunity for self-improvement through a leave of absence. Truly, my sabbatical was a journey of self-improvement at every single step. Reflecting on it, I have come to realize that it was a classic case of progression through

Maslow's (1970) hierarchy of needs: to be able to reach self-actualization (i.e., satisfying academic research and scholarship record), I had to ensure that my physiological (i.e., health), safety (renovations), love and belongingness (family and *shrjapat*), and esteem (self-identity) needs were satisfied. If sabbatical is meant to be a "pause that refreshes" (Reynolds, 1990, p. 90), I definitely had that pause. I was recharged. I was rejuvenated and ready to return to my normal workload at Nipissing University with a better understanding of who I am as a researcher, as a pedagogue, and as a citizen of two countries I call *home*.

Postscript

As I write this chapter, Ontario goes through stage 2 of the gradual reopening of its businesses, services, and public spaces shut down or restricted in the COVID-19 pandemic that put the world in lockdown. I cannot help but feel lucky that my sabbatical happened in what now seems another world and another time—the time and the world when my travels were unrestricted and plans were unlimited. I feel lucky that I was able to have quality time with my family and friends. While I am happy here in the "gateway to the North" (North Bay), with public-health measures mitigating the spread of COVID-19, strangely enough I am also back to my pre-sabbatical feelings of separation from my loved ones as Armenia struggles with the vicious and unpredictable virus, undergoes tremendous political changes, and reckons again with war with Azerbaijan over the Nagorno-Karabakh region.

Endnotes

1. A Scarlett O'Hara moment is a simplistic decision to postpone worry. In the classic film *Gone With The Wind* (Fleming, 1939), Scarlett has a habit of scheduling difficult decisions: "I can't think about that right now. If I do, I'll go crazy. I'll think about it tomorrow."
2. Vilnius University, founded in 1579, is the oldest university in the Baltic states.
3. Block teaching has been defined as "a daily schedule that is organised into larger blocks of time (more than sixty minutes) to allow flexibility for a diversity of instructional activities" (Cawelti as cited in Davies, 2006, p. 3). My course was organized into 3.5 hours of intensive lectures for eight consecutive business days, with the final exam scheduled on the eleventh day.

4   The Erasmus Programme (EuRopean Community Action Scheme for the Mobility of University Students) is a European Union student-exchange program established in 1987.
5   A case-study method is a "discussion-based learning methodology that enables participants, through the use of cases, to learn" (Herreid, 2007, p. 50); a case is a "description of an actual situation, commonly involving a decision, a challenge, an opportunity, a problem or an issue faced by a person or a person in an organization" (p. 50).
6   As concerns the Nagorno-Karabakh region. Heavy fighting broke out in the fall of 2020 leading to a full-scale Nagorno-Karabakh war between Armenia and Azerbaijan. Right now the future of my motherland—my other home—is more unclear than ever; see Council on Foreign Relations (2021).
7   Lithuania, as a former Soviet republic, had seemed to make efforts to distance itself from its recent past. Yet there is still a significant part of population that speaks Russian, which would make my family less dependent on me.
8   You can find the Užupis constitution at Republic of Užupis (2012).
9   Komitas (sometimes Gomidas; 1869–1935) was an Armenian priest, musicologist, composer, arranger, singer, and is recognized as the founder of the Armenian national school of music.
10 Geghard, a UNESCO World Heritage site, is a medieval monastery complex founded in the fourth century by Gregory the Illuminator. It is believed to be the place where the lance that pierced Jesus was kept for about five hundred years (Armenia Discover, n.d.).
11 On Armenia's relations with Turkey, see Republic of Armenia (2021).
12 Article 301 of the Turkish Penal Code states that any person who publicly denigrates "Turkishness, the Republic or the Grand National Assembly of Turkey, shall be punishable by imprisonment of between six months and three years" (Algan, 2008).

References

Algan, B. (2008). The brand new version of article 301 of Turkish penal code and the future of freedom of expression cases in Turkey. *German Law Journal, 9*(12), 2237–2252. https://doi.org/10.1017/S2071832200000845

Armenia Discover (n.d.). Geghard Monastery. https://armeniadiscovery.com/en/place/geghard

Badenhorst, C. (2017). Belonging differently: Immigration, identity, and tenure-track. In T. M. Sibbald & V. Handford (Eds.), *The academic gateway: Understanding the journey to tenure* (pp. 51–61). University of Ottawa Press.

Baldock, C. V. (2000). Migrants and their parents: Caregiving from a distance. *Journal of Family Issues, 21*(2), 205–224. https://doi.org/10.1177/019251300021002004

Barnett, E. D., MacPherson, D. W., Stauffer, W. M., Loutan, L., Hatz, C. F., Matterlli, A., & Behrens, R. H. (2010). The visiting friends or relatives traveler in the 21st century: Time for a new definition. *Journal of Travel Medicine, 17*(3), 164–170. https://doi.org/10.1111/j.1708-8305.2010.00411.x

Baumeister, R. F., & Leary, M. R. (1995). The need to belong: Desire for interpersonal attachments as a fundamental human motivation. *Psychological Bulletin, 117*(3), 497–529. https://doi.org/10.1037/0033-2909.117.3.497

Berg, J. H. (1984). Development of friendship between roommates. *Journal of Personality and Social Psychology, 46*(2), 346–356. https://doi.org/10.1037/0022-3514.46.2.346

Bevan, J. L., & Sparks, L. (2011). Communication in the context of long-distance family caregiving: An integrated review and practical applications. *Patient Education and Counseling, 85*(1), 26–30. https://doi.org/10.1016/j.pec.2010.08.003

Bevan, J. L., Vreeburg, S. K., Verdugo, S., & Sparks L. (2012). Interpersonal conflict and health perceptions in long-distance caregiving relationships. *Journal of Health Communication, 17*(7), 747–761. https://doi.org/10.1080/10810730.2011.650829

Blieszner, R., & Roberto, K. A. (2004). Friendship across the life span: Reciprocity in individual and relationship development. In D. R. Lang & K. L. Fingerman (Eds.), *Growing together: Personal relationships across the life span* (pp. 159–182). Cambridge University Press.

Cardoso-Moreno, M. J., & Tomás-Aragones, L. (2017). The influence of perceived family support on post surgery recovery, *Psychology, Health & Medicine, 22*(1), 121–128. https://doi.org/10.1080/13548506.2016.1153680

Chesworth, N. (2003). The family vacation: A double-edged sword. *International Journal of Consumer Studies, 27*(4), 346–348. https://doi.org/10.1046/j.1470-6431.2003.00325.x

Copeland, A. P., & Norell, S. K. (2002). Spousal adjustment on international assignments: The role of social support. *International Journal of Intercultural Relations, 26*(3), 255–272. https://doi.org/10.1016/S0147-1767(02)00003-2

Council on Foreign Relations. (2021). *Global conflict tracker: Nagorno-Karabakh conflict*. https://www.cfr.org/global-conflict-tracker/conflict/nagorn-karabakh-conflict

Dann, G. M. S. (1997). Tourism conference goers: A serious typology? *Tourism Management, 18*(5), 251–253. https://doi.org/10.1016/S0261-5177(97)00013-7

Davidovitch, N., & Eckhaus, E. (2018). The influence of birth country on selection of conference destination—Employing Natural Language Processing. *Higher Education Studies, 8*(2), 92–96.

Davidson, R. (2003). Adding pleasure to business: Conventions and tourism. *Journal of Convention & Exhibition Management, 5*(1), 29–39. https://doi.org/10.1300/J143v05n01_03

Davies, M. W. (2006). Intensive teaching format: A review. *Issues in Educational Research, 16*(1), 1–21.

Deutsch, M., & Krauss, R. M. (1965). *Theories in social psychology*. Basic Books.

Durko, A., & Petrick, J. F. (2016). Family and relationship benefits of travel experiences: A literature review. *Journal of Travel Research, 52*(6), 720–730. https://doi.org/10.1177/0047287513496478

FASBU CA (2015–2019). *Collective Agreement between Nipissing University and Nipissing University Faculty Association*. Nipissing University.

Fleming, V. (Director). (1939). *Gone with the wind* [Film]. Selznick International Pictures.

Fraser Institute. (2017). *Leaving Canada for medical care*. https://www.fraserinstitute.org/sites/default/files/leaving-canada-for-medical-care-2017.pdf

Good, C. V. (1959). *Dictionary of education*. McGraw Hill.

Griffin, T. (2015). *The experience of hosting friends and relatives for immigrants* [Doctoral dissertation, University of Waterloo]. UWSpace. https://uwspace.uwaterloo.ca/bitstream/handle/10012/9432/Griffin_Tom.pdf?sequence=10&isAllowed=y

Hendrickson, B., Rosen, D., & Aune, R. K. (2011). An analysis of friendship networks, social connectedness, homesickness, and satisfaction levels of international students. *International Journal of Intercultural Relations, 35*(3), 281–295. https://doi.org/10.1016/j.ijintrel.2010.08.001

Herreid, C. F. (2007). *Start with a story: The case study method of teaching college science*. NSTA National Science Teachers Association Press.

Heslop, L. A., Cray, D., & Armenakyan, A. (2010). Cue incongruity in wine personality formation and purchasing. *International Journal of Wine Business Research, 22*(3), 288–307. https://doi.org/10.1108/17511061011075400

Kahneman, D. (1992). Reference points, anchors, norms, and mixed feeling. *Organizational Behavior and Human Decision Processes, 51*(2), 296–312. https://doi.org/10.1016/0749-5978(92)90015-Y

Komter, A., & Vollebergh, W. (1997). Gift giving and the emotional significance of family and friends. *Journal of Marriage and Family, 59*(3), 747–757. https://www.jstor.org/stable/353958

Langer, N., & Ribarich, M. (2007). Aunts, uncles—nieces, nephews: Kinship relations over the lifespan. *Educational Gerontology, 33*(1), 75–83. https://doi.org/10.1080/03601270600894279

Lastovicka, J. L., & Fernandez, K. V. (2005). Three paths to disposition: The movement of meaningful possessions to strangers. *Journal of Consumer Research, 31*(4), 813–823. https://doi.org/10.1086/426616

Lee, R. M., Dean, B. L, & Jung, K-R. (2008). Social connectedness, extraversion, and subjective well-being: Testing a mediation model, *Personality and Individual Differences, 45*(5), 414–419. https://doi.org/10.1016/j.paid.2008.05.017

Liu, J., Guo, M., Mao, W., & Chi, I. (2018). Geographic distance and intergenerational relationships in Chinese migrant families. *Journal of Ethnic & Cultural Diversity in Social Work, 27*(4), 328–345. https://doi.org/10.1080/15313204.2018.1520167

Lourie, S. & Davtyan, A. (n.d.) *Yerevan: Mythology of the modern city.* https://bigliba.com/books/454558

Maslow, A. H. (1970). *Motivation and personality* (2nd ed.). Harper and Row.

Milambiling, J. (2016). *Guilt, trips, and insights.* https://www.aaup.org/article/guilt-trips-and-insights#.XxjCrZ5KiUk

Milardo, R. M. (2009). *The forgotten kin: Aunts and uncles.* Cambridge University Press.

Nesteruk, O., & Marks, L. (2009). Grandparents across the ocean: Eastern European immigrants' struggle to maintain intergenerational relationships. *Journal of Comparative Family Studies, 40*(1), 77–95. https://www.jstor.org/stable/41604262

Okkonen, E., & Vanhanen, H. (2006). Family support, living alone, and subjective health of a patient in connection with a coronary artery bypass surgery. *Heart & Lung, 35*(4), 234–244. https://doi.org/10.1016/j.hrtlng.2005.11.002

Onorato, R. S., & Turner, J. C. (2004). Fluidity in the self-concept: the shift from personal to social identity. *European Journal of Social Psychology, 34*(3), 257–278. https://doi.org/10.1002/ejsp.195

Republic of Armenia. (2021). Bilateral Relations: Turkey. Ministry of Foreign Affairs. https://www.mfa.am/en/bilateral-relations/tr

Republic of Užupis. (2012). Constitution of the Republic of Užupis. http://uzhupisembassy.eu/uzhupis-constitution/

Reynolds, S. J. (1990). Sabbatical: The pause that refreshes. *The Journal of Academic Librarianship, 16*(2), 90–93. https://doi.org/10.1016/j.paid.2010.09.009

Segal, N., & Marelich, W. D. (2011). Social closeness and gift giving by twin parents toward nieces and nephews: An update. *Personality and Individual Differences, 50*(1), 101–105. https://doi.org/10.1016/j.paid.2010.09.009

Sima, C., & Denton, W. (1995). *Reasons for and products of faculty sabbatical leaves* [Paper presentation]. Annual meeting of the Association for the Study of Higher Education, Orlando, FL. ERIC. https://files.eric.ed.gov/fulltext/ED391420.pdf

Shaw, W. (2010). Serendipitous coffee experiences in Papua New Guinea. In J. Lee (Ed.), *Coffee culture, destinations and tourism* (pp. 138–158). Channel View.

Taylor, A. C., Robila, M., & Lee, H. S. (2005). Distance, contact, and intergenerational relationships: Grandparents and adult grandchildren from an international perspective. *Journal of Adult Development, 12*, 33–41. https://doi.org/10.1007/s10804-005-1280-7

Vroman, K. G., Arthanat, S., & Lysack, C. (2015). "Who over 65 is online?" Older adults' dispositions toward information communication technology. *Computers in Human Behaviour, 43*, 156–166. https://doi.org/10.1016/j.chb.2014.10.018

Yoo, H., McIntosh, A., & Cockburn-Wootten, C. (2016). Time for me and time for us: conference travel as alternative family leisure. *Annals of Leisure Research, 19*(2), 444–460. https://doi.org/10.1080/11745398.2016.1147361

Yoon, E., Lee, R. M., & Goh, M. (2008). Acculturation, social connectedness, and subjective well-being. *Cultural Diversity & Ethnic Minority Psychology, 14*(3), 246–255. https://doi.org/10.1037/1099-9809.14.3.246

CHAPTER 7

Academic Sabbatical Journey: The Crossovers between Research and Cultures

Pei-Ying Lin

This chapter describes my first sabbatical experience, centred on a research project carried out in an international context. A twelve-month sabbatical application was prepared, as per the requirements of sabbatical leaves at the University of Saskatchewan. It outlined the objectives of the proposed project, the benefits to both me and the university, a plan explaining how I would achieve the objectives, the importance of the research, and the anticipated outcomes from this project.

Leading up to the sabbatical, along with colleagues I had conducted an array of studies on student achievement using large-scale data sets; however, our results were mixed. This is not surprising; the inconsistent results reflect the variations among data sets and studies, such as the size of samples, heterogeneity of student characteristics, subject domains, the age of the studied groups, and the research methods employed (Laitusis, 2010; Lewandowski et al., 2008). Due to the complexity of these variables, the effects of accommodations for classroom tests and high-stakes assessments remain inconclusive. Accommodations, if used properly, can help students with special needs bypass their disabilities and demonstrate what they have learned and can do with that knowledge. To address the methodology issues, my colleagues and I narrowed the focus to foundational cognitive skills for classroom learning among children with intellectual disabilities.

The sabbatical project suited my interests because it was designed to test an innovative educational neuroscience methodology and explore its capabilities, using functional near-infrared spectroscopy (fNIRS) that can used to measure cognitive skills of students with intellectual disabilities. My collaborator, Dr. Hsin-Chin Chen at the National Chung Cheng University in Taiwan, is an expert in the use of fNIRS, and he invited me to conduct a project in Taiwan during my sabbatical year. After completing the preparation work, I recruited several children with and without special needs through a number of visits to local school in Taiwan.

I begin this chapter begin by laying out the background of this research and describing the activities pertaining to my sabbatical project. I also share the conversations and negotiations that took place between researchers in different disciplines (special education, experimental psychology, and neuroscience). Self-reflection, observations, and conversations with local schoolteachers and administrators are also shared and discussed with reference to the crossovers between cultures and research.

The Research Focus

It is clear that conducting intensive research activities at local schools in an international context and working closely with experts in the field, who kindly offered the use of expensive fNIRS equipment (figure 7.1), could not be done without a sabbatical. The research process thus highlighted the importance of sabbatical opportunities. Research activities that occurred during the sabbatical substantially facilitated and strengthened the international research partnership, as well as interdisciplinary knowledge exchange and mobilization. The primary focus of this chapter is on the collaborative research process and lessons learned from the project. The results of the research will be reported in different scholarly venues in the following years.

Conducting the fNIRS study required expertise in multiple disciplines, including experimental psychology, radiology, and special education. Multidisciplinary collaboration often creates interesting conversations and sparks new ideas among researchers. My sabbatical project provided excellent opportunities for sharing knowledge, techniques, and facilities, as well as allowing the team to share expensive equipment, such as the fNIRS system (e.g., Bozeman & Youtie, 2016; Coccia & Bozeman, 2016; Hackett, et al.,

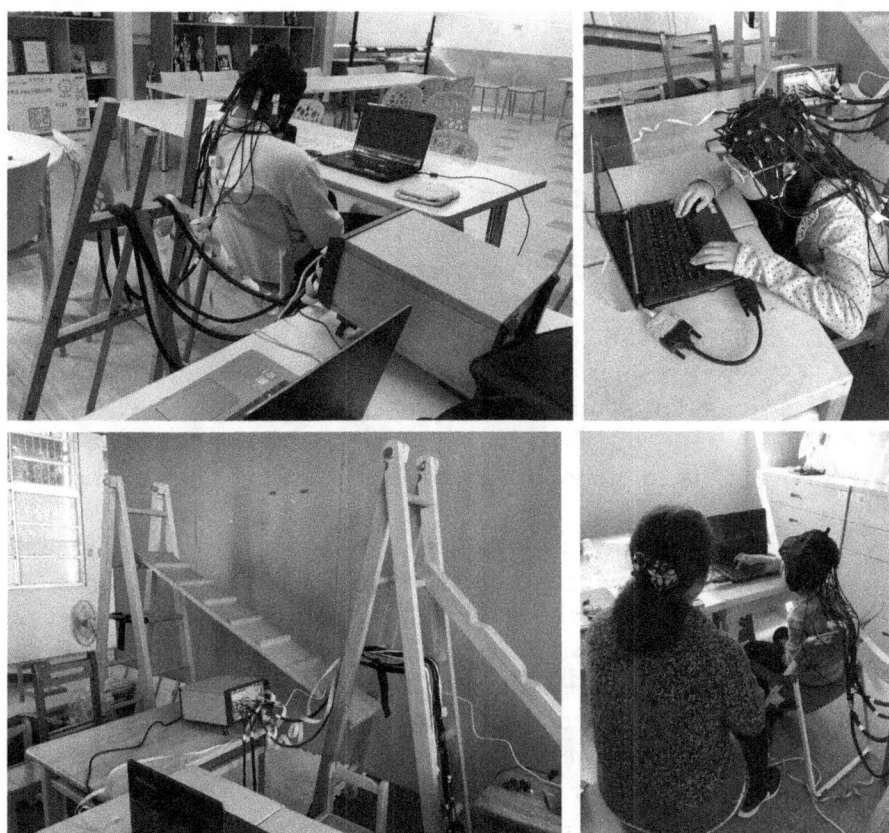

Figure 7.1. *Functional near-infrared spectroscopy system and data collection.*

2008). The fNIRS system is the property of the partner institute and cannot be transported to Canada, so I could not conduct this research without being at the partner institute, in person.

The fNIRS is a light-based technology designed to explore specific brain functions by positing multiple sources and detectors over the scalp to measure changes in blood flow to varied regions of the brain. The light-intensity signals were recorded by fNIRS and then converted into relative concentrations of oxyhemoglobin, deoxyhemoglobin, and the summed total (Strangman et al., 2002). This provides precise information about anatomical locus of brain activation (Dieler et al., 2012; Kovelman, 2012). It is more tolerant of physical-movement artifacts than other neuroimaging equipment, such as functional magnetic-resonance imaging or electroencephalography (Gallagher et al., 2012; Sela et al., 2014; Yang & Chen, 2013). Recent advances in fNIRS technology have drawn international interest in extending its application to different fields, including neurology, psychiatry, and psychology, because it is non-invasive, safe, portable, and relatively inexpensive (Dieler et al., 2012; Ferrari & Quaresima, 2012; Gallagher et al., 2012). In particular, teachers and students always have dynamic interactions in a non-clinical environment; the fNIRS is wearable and relatively insusceptible to physical movement, making it well suited to the goals of this project.

As we were developing experimental trials and writing transcripts that allowed software to properly communicate with the system, it was not possible to continuously troubleshoot errors without having the equipment at hand and professional consultations offered by my collaborator. This is the novelty of the opportunity that contributed to my sabbatical leave. Moreover, it is unusual for a faculty member to oversee a laboratory in a faculty of education, so it was interesting to closely observe the supervisory approach taken by psychology professors. For instance, Dr. Chen managed at least one laboratory where he supervised several teams of graduate students who were assigned to different research projects. In addition, his doctoral students were trained to take up the leadership role to oversee the progress of projects on behalf of Dr. Chen. Given that students on different teams performed an array of research activities, completed paperwork, and handled miscellaneous chores, the students I worked with at Dr. Chen's laboratory effectively helped one another to get their projects running and to meet deadlines. It was amazing to witness how thoroughly they did their due diligence, and to take in their strong work ethic and motivation. It is worth noting that these students put in considerable work to earn skills and degrees, rather than research stipends. Such supervisory approaches may be different from the field of education generally, which, in my experience, emphasizes academic writing and research processes.

Throughout my sabbatical year, there was a mutual benefit from open, positive, respectful, and healthy formal and informal communications among team members on an ongoing basis. Our communication was usually concentrated around each team member's expertise and research experience. Our formal communications occurred through fNIRS workshops, project seminars, and weekly laboratory meetings, while informal communications occurred on an individual basis. Mutual understanding and subject-matter knowledge also played a key role in successful team collaboration. Our weekly laboratory meetings, which covered a broad range of topics, included the theories underlying fNIRS, techniques for equipment installation, experimental designs and paradigms, probe design, data-collection techniques and procedures, data management and analysis, and interpretation of fNIRS brain-activation data.

In addition to my sabbatical project, I also worked closely with Dr. Chen's three doctoral students and five master's students, who were also responsible for other research projects. At weekly laboratory meetings, we had a great deal of focused and dynamic discussions as they were required to report on the progress of their projects. Students were encouraged to use the data they collected to write their theses or dissertations. Our meetings provided ample opportunities for student training and mentorship. Our team substantially benefitted from members who provided timely information and updates, as well as orchestrated and synchronized actions taken by different members. It was especially true as different projects were run by team members simultaneously and there was only one fNIRS system available in the laboratory.

On top of my research at the partner institute, I was excited to be able to travel to present at several international conferences that I would not be able to attend without sabbatical leave. In August, I travelled to Bangkok to give a presentation at the Asia Pacific Conference on Giftedness about Canadian gifted students' use of accommodations for a large-scale assessment. The scorching hot summer, spicy food, and friendly presenters made the academic conference even better. At the conference, I was invited to present at the International Research Association for Talent Development and Excellence, in Taipei. Furthermore, on behalf of my research group, I presented a paper on teacher candidates' beliefs about inclusive education in Taiwan and the US at the conference of Special Education Across Taiwan Strait in Taipei. Throughout the conferences, I was able to connect with colleagues and friends who shared similar research interests. Finally, the conference of the Organization for Human Brain Mapping in Rome in June concluded my sabbatical year. By attending these conferences, I was able to disseminate research results, network with professionals and stakeholders, generate new ideas, and note new advancements in the fields.

Overall, the unique experiences I gained over the sabbatical year helped to refine knowledge and skills that enhance my teaching of undergraduate and graduate students. The innovative research approach I employed for the sabbatical project has become a first-hand example I provide in research-methods courses. I share with my students those "aha" moments I had with my team members. The experiences are certainly valuable as an instructor. As I frequently interacted with elementary and secondary special-education teachers and their students at schools in Taiwan throughout the sabbatical leave, those stories gleaned from classroom experiences can then be shared with students in special-education courses I teach in Saskatchewan. My sabbatical project is tackling some practical questions shared by many participating teachers, such as: Do my students really respond to my instructions? If so, how do they respond to them? I believe that graduate and undergraduate students at the University of Saskatchewan benefit from our knowledge-creation activities and professional techniques shared by team members at international institutes.

Regaining a Cultural Connection

I was born and raised in the cultures of Taiwan and speak both Mandarin and Taiwanese (Min Nan) as mother tongues. Related memories, self-identity, and heritage have been deeply rooted in my life since childhood. Because the sabbatical project was in Taiwan, I was able to reconnect to my cultural heritage and regain a cultural connection with people on this tropical island.

My partner institute is located on a hill surrounded by pineapple fields. I was required to travel two hours by bus, commuter train, and then drive the last leg home if I chose to commute to work. As such, it made sense to rent accommodations near the university for the year. Many apartments nearby were rented out to students, which made me feel like a university freshman staying at a dormitory again. The huge campus includes several bike lanes, walking trails, parks, gyms, a golf course, and a track-and-field facility where Olympic athletes train. It was enjoyable and relaxing for me to jog, bike, and walk along the walking trails after a long day of work.

Compared to the harsh winters in a prairie province, the country has mild and shorter winters, and hot and humid summers. The autumn and spring months are nice and enjoyable. People can enjoy a variety of outdoor activities all year around as they can be at beaches or mountains within an hour or less. Thanks to the tropical weather, Taiwan is a paradise for fresh fruits, vegetables, and seafood.

In my leisure time I enjoyed biking, aerobic exercises, and grocery shopping at a traditional farmers' market. This market attracts huge crowds as it has more than a hundred street vendors selling a wide range of fresh local produce, plants, seafood, Taiwanese deli food, clothing, and miscellaneous items. It was fun to be part of the crowd and shop for good deals. The scenes and the street food brought back childhood memories. These lived experiences enriched my sabbatical year abroad by rebuilding a stronger sense of belonging to community, cultures, and social groups.

After studying and working in Canada for several years, I truly appreciated every moment that I shared with close family and friends. I regained the opportunity to take part in the important life events of people I care for, such as a wedding and a funeral. I was thrilled to be able to barbeque with families at the mid-autumn festival night, watch firework shows at the beehive festival in my hometown, help prepare a reunion dinner on the Lunar New Year's Eve, pay respect to ancestors on Tomb Sweeping Day, and wrap rice dumplings for the celebration of the dragon boat festival. These were the special occasions and activities I had missed for many years.

Being an associate professor working overseas (in Canada) for several years, I found it was challenging to reach out to the local school communities when recruiting target participants, and to collect experimental data in school settings. Throughout the entire project, I realized and learned that I had become a cultural outsider to the teachers and school administrators who would determine the acceptance or rejection of my invitation to participate in the research project.

I paid several school visits to explain the project to various stakeholders, including general- and special-education teachers, principals, and students. These face-to-face meetings provided opportunities to communicate the nature, purposes, and procedures involved in this project with the stakeholders in each school. Although many meetings were fruitful for attracting participating teachers and students, some meetings were quite disappointing, even unpleasant, for me as a researcher and teacher educator. It was difficult for an outside researcher to build trustful, positive, and respectful relationships with local school communities in one sabbatical year.

It was interesting to see that my years of overseas teaching experience somehow disconnected me from the local culture of Taiwanese principals and teachers, even though I was born in the country. It is also thought-provoking to observe that professors at local normal universities or colleges of education in Taiwan were often considered authorities of knowledge and respected sources, whereas I found myself involved in power struggles with school administrators in particular. I also received ambiguous responses from teachers; some would agree to participate, then I would not hear back from them. Such ambiguity truly confused me as it added unpredictability to the research. This is, perhaps, part of the challenge of the dynamic relationship between cultures and research.

My understanding is that sabbaticants are expected to take up a sabbatical project that may well involve all the key elements of a quality study, such as data collection, analyses, and dissemination of findings. It is common that sabbaticants may choose to carry out studies overseas, in otherwise local contexts. Based on what I have learned from my sabbatical project, it is worthwhile planning the study one or even two years ahead to better facilitate the research process in an international setting.

Concluding Thoughts

When it comes to a sabbatical leave, what excites or motivates faculty the most is to be on top of our own schedules, regain the balance between work and life, reenergize ourselves, and enhance our mental, emotional, physical, and spiritual well-being through intended and unintended activities. The hustle and bustle of our academic careers keeps many of us on the go. Most struggle to keep their heads above water. Besides doing full-time research activities, I also took the opportunity to reflect on my relationships with family, friends, and others by looking back at my life and career trajectories.

As tenure-track faculty members of universities, we are expected to jump through hoops to follow a collegial process and meet the standards for promotion and tenure. Relationships with families and friends living out of the country are often compromised by the long distances. During the sabbatical leave, I had more opportunities to visit and look after my elderly parents while working on my sabbatical project. My dear father passed away less than one year after the completion of my leave. I believe that the leave helped mitigate some of my anxiety, stress, and sorrow resulting from family crisis.

My first sabbatical leave was an amazing gift to my professional career as well as to my personal life. It allowed me to explore a brand-new multidisciplinary research territory—educational neuroscience in special education—with experts in the field through international collaboration. It was exciting, overwhelming, and rewarding to work with skilled colleagues and students using cutting-edge technology and applying that in my research regarding children with intellectual disabilities. Throughout my sabbatical project, I came to appreciate different ways of thinking and doing among team members. We found ways to transform ideas into practical research activities and troubleshoot technical problems for better outcomes.

This project required me to translate the multidisciplinary knowledge of special education, experimental psychology, and neuroscience into feasible practices. It was demanding and time-consuming for everyone involved to complete such a project within a year. It took efforts to navigate cultures and maintain research partnerships over time, especially when no financial incentives were offered to collaborators or school partners. Overall, the professional development that occurred during this sabbatical year allowed me to continue my commitment to teaching, research and scholarly work, and service to educational communities. Just as a substantial amount of time, commitment, and effort went into each piece of my sabbatical work, so too am I committed to disseminating the collective output from team members, so it can be read and heard as well as further transformed into teaching practices. My sabbatical leave was a bumpy journey, but it is the one that has enhanced my overall academic journey, and thus those of my students and team members.

References

Bozeman, B., & Youtie, J. (2016). *The strength in numbers: How to create science collaboration dream teams*. Princeton University Press.

Coccia, M., & Bozeman, B. (2016). Allometric models to measure and analyze the evolution of international research collaboration. *Scientometrics, 108*, 1065–1084. https://doi.org/10.1007/s11192-016-2027-x

Dieler, A. C., Tupak, S. V., & Fallgatter, A. J. (2012). Functional near-infrared spectroscopy for the assessment of speech related tasks. *Brain and Language, 121*(2), 90–109.

Ferrari, M., & Quaresima, V. (2012). A brief review on the history of human functional near-infrared spectroscopy (fNIRS) development and fields of application. *Neuroimage, 63*(2), 921–935.

Gallagher, A., Béland, R., & Lassonde, M. (2012). The contribution of functional near-infrared spectroscopy (fNIRS) to the presurgical assessment of language function in children. *Brain and Language, 121*(2), 124–129.

Hackett, E. J., Amsterdamska, O., & Wajcman, J. (2008). *The handbook of science and technology studies.* MIT Press.

Kovelman, I. (2012). Neuroimaging methods. In E. Hoff (Ed.), *Research methods in child language: A practical guide.* Blackwell Wiley.

Laitusis, C. C. (2010). Examining the impact of audio presentation on tests of reading comprehension, *Applied Measurement in Education, 23,* 153–167.

Lewandowski, L. J., Lovett, B. J., & Rogers, C. L. (2008). Extended time as a testing accommodation for students with reading disabilities: Does a rising tide lift all ships? *Journal of Psychoeducational Assessment, 26,* 315–324.

Sela, I., Izzetoglu, M., Izzetoglu, K., & Onaral, B. (2014). A functional near-infrared spectroscopy study of lexical decision task supports the dual route model and the phonological deficit theory of dyslexia. *Journal of Learning Disabilities, 47*(3), 279–288.

Strangman, G., Boas, D. A., & Sutton, J. P. (2002). Non-invasive neuroimaging using near-infrared light. *Biological Psychiatry 52*(7), 679–693.

Yang, Z.-H., & Chen, H.-C. (2013). Applying Near-Infrared Spectroscopy in Cognitive Neuroscience. *Journal of Neuroscience and Neuroengineering, 2,* 231–242.

CHAPTER 8

Place Making

Lee Anne Block

My academic career has developed through a continuing effort to balance family and work, the personal and professional. Finding that balance is both difficult and joyful. My first sabbatical was shaped by the birth of twin grandchildren. In an earlier chapter in this series, I noted that "although they bring wonder and wisdom, grandchildren are not part of one's curriculum vitae" (Block, 2017, p. 41). The wonder of the tiny sister and brother also produced some difficulty in time management for research and writing. My research on place-based learning was supported and reduced by the experience of living and learning with the twins. I sought a place to focus my research and found it in Navdanya, an organic farm and learning centre in northern India. There, place-based learning developed into an understanding of "place making," how we impact places. That understanding led to a community-based reconciliation project, the Kapabamayak Achaak Healing Forest, where the twins planted fingerling spruce when they were four.

Breathing Space and Births

After ten years in the academy, I was fortunate enough to be granted a study leave, a breathing space, from July to January. For part of that leave, I positioned myself for place-based learning in a far-from-local place. I travelled from Winnipeg, Canada, to

Navdanya, an agroecology and biodiversity conservation centre, in Ramgarh, India. As well as being an organic farm, Navdanya is the site of Bija Vidyapeeth, or Earth University, which offers a variety of courses on ecology (see https://www.navdanya.org). For ten days, I was a resident student taking a course, Gandhi, Globalization and Earth Democracy. Navdanya was founded in 1994 by Vandana Shiva, a physicist, feminist, and environmental activist whose family owned land in northern India. Shiva had been working on seed saving since the late 1980s. Navdanya means "nine seeds" (symbolizing protection of biological and cultural diversity) and "new gift." Navdanya was a gift of learning, which I still value years later.

The decision to travel to Navdanya for the course was complicated by the birth of the twins just six weeks prior to my study leave (the University of Winnipeg's term for sabbatical). When my daughter was seven months pregnant, she left her career, her friends, and her home in a large American city, where she had lived and worked for almost ten years. In her late thirties, having been independent and self-supporting since age twenty-one, she moved into our home in Winnipeg, the city where she had grown up, focused on bringing the twins as close to term as possible. My partner of fifteen years, her stepfather, and I had a large house that could accommodate her and the twins without crowding. Emotionally we also had room for her, the babies, and a nanny—although it was a stretch.

I earned my PhD at the University of North Dakota and, after term positions there and at the University of Manitoba, was hired into a tenure-track position at the University of Winnipeg. After three years, I was entitled to apply for a half year of study leave. The study-leave committee accepted my application and the leave was scheduled from July 1 to December 31. By the time the twins were born, I had finished teaching and had most of my marking completed for the May grades deadline. In the month of May, my primary focus was on the twins and their mother. I submitted my grades and kept up with email but did no research or writing. It will come as no surprise that June was much the same.

Our first grandchild had been born two years earlier in Toronto, with a second arriving two months later in Montréal. I had spent most of that winter break in Montréal helping the new parents with the baby. With the twins it was different from the other grandchildren, I was not simply helping; I was co-parenting. Their mother and I had agreed to that term. However, I was the working co-parent and my partner was also working full time. My daughter hired a part-time nanny who came in daily and did some cooking and light housework for the family as well. There had been a night nanny for the first three weeks. During evenings all three of us were on call—rocking, singing, walking, and talking the babies to sleep. Nights were also busy. Our community of friends and relatives was very supportive. Despite that help, it was nonetheless intense. Without the structure of teaching in September, I had to find time and space to work, to research, and to write.

Research

In my faculty, one's first study leave usually comes after earning tenure. However, I had negotiated with the associate dean to take my study leave before tenure to improve my prospects by having time and space to write. I had anticipated having eight months to deepen my research agenda, and time to write without interruptions. My research encompassed teacher education, cultural sustainability, school gardens, and place-based learning, all emerging from my lived experience. Life experience supports learning, but life circumstances can obstruct the writing process. At the time of my application, I did not know I would be living with and caring for twin grandchildren and their mother during my study leave. It was a context that required an intricate balancing act.

My academic career has evolved through a series of similar balancing acts, and from integrating the personal and professional. My research emerged from problematizing my teaching and from an individual commitment to sustainability. In my four years at the University of Winnipeg, I had presented and published papers on teacher education and on internationally educated teachers and had begun a school gardening project. I was collaborating with Dr. Laura Sims, a colleague at Université de Saint-Boniface, on a paper on teacher education and sustainability. It was with her that I first discussed going to study and work at Navdanya. I was concerned it might not be seen as legitimate research. Laura told me to go for it and learn from it. After some soul searching, I applied to Navdanya, was accepted for the course, and bought the plane tickets. The course description as posted in 2014 on the Navdanya website read:

> Gandhi, Globalization and Earth Democracy
> November 21st – 30th, 2014
> Faculty: Sri Satish Kumar, Venerable Samdhong Rimpoche, Dr. Madhu Suri Prakash and Dr. Vandana Shiva, Arun Gandhi
>
> We live in the midst of multiple crises—ecological, economic, social, political. The current economic model has pushed most ecosystems to the verge of collapse. Species are disappearing, and climate catastrophe is overtaking people's lives from the Himalaya to the Rockies, from the Bay of Bengal to the Philippines.
>
> Not only are ecosystems collapsing, economies are collapsing. People are suffering from a delusion in which it is believe[d] that this economic downturn is only a small hiccup and all will be back to business as usual. This is not the case; we are at a turning point of a crisis. A crisis is also an opportunity and during this course we will discuss how this crisis can be turned into an opportunity. The course is not only about information and knowledge but also complemented with experience, by being on the Navdanya Biodiversity Conservation Farm and participating by doing.
>
> Globalization has also led to the unprecedented concentration of power in the hands of a few global corporations. The course explores the relevance of the four Gandhian principles of swaraj (self-governance), swadeshi (local production), sarvodaya (well-being of all) and satyagraha (non-violent civil disobedience based on the force of truth) to create and defend people's economic and political freedom.

Examining the political context of sustainability was important to me, as was consideration of how to take action. I believed the course at Navdanya could intensify this learning.

In the interim, from August until my departure in November, I spent full days on the Winnipeg campus, away from the babies and continuing my research and writing. I would arrive home as the nanny was leaving and be kept busy with the twins. The house would be covered in baby equipment and there would often be visitors. My partner's son, his wife, and their dogs stayed with us for a couple weeks in October, adding their energy to the home. We did not always recognize home as the place it had been—it was altered and overtaken by kids, grandkids, and dogs. Home was a mixture of the familiar and the unfamiliar. The babies were new, but caring for babies was familiar. Living with my daughter had happened before, but now it was different:

> No place is to be learned like a textbook or a course in a school. And then turned away from forever on the assumption one's knowledge is complete. What is to be known about it is without limit, and is endlessly changing. Knowing is therefore like breathing; it can happen, it stays real, only on the condition that it continues to happen. (Berry, 1991, p. 75)

Change was the fabric of my life during my study leave. Balancing attention to my research with caring for the twins was ongoing. The babies' needs were changing; our home was changing to meet those needs, and my research direction was changing as I prepared for Navdanya. I was concentrating on place-based learning.

Place-Based Learning

Place-based learning has become part of my practice and grounds my pedagogy as a teacher educator. I examine how place is central to the educational process; this learning begins within the local, the places we inhabit. Place-based learning connects us to places, spaces, sites, environments, ecosystems; none of which are empty of human intervention, of the learner. The learner is, in turn, situated and positioned by those places and by the cultures that emerge within them (Chawla, 2007; Gruenewald, 2003; Sobel, 2008). Constructing a pedagogical space (Stevenson, 2008) within which it becomes possible and necessary to act with intention and address socio-environmental issues is inherent in place-based learning.

Place-based learning is an orientation, not a strategy. It orients us to a way of knowing that embraces the changeable, the emergent (Kentel & Karrow, 2010; McKenzie, 2004), and the possibility of transformation. For a teacher, it is a repositioning, from one who produces and delivers knowledge to one who facilitates knowing (Anderson et al., 2017; Davis et al., 2008; Freire, 2005). Familiar and unfamiliar places are both sources of learning. The teacher must adjust the mix of the familiar and the unfamiliar to the teaching and learning context.

The focus on place-based learning is infused in the social-studies-methods courses I teach. I emphasize that place-based learning is embodied (Kimmerer, 2013) and requires action (Chawla, 2007; Hampton, 1993). Students' agentic potentials can be realized through interaction with the place, its biotic and abiotic components. These interactions, in turn, can shape the place they are experiencing. Studying the particulars of place involves understanding systems and thinking systemically (Laszlo & Clark, 1972; von Bertalanffy, 1968).

Place-based learning moves through past, present, and future. In connecting to a place, students discover its history and its potential, and thus the potential to act for change. Teaching respect of place and how to live within ecological limits (Shiva, 2016; Suzuki & Boyd, 2009) necessitates addressing the inequities in our places, both local and global. Thus place-based learning encompasses place making—"from the perspective of democratic education, schools must provide opportunities for students to participate meaningfully in the process of place making, that is, in the process of shaping what our places will become" (Gruenewald, 2003, p. 627). Place shaping or making is collaborative, grounded, and enacted in both teaching and community activities. Place making requires more than studying a place; it requires intentional interaction with the place and its living and non-living components, human and other than human. This intentional interaction involves taking one's place within a place and taking it in relationship. Place-based learning can be transformed to place making when it becomes possible and necessary to act with intention to address socio-environmental issues (Gruenewald, 2003; Stevenson, 2008). By teaching through the interactions of persons, places, and the relationship to the land, we may understand the agentic potential to act collaboratively for change in classrooms, schools, or communities.

Navdanya: Learning Contextually

Navdanya is a small organic farm that serves as a model to local farmers in the northern state of Uttarakhand (formerly Uttaranchal) at the foothills of the Himalayas. Practices at Navdanya are also shared with small farms elsewhere in India. The farm also houses

Bija Vidyapeeth, which offers courses and workshops related to seed saving, organic farming, and paradigm shifts. The course I studied was taught by Dr. Vandana Shiva, Satish Kumar, and the Venerable Samdhong Rinpoche over a ten-day residence.

The formal course was lecture based, with Kumar, Shiva, and Rinpoche speaking sequentially a few days each. Shiva and Rinpoche also taught together. Our teachers were learned scholars and activists, well known in ecological movements. There was time for questions and discussion after the lectures. During the day we met outside; in the evenings we met in a hall. We were literally sitting at the feet of the master for much of our course work. That traditional modality was both connected and in counterpoint to the place we inhabited. Studying with a guru is a tradition in India. Within that study there is the possibility of transformative learning. The Navdanya experience has been characterized as transformative: "One reason I created this space was for cultural transformation" (Vandana Shiva, lecture, November 28, 2014). In counterpoint to the traditional lecture format was the collaborative and intergenerational learning process at Navdanya.

The *bijaks* (literally "the sower of seeds") were an example of how learning at Navdanya encompassed the traditional, the modern, and the postmodern. They were interns—mostly young adults, late teens to late thirties, from Europe, the Americas, and Asia—who had found their way to Navdanya with an intention to live the change. In contrast to students like me, the *bijaks* were at Navdanya for extended time periods. They stayed in dorms, worked and played on the farm, pursued their individual studies, and took courses. Those I studied and worked with during my stay were examining and advocating for a range of issues, from organic gardening and farming to peace studies, community organizing, and economics. The direction of their work was shaped by their communal life. There was ongoing discussion and debate, very different from the formal classes, yet an extension of them. At Navdanya, the *bijaks* were producing knowledge in relation to specific projects in their local settings. Moreover, they were exchanging knowledge among each other, their teachers, staff, and students on the farm, and people in the surrounding villages. One evening of the course students and *bijaks* presented their individual research.

This collaborative process was also intergenerational. Teachers, students, and *bijaks* ranged in age from fifteen to eighty. All benefited from the different experiences and the different historical periods lived through. In one presentation, a student, otherwise a professor of education, referenced her experiences as a student and teacher in the seventies, connecting the environmental movement of then to the present. This student's cross-cultural experiences also enriched the conversation, as did the student studying peacemaking in Israel-Palestine. Those intergenerational and cross-cultural experiences were woven through the ongoing dialogue during the course.

The experience at Navdanya was of place-based learning. Had I been taught by the same three teachers in another location, I would have learned differently. Their teachings resonated with the place and context they taught in, learning outside in a garden, learning in collaboration, cross-cultural learning, intergenerational learning, and learning bracketed by service, *swadeshi* (self-reliance through working with one's hands). The Navdanya experience rooted my focus on ecology and sustainability, and from those roots grew an understanding of place making. I experienced the balancing of diverse perspectives produced by intentional use of place-based, collaborative intergenerational learning in counterpoint to traditional lectures. Working in place, *swadeshi*, is directly experienced at Navdanya and is integrated into the learning process. Grounded in this experience, I began a consideration of how the design and practice of Navdanya could inform place-based teaching and learning in schools and in my teacher-education courses.

Another traditional aspect of the teaching and learning at Navdanya was the absence of personality or individualism. As students, we were able to access what was offered by our teachers and the place and work with it. The milieu was one wherein the group attended to the teaching. There was no tailoring of instruction to our personal needs, nor were we invited to "share our thoughts and feelings" on a regular basis. It was energizing to connect to the teaching and work collaboratively, with one's personal agenda withheld for the interim. The teaching could become a place from which to build individual or collective inquiry (Whyte et al., 2016).

At Navdanya, place-based learning is both local and more than local. It is extended through time and space as *bijaks* and students in the courses maintain relationships with one another when they return to their home countries and continue to generate cultures of sustainability. These aspects of Navdanya construct a culture of sustainability: a community of shared work and shared values, respect for differences, respect for place, living and working in interaction with animals and vegetation, an ecological perspective. Navdanya was designed to facilitate a specific kind of learning, particular to its mission and its place, and yet transformable to other places. Similarly, place-based learning is embedded in the familiar to expand into the unfamiliar (Chawla, 2007; Kimmerer, 2013).

As Shiva explained (lecture, November 28, 2014), we need allies in changing the paradigm, in transforming a mechanistic worldview to an understanding of the web of life and the relationships that shape it. At Navdanya, the relationships between people and place are foregrounded. Place making emerges from these relationships.

My position at Navdanya encompassed both student and teacher, both foreigner and fellow, and within that merging of relationships transformative learning became possible. What was transformative came from both the familiar and the unfamiliar, from the place and from within. Authorizing time for study is itself a powerful choice and experience. Having Navdanya as a place to study, reflect, and regenerate placed me within a tradition and among like-minded people. The conversations that emerged from the intersection of place and people affirmed some of my convictions and unsettled some of my assumptions.

Positioning Oneself and Perspectives

How does one construct possibilities for exploratory dialogue in familiar places? It begins by teaching through the interactions of persons and places and the relationship of culture and place: "the land shows the bruises of an abusive relationship. It's not just the land that is broken; but more importantly, our relationship with land" (Kimmerer, 2013, p. 9). Indigenous perspectives on place, on land, and on those relationships offer alternatives to the subject/object dichotomy of scientific materialism. Our teachers at Navdanya also proposed alternatives to that dichotomy. Kumar (lecture, November 24, 2014) explained that caring is not attachment; rather, caring is engaged action, that love is freedom from attachment and engagement is a participatory relationship, not an ownership. The emphasis on relationship was both familiar and unfamiliar for me. Differences in Indigenous, Asian, and Western perspectives are not incompatible. Cultural hybridity includes many perspectives and their influence on each other (Donald, 2009; Simon, 2013).

My position at Navdanya also included my role as grandmother, Baba. Every evening after dinner, I would take my iPad to the best WiFi zone and FaceTime with the twins, who were six months old, their mother, and my partner. Those relationships were cherished; part of my learning at Navdanya was holding onto and letting go of those relationships simultaneously. My understanding of how to connect, how to relate with generosity rather than possessiveness, has deepened over time and from learning from Indigenous perspectives as I worked with Indigenous activists in Winnipeg on the Kapabamayak Achaak Healing Forest, a reconciliation project. Understanding we are all related, and trusting relationships, allows for letting go.

My first journey to India was in 1973, when I was twenty-one. I was hired to teach at a school in Ootacamund (now Udhagamandalam), Tamil Nadu, in southern India. I had joked that the only way I could leave my parents' home was to go all the way to India. Certainly, I am a person for whom relationships are a priority. Leaving my role as co-parent/Baba for three weeks in India and Sri Lanka was not an easy decision. Yet my role as a researcher was also a priority. Study leave is a privilege that comes only every several years, and I wanted to utilize the time to gather new understandings. I believed Navdanya would nourish new ways of thinking and teaching about sustainability, and it did.

Understanding one's relationships as part of the web of life (Simpson, 2014; Kimmerer, 2013) is central to Indigenous teachings. These teachings, and Indigenous history and cultures, have been missing or misrepresented in Canadian social studies and science curricula (Borden & Wiseman, 2016; Greenwood, 2009; Scully 2012). Like many other teacher educators (Tupper, 2011; Sims, 2015), the investigations of the Truth and Reconciliation Commission had incited me to rethink how I taught Indigenous perspectives. I wanted to do better. During my research on Indigenous history, I initiated the community-based project Kapabamayak Achaak Healing Forest. This place-making project was produced in part through what I had learned in Navdanya. It included *swadeshi*, and is intended for transformative learning.

Kapabamayak Achaak Healing Forest and Place Making

The Kapabamayak Achaak Healing Forest is a response to the Truth and Reconciliation Commission's calls to action (Canada, 2015). It is a place for learning and healing located within St. John's Park in the North End of Winnipeg. This park is built on the site of the landing of the Scots Selkirk settlers. It was the meeting place for those settlers and Indigenous people. Many statues and memorials to settler history and war heroes were installed, but there was no recognition of Indigenous history or peoples. Kapabamayak Achaak (Ojibway; "Wandering Spirit") rectifies this omission. It is a living memorial to Indigenous children lost to or affected by the residential school system. It provides a culturally specific urban greenspace for the community, for ceremony or simple reflection. The architect, Ryan Epp, describes Kapabamayak Achaak as a spiritual landscape, built to remind us all that Mother Earth and her inhabitants are sacred.

It is an outdoor learning space where place-based learning and intergenerational learning connect students to their histories, and cultivates citizenship and sustainability; where place making becomes possible. There is a teaching circle of oak logs around a granite medicine wheel, with additional stone seating. Métis-Anishinaabe artist Natalie Rostad-Desjarlais painted designs with animal and human figures on boulders in the four directions. Trees and shrubs were planted. In the next phase of construction there will be a garden of medicinal plants adjacent to the circle.

Visits to the site are not intended to be singular experiences. Teachers are encouraged to plan a series of visits, which allow students to see changes in the environment and build relationships with the place. A living curriculum is being constructed with teachers and students. Kapabamayak Achaak Healing Forest curriculum emerges from our focus on sustainability and thus is designed for transformational learning: "All education is environmental education. By what is included or excluded, students are taught that they are *part of* or *apart* from the natural world" (Orr, 2004).

Kapabamayak Achaak is a collaborative partnership between public school, post-secondary educators, and community members, Indigenous and non-Indigenous, who formed the Healing Forest planning group, with the support of Cathedral Church of St. John the Evangelist, located adjacent to St. John's Park. My role was lead of the planning group, which recently incorporated as a non-profit agency. Kapabamayak Achaak has received private donations from community members and has received grants from the University of Winnipeg, the Province of Manitoba, the City of Winnipeg, the United Way, and the Winnipeg Foundation. These grants have been directed to constructing the site within St. John's Park, and for the learning taking place there. One example of an education project is the commemoration of Orange Shirt Day, which remembers survivors of residential schools through the story of Phyllis Webstad, who was stripped of the new orange shirt she wore the first day at her residential school. On site, the schoolchildren hear stories from Indigenous Elders or survivors of the residential schools. They also explore the site and the park it is situated in.

Collaborating on the construction and the curriculum development of Kapabamayak Achaak is compelling place making. Community engagement through the project has connected me to current activism and to tradition in parts of Indigenous communities in Winnipeg. Working with Indigenous community activists and studying Indigenous worldviews foregrounded how relationships and relationship building are valuable for learning. This influences how I work with partners in the Kapabamayak Achaak Healing Forest. My concerns about myself, a non-Indigenous person, as "lead" of the project were ameliorated. This work directed me to reconsider how I build relationships within my teacher-education practice. I also reconsidered my relationship to the land and how that infused my living and learning.

I grew up in a garden and keep that tradition for my children and grandchildren. We observe growth, climb, and talk to trees; study insect life and feed the birds. As a young adult I moved back to the land; as an older woman I understand the land is everywhere. Working on the Kapabamayak Achaak Healing Forest has awakened my awareness of sacred spaces. Bringing students into that space, I witness their connection to the other than human world, to the land. Kapabamayak Achaak, akin to Navdanya, can become a place for transformative learning, where place making is integrated with the learning and where the past informs the future. My experiences at Navdanya shaped my understanding of how place-based learning is transformed to place making. I attempt to enact this understanding in teaching and in community-based research in Kapabamayak Achaak.

Studying in Navdanya was an honour and a gift. Leaving Navdanya was easier than leaving the babies had been. In mid-December I returned to Winnipeg, having completed the course and after meeting my partner in Sri Lanka for ten days. In Jaffna, Sri Lanka, we revisited his past as a student there in the 1970s, and imagined a possible future of wintering and volunteering in the island country. Winnipeg was cold in December and there were no flowers blooming, except the roses in the babies' cheeks as we walked with them in the snow. In January my study leave was over; the twins were sitting up and teaching recommenced—with a promise to build on what I had learned in Navdanya and a commitment to place making and relationships. Enacting that commitment in my teaching is an incomplete and continuing task, as is making places for learning. The Kapabamayak Achaak Healing Forest is a place where relationships are made.

References

Anderson, D., Chiarotto, L., & Comay, J. (2017). *Natural curiosity 2nd edition: A resource for educators: The importance of Indigenous perspectives in children's environmental inquiry*. Laboratory School, Dr. Eric Jackman Institute of Child Study, Ontario Institute for Studies in Education, University of Toronto.

Berry, W. (1991). *Standing on earth: Selected essays*. Golgonooza Press.

Block, L. A. (2017). Relocating: Moving between the field and the university. In T. Sibbald, & V. Handford (Eds.), *The academic gateway: Understanding the journey to tenure*. (pp. 41–50). University of Ottawa Press.

Borden, L. L., & Wiseman, D. (2016). Considerations from places where Indigenous and Western ways of knowing, being, and doing circulate together: STEM as artifact of teaching and learning. *Canadian Journal of Science, Mathematics and Technology Education, 16*(2), 140–152.

Canada. (2015). *Truth and Reconciliation Commission of Canada*. Queen's Printer. See https://nctr.ca/about/history-of-the-trc/trc-website/

Chawla, L. (2007). Childhood experiences associated with care for the natural world. A theoretical framework for empirical results. *Children, Youth and Environments, 17*(4), 144–170.

Davis, B., Sumara D., & Luce-Kapler, R. (2008). *Engaging minds: Changing teaching in complex times*. Routledge.

Donald, D. (2009). Forts, curriculum, and Indigenous Métissage: Imagining decolonization of Aboriginal-Canadian relations in educational contexts. *First Nations Perspectives, 2*(1), 1–24.

Freire, P. (2005). *Teachers as cultural workers* (Expanded edition). (D. Macedo, D. Koike, & A. Oliviera, Trans.). Westview Press.

Greenwood, D. A. (2009). Place, survivance, and White remembrance: A decolonizing challenge to rural education in mobile modernity. *Journal of Research in Rural Education, 24*(10), 1–6.

Gruenewald, D. A. (2003). The best of both worlds: A critical pedagogy of place. *Educational researcher, 32*(4), 3–12.

Hampton, E. (1993). Toward a redefinition of American Indian/Alaska Native Education. *Canadian Journal of Native Education, 202*(2), 261–310.

Kentel, J. A., & Karrow, D. (2010). Living (Ek) statically: Educating-within-place and the ecological imagination. *Journal of the Canadian Association for Curriculum Studies, 7*(2), 6–30.

Kimmerer, R. W. (2013). *Braiding sweet grass: Indigenous wisdom, scientific knowledge and the teachings of plants*. Milkweed Editions.

Laszlo, E., & Clark, J. W. (1972). *Introduction to systems philosophy*. Gordon and Breach.

McKenzie, M. (2004). The "willful contradiction" of poststructural socio-ecological education. *Canadian Journal of Environmental Education (CJEE), 9*(1), 177–190.

Orr, D. W. (2004). *Earth in mind: On education, environment and the human prospect*. Island Press.

Scully, A. (2012). Decolonization, reinhabitation and reconciliation: Aboriginal and place-based education. *Canadian Journal of Environmental Education, 17*, 148–158.

Shiva, V. (2016). *Earth democracy: Justice, sustainability and peace*. Zed Books.

Simon, R. (2013). Towards a hopeful practice of worrying: The problematics of listening and the educative responsibilities of Canada's Truth and Reconciliation Commission. In J. A. Henderson & P. Wakeham (Eds.), *Reconciling Canada: Critical perspectives on the culture of redress* (pp. 129–142). University of Toronto Press.

Simpson, L. B. (2014). Land as pedagogy: Nishnaabeg intelligence and rebellious transformation. *Decolonization: Indigenization and Society, 3*(3), 1–25.

Sims, L. (2015). Inspired to face the hurdles: A non-Indigenous educator's experience facilitating the integration of Aboriginal perspectives into education. *MERN Indigenous Education Research Monograph, 1*, 1–9. http://mbtrc.org/data/documents/occ-1.pdf

Sobel, D. (2008). *Childhood and nature: Design principles for educators*. Stenhouse Publishers.

Stevenson, R. B. (2008). A critical pedagogy of place and the critical place(s) of pedagogy. *Environmental Education Research, 14*(3), 353–360.

Suzuki, D., & Boyd, D. R. (2009). *David Suzuki's green guide*. Greystone Books.

Tupper, J. (2011). Disrupting ignorance and settler identities: The challenges of preparing beginning teachers for treaty education. *In Education, 17*(3), 38–55.

von Bertalanffy, L. (1968). *General system theory: Foundations, development, applications*. Braziller.

Whyte, K. P., Brewer, J. P., & Johnson, J. T. (2016). Weaving Indigenous science, protocols, and sustainability science. *Sustainability Science, 11*(1), 25–32.

SECTION 3

Perspectives Based on More Than One Sabbatical

Academics who have had more than one sabbatical represent a small portion of the academy, yet they clearly find sabbaticals beneficial as they have chosen to take more than one. In this section, the focus is on the long view of personal experiences. What are the commonalities academics see in their own taking of multiple sabbaticals? These may have commonalities with the earlier chapters and, perhaps, elements that are absent reflecting features that either are not enduring or not found among the few authors in this section. While the small sample constrains generalization, our sense is that there is likely an evolution of individual sabbatical experiences as one takes more sabbaticals and learns from prior experiences.

The section begins with Lloyd Kornelsen comparing the experience of an academic sabbatical with a study leave he had while a practicing teacher. The former involved travel, research, and academic events, while the latter emphasized personal restoration. The chapter is an interesting comparison because both approaches appear, in the academic literature, as sound approaches to the sabbatical.

The second chapter here, chapter 10, brings together a writing group from Memorial University who conducted a thematic analysis of their collection of sabbaticals. Each had only had a first sabbatical, but it is included in this section because of the collective voice of seven first sabbaticals. They observe that goals were lofty and actual achievements sometimes developed in unanticipated directions. Whether these details are a consequence of the first sabbaticals is something to consider while reading the rest of the section. They also draw out other issues such as graduate supervisions.

In chapter 11, Merridee Bujaki recounts her three sabbaticals. She notes gendered challenges, and that plans had to change to address some unexpected challenges. Given her disciplinary focus of accounting, her approach to addressing neoliberal expectations of the institution speaks volumes about work-life balance.

The section closes with Don and Shelleyann Scott writing about several sabbatical experiences, which include challenges unique to an academic couple. In their chapter, one can see a careful weighing of options and choices. It is fitting that they offer advice since they have experienced both the travel sabbatical and the "staybatical."

Note: Among the authors in this section, Lloyd and several members of the Memorial University Writing Group have contributed to two earlier books about academic experiences during the tenure-track stage and around the time of tenure, allowing the interested reader to connect these chapters to their longitudinal history.

CHAPTER 9

Practitioner Study Leave and Academic Sabbaticals: An Unsettling Reflection on Both

Lloyd Kornelsen

I completed a six-month sabbatical, in July 2018, as a tenured associate professor of education. My memories of that time are of hard work, reflective silence, contented okay-ness, and laughter with friends and family. At the outset, I felt confident in achieving my academic and research goals in part because they served as culmination of important life-long research-teaching interests and activities. My partner and I travelled across Canada, from west (Vancouver) to east (Montréal) and north (Gillam, Manitoba). I took my books and laptop everywhere, participating in conferences, starting a book project, and meeting with colleagues from across the country. By the end of the sabbatical, I had accomplished what I said I would—to what I had agreed with the university research/study-leave committee (RSLC)—eighteen months previously.

Two months after the sabbatical ended, I was back teaching, feeling energized and engaged—but puzzling about how different this felt from the end of a study leave I had taken eighteen years earlier as a high-school teacher. I expected to feel the same at the end of the academic sabbatical as I had felt at the end of my practitioner sabbatical. As then, I thought I would feel a marked difference between beginning and end of leave, between feelings of un-mitigating fatigue at the start and a sense of rested rejuvenation at the end. I did not feel that, and it surprised me. Rather, I realized that I had felt mostly energized and engaged (and happy) seven months previously, at the beginning of the academic leave; and that the whole sabbatical had felt different—easier and less fraught—from the practitioner study leave. In the two years since, I have struggled to find words or envisage conceptions to name and understand the difference. Thanks to multiple conversations with Timothy Sibbald and Victoria Handford, the editors of this volume, I have begun to understand the difference. This chapter is an outcome of those conversations, one where I briefly chronical the two, the academic sabbatical and the earlier practitioner study leave, propose several reasons for my differing experience, and muse, briefly, about an arising question about study leaves, elicited by a conference I attended during my academic sabbatical.

The Academic Sabbatical

The sabbatical was granted by the RSLC following a six-month peer-review process. I had been appointed to an academic position in the university's faculty of education five years previously (following twenty-four years of high-school teaching). I had enjoyed those years of academic work immensely (teaching, research, and service), since it represented a continuation, an outgrowth, and a culmination of my twenty-four years as a high-school social studies teacher. It freed me to build on relationships, knowledge, and insights in ways and by means previously not possible, nor imagined.

I wanted the sabbatical to be an opportunity to work on those things I had found most worthwhile during the previous five years—projects that I saw as extensions of my work as a high-school teacher. In my application to the RSLC, I proposed editing a volume/book on how social studies teachers, from across the country, talk and write about the experience of teaching for global citizenship. Additionally, I proposed investigating international practicum programs in the areas of global citizenship and human rights and write best-practices manuals for the international practicum program in the human rights department at the university.

I pitched the idea for the book to a national academic publisher (who endorsed the idea) midway through the sabbatical, and then asked two colleagues to help co-edit the book. In developing the book's rationale, I wrote a paper (peer-reviewed and published in 2020) and presented on the topic at a national education conference. At the end of June, we sent out a national call for proposals for chapter contributions. In October, fifteen months later, a completed manuscript was sent out for peer review.

I wrote two practicum manuals for the human-rights department, one for the practicum coordinator, the other for students. The manuals built on my original research (Kornelsen, 2014) and included recent literature on international human-rights/education/global citizenship practicums. I presented a paper derived from the project at an international education conference in Mexico City. I shared it with colleagues at my university and with university researchers doing a pan-Canadian study on international practicum programs.

When the sabbatical ended, I was satisfied that I had met my commitments to the RSLC. In the two years since the leave, the book has been published and the manuals adopted by the human-rights practicum coordinator and used by numerous practicum students.

The Professional Study Leave (Eighteen Years Earlier)

The study leave was granted by the study-leave committee of the high school where I was teaching. At the time, I had been teaching for twelve years. I was physically exhausted, mentally depleted, and emotionally bereft. Several years previously, I had been diagnosed with clinical depression. I assumed it was connected to teaching. As a part of my professional-development plan, I agreed to start a master's degree in adult education; however, I spent much of the study leave reading, writing, and resting at a cabin I built, on an island in a lake. I did not travel.

The questions I dealt with that year—and the ones that would eventually form the basis of my thesis research—were about my teaching life. They had to do with what I feared might end my professional teaching practice (burn-out and depression) and with what still attracted me to teaching (experiencing "flow": forgetting about time, sensing greater inner clarity, and experiencing heightened mindfulness). Six years later, upon completing the thesis, a respected adult-education scholar invited me to submit my research findings in a chapter for a book on teaching with authenticity, to be published by an international academic publisher (Kornelsen, 2006). Subsequently, thirteen years later, as an academic, I was contacted by a university in Australia, asking whether I would serve as an external examiner for a PhD dissertation entitled "Australian higher education counselling educators' conceptualisation of presence within the context of the teacher-student relationship." I agreed; and as it turned out, my master's thesis was referenced extensively in the dissertation.

During my practitioner leave, I did not expect to return to teaching. I believed that I had reached the end of my teaching career, thinking that my mental, physical, and emotional well-being could no longer sustain the rigours of classroom teaching. I thought of returning to carpentry or corporate consulting, work that I had done previously. However, I was contractually obligated to return to the school for one year. Upon returning to the classroom, not ten minutes into the first class, I changed my mind. I felt at once restored and confident, connected, and exhilarated—in ways I had not experienced in a long time. The difference between how I felt at the beginning of the leave and at the end was striking and stark: At the end of the school year ahead of my practitioner sabbatical, I had felt defeated, exhausted, and depressed. But, when it was over in September of the following year, I felt hopeful, energized, and engaged (the very things that had drawn me to teaching in the first place). I taught school for many more years.

In the years following the leave, I started an international practicum at my school; several colleagues nominated me for a national teaching award; I was asked to help develop a human-rights program at a nearby university; I joined a team working on a new provincial Grade 12 social studies curriculum; and I completed a PhD in peace education. Even though the post-leave years were not free of depression or self-doubt, I have not since yearned to leave the profession as I did at the beginning of my practitioner leave.

The Question of Difference

So, why the difference between the two, the practitioner study leave and the academic sabbatical? Both clearly signaled professional and academic productivity, by all customary and quantifiable standards. However, the study leave restored me in ways, as I remember, that the sabbatical did not. I did not need the sabbatical in ways that I needed the study leave, to rest, repair, and renew. It is beyond the scope of this chapter to present a comprehensive comparative account of the two. However, several possibilities resonate: (1) It had to do with the nature of my work, teaching; (2) it had to do with my teaching style and disposition; and (3) it had to do with life circumstances and the particular arc of my career.

1. Was it my teaching? Is the work that schoolteachers do such that they benefit from rest and time away, more than many other professions? I have worked at many things. I have been a postmaster, carpenter, business owner, corporate consultant, university administrator, and truck driver. None of these have been as draining or depleting, as teaching—mentally, physically, or emotionally. And so, the question, is there something unique about the work that teachers do, that requires time away from that work, to restore and renew? Possibly.

Peter Jarvis (critical theorist) and Max Van Manen (hermeneutical phenomenologist) write about how teaching requires an ongoing openness to the call and vulnerability of the other (Van Manen 2015), and a continual accessibility to, and care for, the student or student group (Jarvis 1995). Andres Vercoe (1998), a constructivist learning theorist, says that to teach dialogically, teachers need to approach reoccurring topics afresh, allowing for the potential to always relearn and recreate the subject anew with students; it is necessary for the teacher to remake the subject in dialogue every time, with each new student or student group. To teach this way can be exhausting and discouraging—because as Donald Schön said (1987)—to teach well calls for ongoing reflection in action. When I took my practitioner leave, I had been teaching four to five hours a day, five days a week, ten months of the year for twelve years. Whereas, when I took the sabbatical in 2018, I had been teaching an average of three hours a day, three days a week, seven months of the year for five years.

2. Or had it to do with my teaching style and disposition, one that could not continence teaching in ways that were not dialogic as conceived by pedagogues like Vercoe? I believed that as a social studies teacher, teaching for democracy, I had no choice. If I were to engage young people in dialogue about their world, about political responsibilities and shared obligations, I needed to teach "democratically," respecting the subjectivities of every student in the class. That, and I really did not know how to teach any other way. Perhaps this is why I was drawn to social studies in the first place; my teaching style necessarily predisposed me to teach what I taught. According to Yaroslav Senyshyn (1999), in the long term, teaching dialogically can be exhausting, and it is easy to fall into a habit of top-down, technique-driven teaching that objectifies and dehumanizes students. I was determined not to do so, resulting in my fatigue and need for rest as a reasonable response.

3. Or had it to do with life circumstances and the arc of my career? At the beginning of my practitioner leave, my partner and I were parenting two adolescent children. To supplement my income, I worked evenings, weekends, and holidays as a corporate consultant. At school, I was teaching four sections of the same course, world issues. The course had started to tire me, and its topics depressed me (war, genocide, global injustices, and atrocities). My dad died late in the year prior to the leave. A reasonable explanation for my fatigue and feelings of burnout had to do with life's circumstances, shaped by the particular arc of my career. In fact, studies of teacher-retention rates show a spike in teachers leaving the profession after eleven to fourteen years of teaching, for reasons similar to mine (e.g., Guarino et al., 2011). My life circumstances at that time may not have been unique. (When I took the academic sabbatical, our children were living away from home. I was no longer consulting. I found my work engaging, challenging, and satisfying. No one close to me had recently died.)

All three explanations make sense. All could account for the difference, and all probably contribute. Given the inter-related contingencies of cause and effect and the storying nature of memory, it is impossible to know exactly how much each accounted for what. Perhaps it really matters not; the practitioner leave was critical to my survival as a teaching professional in ways that the academic sabbatical was not. Both, study leave and sabbatical, freed time, space, and energy to contribute to field and academy; but only one, the study leave, restored me in a way where I could continue my work, teaching. If this is so, and if I am not alone, then I am led to a question:

An Ending Question and Observation

Teaching is hard work. It can be energizing and euphoria-inducing; it can be draining and depleting. A study leave may be critical to renewing, restoring, and rejuvenating teachers. So why is it easier to earn sabbaticals from universities than study leaves from schools? In my experience, it is understood that the sabbatical is a customary part of academic culture for tenured professors in universities. A common phrase echoing in halls of my university is "When are you going on sabbatical?" or, as overheard at committee meetings, "Sorry, I'm on sabbatical next term." This is not the case in the K–12 system. Here the study leave is often deemed a privilege or unaffordable luxury, and sometimes viewed as professional infidelity.[1] The reasons for the difference are complicated, of course, having to do with history, culture, and politics. It is far beyond the scope of this chapter to offer a critically definitive or analytical response.

However, the memory of an international conference on education in Mexico City during my academic sabbatical may signal a reason.

> Over 1000 participants were attending this conference on education—presenting papers, displaying posters, facilitating workshops, and participating in roundtable discussions, and all the other usual conference activities. We expected our offerings would inform public policy, curriculum development, teaching practice, and education research and philosophy. Yet, at this meeting of educationists, I had not met one practicing K-12 teacher (not unlike other conferences on education I have attended), neither as presenter nor as audience member, persons with indispensable knowledge and critical insight into the issues about which we had gathered to talk, those persons who could temper, nuance, enrich, and challenge our findings. Where were those people; and why were they not here? (Kornelsen, 2020, p. 132)

Thinking about it now—and seeing so few K–12 teachers at other conferences on education—it is difficult to believe that we, conference participants, education academics, and stewards of the public purse, value or respect teacher voices. For if we did, would we not find ways to include them in conferences on education; and would we not find the where-with-all to offer them time away from work so that they might think about their craft, reflect on their practice, rest from their work, and perhaps engage in discussions with researchers? I think we would; and I submit that that is why study leaves for teachers are less common than the sabbaticals for professors. (As Aulls & Shore [2008] and Kincheloe et al. [2011] contend, K–12 teaching work has lower academic status than that of tenure-track professors.) But why this is so? I do not know. The issue is not without educational significance or consequence. For as Pasi Sahlberg (2015), in a book exploring reasons for Finland's successful education outcomes, suggests, Finland's success may come down to teachers having time away from the classroom to rest and reflect.

However, and finally, my experience beckons more study, research, and introspection. Were my feelings of contentedness after my academic sabbatical related to my life and career trajectory, doing work that I found engaging, worthwhile, and meaningful (Kornelsen, 2020)? Was the practitioner study leave critical to putting me on a path to more interesting and challenging work; indeed, providing the trajectory to a tenure-track professorship in education? Is my experience generalizable to experiences of other teachers and professors? In what ways? How does K–12 education benefit from teachers taking study leaves? In Canada today, why is there such a stark difference in how sabbaticals and study leaves are treated by universities and schools (e.g., why the difference in terminology: study leave vs. sabbatical)? And so on.

Endnote

1   Based on conversations with teaching colleagues.

References

Aulls, M. W., & Shore, B. M. (2008). The experienced teacher and action research. In M. W. Aulls, & B. M. Shore (Eds.), *Inquiry in education, volume 1: The conceptual foundations for research as a curricular imperative* (pp. 69–81). Routledge.

Guarino, C. M., Brown, A. B., & Wyse, A. E. (2011). Can districts keep good teachers in schools that need them most? *Economics of Education Review, 30*, 962–979.

Jarvis, P. (1995). Teachers and Learners in adult education: Transaction or moral interaction? *Studies in the Education of Adults, 27*(1), 24–35.

Kincheloe, J. L., McLaren, P., & Steinberg, S. R. (2011). Critical pedagogy and qualitative research. In N. K. Denzen & Y. S. Lincoln (Eds.), *The Sage handbook of qualitative research* (pp. 163–177). Sage.

Kornelsen, L. (2006). Teaching with Presence. In P. Cranton (Ed.), *Authenticity in teaching* (pp. 73–82). Jossey-Bass.

Kornelsen, L. (2014). *Stories of transformation: Memories of a global citizenship practicum*. The International Centre for Innovation in Education.

Kornelsen, L. (2020). For academy's sake: A former practitioner settles in academe. In T. M. Sibbald & V. Handford (Eds.), *Beyond the academic gateway: Looking back on the tenure-track journey*. University of Ottawa Press.

Sahlberg, P. (2015). *Finnish lessons: What can the world learn from educational change in Finland?* Teachers College Press.

Schön, D. (1987). *Educating the reflective teacher.* Jossey-Bass.
Senyshyn, Y. (1999). Perspectives on performance and anxiety and their implications for creative teaching. *Canadian Journal of Education, 24*(1), 30–41.
Van Manen, M. (2015). *Pedagogical tact: Know what to do when you don't know what to do.* Left Coast Press.
Vercoe, A. (1998). The student–teacher relationship in Freire's pedagogy: The art of giving and receiving. *The New Zealand Journal of Adult Learning, 26*(1), 56–73.

CHAPTER 10

Sabbatical Tales: Expectations and Experiences

Cecile Badenhorst, Antoinette Doyle, Jackie Hesson,
Xuemei Li, Heather McLeod, Sharon Penney, and Gabrielle Young

Sabbatical leave is one of the greatest privileges tenured academics receive. At Memorial University of Newfoundland, a mid-sized public university in easternmost Atlantic Canada, after achieving tenure in the sixth year of work, faculty may apply for sabbatical in the seventh. Officially, the sabbatical year is to undertake dedicated, focused work. Deciding to take a sabbatical is not an automatic decision, and sabbatical leave can be fraught with complexity. For us, sabbatical leave is provided to enable faculty to engage in research, scholarship, or critical-creative professional or developmental work, "to foster their academic or professional effectiveness" (MUNFA, 2019, Article 22.14, 77). Sabbatical leave is only granted after achieving tenure, and faculty can choose to take a short sabbatical of four months after four years of service or twelve months after six years of service. If faculty take a sabbatical during these stipulated time periods, they receive 80 percent of their annual salary. If they delay the start date of their sabbatical, the remuneration percentage increases. For example, if the year-long sabbatical is delayed by twelve months, the salary paid increases to 85 percent; if by twenty-four months, the pay increases to 90 percent.

Those wishing to take sabbatical leave apply in writing to their administrative heads at least ten months before the start of the leave. The application "shall be supported by adequate documentation which outlines the scope and aims of the proposed sabbatical activity and shall include a copy of the report of the last sabbatical" (MUNFA, 2019, Article 22.21, 78). For all of us, this was our first sabbatical leave, and many found that sabbatical leave can be complicated as intentions often do not equate with achievements. A year without being anchored by teaching or service commitments can cause the faculty member to project unrealistic, idealized goals which are difficult to achieve. Others miss the structure of faculty life and find themselves squandering their time. Some overbook their time and find themselves busier than when not on leave. In this chapter, we present the narrative study of our experiences of these complexities. We found that reflecting on our sabbatical experiences was fruitful, and that contemplating the micro and macro aspects of our experiences may well help us negotiate the next sabbatical.

What Is a Sabbatical?

Academic sabbaticals have existed since 1880, when the concept of offering faculty every seventh year off was introduced by the president of Harvard University, Charles W. Eliot (Zahorski, 1994). Currently, the majority of North American universities offer their faculty (particularly tenured or tenure-track faculty) sabbatical leaves (Lundquist & Misra, 2017). Sima (2000), using Good's 1959 definition, stated: "The sabbatical leave is a plan for providing teachers with an opportunity for self-improvement through a leave of absence with full or partial compensation following a designated number of years of consecutive service (originally after six years)" (p. 69).

There is general consistency around the definition of a sabbatical leave in terms of length and compensation; however, as noted by Sima (2000), there is "less agreement regarding its purposes" (p. 69). This was also true when we searched Memorial University's faculty websites and our collective agreement. There were no clear, published guidelines of institutional expectations of sabbatical leaves; nor were there clear guidelines regarding what can be asked of faculty while they are on such leave. Jarecky and Sandifer (1986) reported that fewer than a third of medical-school faculty returning from sabbatical were required to submit a report, and that "sabbatical accomplishments were infrequently given exposure in their institution, and thus were not shown to advance the teaching, patient care, or the research objectives of the medical school" (p. 806). More recently, Mamiseishvili and Miller (2010) reported that there is limited empirical research to examine the structures, processes, and outcomes of sabbatical leaves. They suggest that "one of the reasons for this lack of empirical literature on this subject might be associated with the difficulty to measure or somehow quantify the value or the benefits of a sabbatical in any particular area of faculty work" (p. 12).

Iravani (2011) classified the sabbatical leave into five categories, using an author-developed survey to determine purpose and impact. Analyzing data from 120 participants, the author suggested that sabbaticals are provided for the following purposes: (1) professional (writing articles and books), (2) cultural/psychological (vocational peace of mind, family peace of mind), (3) capacity building (creative endeavours, developing ideas, improving teaching), (4) institutional productivity (research contacts, national and international), and (5) for personal motivation (i.e., spiritual renewal). Some of Iravani's purposes, such as research, creative activities, and professional activities, are also reasons put forward in Memorial's collective agreement for granting sabbatical leaves; however, cultural/psychological and personal motivation are not included.

Purpose of Sabbaticals

Most of the research published on sabbatical leaves has been qualitative in nature, consisting of personal narratives and opinion pieces (Kang & Miller, 1999). The leave appears to serve two main purposes. The first purpose is to engage in academic and professional development, such as writing manuscripts, book chapters, and grant proposals; presenting at conferences; and revising courses (Iravani, 2011; Maranville, 2014; Miller, et al., 2012). In a rare, quantitative study, Franklin (as cited in Carraher, et al., 2014, p. 297) reported on the sabbatical productivity of 288 faculty at the University of Wisconsin, noting that the group produced 256 articles and 61 books, made 271 presentations at professional meetings, and revised or developed 165 courses or programs.

The second purpose of the sabbatical is to enhance or re-establish faculty members' personal well-being. Several qualitative papers refer to such leave as an opportunity for re-energizing, preventing burnout, and regaining health and wellness (Hubbard, 2002; Iravani, 2011; Kang & Miller, 1999). Burnout is, "a prolonged response to chronic emotional and interpersonal stressors on the job, and is defined by the three dimensions of exhaustion, cynicism, and inefficacy" (Maslach, et al., 2001, p. 397). While limited, the data from quantitative studies also support sabbatical leave as a time to support wellness. For example, Franklin (as cited in Carraher et al., 2014) found that 82 percent of 288 faculty members reported renewed vitality and 68 percent reported a reduction in stress because of sabbatical. Additionally, Davidson and colleagues (2010) compared the well-being of 129 faculty members before, during, and after sabbatical to that of 129 matched controls who did not take leave during the same time frame. Those on sabbatical experienced a decrease in stress along with increases in positive affect and life satisfaction.

Although sabbatical leaves are not meant to free faculty members from all regular work duties, they are meant to free them from teaching, committee services, faculty meetings, and other administrative work. Flaxman et al. (2012) noted that faculty on sabbatical are relieved from usual day-to-day demands, allowing them to detach from their duties, replenish their resources, develop new resources, and receive the benefits of respite. Nevertheless, they noted that upon return to regular duties well-being benefits deteriorated more rapidly in faculty who exhibit "perseverative cognition" (worry and rumination) about work during the respite. Others also noted a similar relationship between the ability to detach from normal responsibilities and benefits to well-being. Studying 129 faculty members on sabbatical, Davidson and colleagues (2010) noted: "To obtain the full benefit of a respite, workers must detach from their workplace and experience a positive respite" (p. 961). Consequently, it appears that detachment from regular duties and respite are two key characteristics of sabbatical leave.

Methodology

In choosing a narrative approach, we assume that the sense an individual makes of an experience is important (Riessman, 2008). Experience is ordered through narrative, thereby giving it reality. Our focus is on what was chosen to tell, what language was used and what was emphasized, all of which contributed to the bigger picture (Merriam & Tisdell, 2016). Analyzing narratives is complex, and people telling their stories are involved in the fluid process of producing identities. Narratives are the way we develop "processes of being and becoming, belonging and longing to belong" (Riessman, 2008, p. 8). These are not single or stable identities. Sometimes our stories project a preferred self. Riessman (2008) identifies three levels to narrative research: the storyteller and the stories told (interpretations of memory and experience), the narrative data (objects for scrutiny), and narrative analysis (systematic study of the data). Using Riessman's thematic model and Merriam and Tisdell's (2016) analysis scheme, we took a systematic approach to analyzing narratives, where questions and written responses to the questions are "narrative occasions" (Riessman, 2008, p. 23). In thematic analyses of narrative, although the content is the key focus, the "case" is kept intact. The micro context of the case is important and themes are drawn from the case before being compared across other cases. The focus is on "what" was said rather than how it was said, to whom or its purpose. Meanings beyond individual storytellers are revealed, which point toward broader social implications. The purpose is to generate "a set of stable concepts that can be used to theorize *across* cases" (Riessman, 2008, p. 74).

We, the authors of this study, are also the participants. We are all tenured and affiliate with different subdisciplines within education: counselling psychology, TEFL/TESL education, arts, special education, and adult/post-secondary education.

We each wrote narratives in response to the following questions:

1. What do you think is the purpose of a sabbatical?
2. What did you expect?
3. What did you do on your sabbatical?
4. What surprised you?
5. What would you do differently?
6. Was the sabbatical worthwhile and why?
7. What advice would you give to others about sabbatical leave?

In our first round of open coding, we read the narratives and made notes on keywords and observations. Then we worked sentence by sentence before examining the whole response. In our second round of analytical coding, we grouped keywords into categories. We reduced the keywords by continually grouping, until we finalized and named the analytical codes. We created categories that were both sensitive to what was emerging from the data and conceptually congruent (Merriam & Tisdell, 2016, p. 213), where all categories are at the same level of abstraction. In our third round, we combed through the narratives and found evidence for the analytical codes, which were extracted as quotes. In the fourth round we took the results back to the group for member-checking. In the fifth round, as a group, we moved into levels of abstraction that explain these experiences by drawing conclusions and micro-theorizing from the data.

It is worth noting is that we all took one-year sabbaticals between 2017 and 2019. During this period, our university experienced extensive financial cutbacks. Tensions within our faculty increased tremendously as resources were competed for by subdiscipline groups within the faculty. Fewer per-course instructors were hired, and units within education were under pressure to be seen as thriving through increasing student enrolments. Consequently, some of us were asked to continue teaching or to develop new courses despite being on sabbatical, and, because of program loyalties, individuals felt obliged to agree. In what follows, we provide assessments of each of our sabbatical experiences.

Cecile found that it was difficult to extract herself from the faculty tension during her sabbatical. She was awarded a fellowship to conduct guest teaching in South Africa. This proved to be beneficial to her professional interests; it was enjoyable but exhausting. During her leave, she continued to supervise graduate students and provide academic service. Nevertheless, she found the sabbatical to be a positive and productive experience. She felt less fragmentation in her work because she could focus on one aspect of the job at a time. Overall, Cecile felt her sabbatical allowed her to balance work and personal life. It was worthwhile.

Gabrielle maintained graduate supervision, editorial duties, and academic service during her leave. And yet, she made extensive progress with new projects. Her goals were (over) ambitious and she felt she underachieved. She also saw the sabbatical as a way to reconnect with friends and family after many years apart. Leave provided the space to reconnect emotionally and physically, which was energizing. Gabrielle felt collaborative work was a highlight and she spent sabbatical time nurturing both personal and work relationships. Overall, the sabbatical allowed her to regroup. It was worthwhile.

Heather's sabbatical goals were overshadowed by the death of her mother and the grieving process afterward. She felt she had to be flexible as she coped with the situation as it unfolded. She was grateful to have the time to put family needs ahead of work needs. She continued to supervise doctoral students and edit a national journal.

She also used the leave to apply for an award and promotion. Even though her sabbatical didn't happen as expected, and some of her plans were put aside, she believed her sabbatical was worthwhile.

Jackie felt that the preceding years had worn her out and she wanted the sabbatical leave as a time to recharge. She planned to travel but family obligations caused her to stay at home, where she continued supervising several students and, because of programming demands and a lack of replacement, was obliged to teach a course. For her, being on campus felt like a continuation of regular work, but it also felt isolating. Although Jackie was very productive, she was not able to disentangle herself from the faculty and she did not feel rested at the end of her leave.

Sharon delayed her sabbatical because of faculty obligations. A heavy graduate-supervision load left her feeling behind in her work, and computer problems as well as faculty tensions and commitments added to her sabbatical woes, such that she returned to work feeling she had not had a break or time for personal rejuvenation or professional development. Yet she took on unplanned new projects and found collaborative work enjoyable. Therefore, despite many reservations, she felt the sabbatical was worthwhile.

Toni believed she set realistic goals for her sabbatical but achieved more. She applied for grants, continued to supervise graduate students, continued editorial duties and academic service, and felt obliged to redevelop a course. She found it difficult to refuse professional requests, however, and she also felt a sense of isolation even though she followed a disciplined routine. She felt that in a shorter sabbatical leave it may be easier to set boundaries and refuse faculty work. Looking back, she considered the sabbatical worthwhile but advocates being more "selfish" with one's time in future sabbatical leave.

Xuemei began her sabbatical in need of recuperation after years of overwork and burnout. She intended to spend more time with family. She continued with academic service, editorial work, and graduate supervision, including teaching one student in a reading/seminar course. While travelling and teaching in China was enjoyable, she felt it was also exhausting. Family responsibilities, illness, and ongoing faculty tensions meant she felt worn out and unwell by the end of the sabbatical. Nevertheless, she developed an online course and felt she was productive with her research. Thus, despite caveats, she felt that the sabbatical was worthwhile.

Our Experiences of Sabbatical Leave

Many of our narratives described the purpose of the sabbatical in almost idealistic, fantasy-like terms. Most hoped for uninterrupted hours of reading, long periods of time immersed in scholarship, and undivided attention paid to research. Toni, for example, sought "an uninterrupted period of scholarship, a period of reflection on academic activities for the purpose of goal setting for future academic work." Jackie reflected, "sabbatical is a time to move away from teaching and service obligations in order to focus on research." As well, our narratives highlighted the importance of taking time for professional development, to reflect and set goals. Sharon wrote about "time for self-reflection, self-rejuvenation, reading in your content areas, and time for professional development." Yet these expectations, while highly anticipated, were often unmet.

Tensions between Goals and Realities
Similarly, when it came to goal setting, what we wanted to achieve ended up being far from what we were able to achieve. Sharon said, "I had expected to feel a sense of freedom from the everyday responsibilities of a faculty member. No teaching responsibilities, no office hours, not being asked to serve on committees, and no requirements to attend faculty meetings." Cecile added, "I was determined to slow down and to enjoy my sabbatical." However, as Cecile indicates, the unpredictability of academic work often undermines plans and goal setting:

> Unexpectedly, a new grant became available and I applied for it because it was directly related to my sabbatical goals. The grant was on a one-year cycle so everything had to be set up, produced, and completed in one year.

These unintended opportunities, as well as the sense of responsibility to ongoing faculty demands, were pervasive throughout the narratives, and framed the reality of how our time was spent.

Toni was surprised by the number of requests for her attention, many of which were time sensitive and involved ethical responsibilities to the profession. She noted, "I felt I could or should not say 'no' because of a sense of care and duty to the programs to which I belong." Such work included responding to students' requests for references for scholarships and requests for support for colleague's promotion and tenure applications, as well as attending meetings about program development. While these tasks are small on their own, they add up and end up whittling away at sabbatical time and goals.

Sharon felt the pull of the ongoing tensions in the faculty that resulted in many hours of meetings. As she further commented:

> There were a number of other difficulties that occurred during my sabbatical, particularly around staffing (faculty) that I also felt I needed to be a part of so that I could have a voice in the decision-making process. I did not feel like I could remain away from faculty council, so along with everything else on my plate I also attended faculty meetings, staffing meetings, and faculty forums.

The internal politics dividing the faculty did not allow us to absent ourselves. Although Xuemei hoped to return to "a restored workplace culture, free from politics and mistrust," she found undercurrents of "continued hostility and isolation." Since Cecile was involved in a job replacement in her unit, she "was extremely worried about being away for travel." She wrote, "it's hard to explain how taxing this was. I felt like I was at a breaking point."

The narratives also highlighted how subject-area expertise also affected the ability to remove oneself from regular work, because of the need to be involved to provide extended expertise. Xuemei said,

> I could not help volunteering my service to Teaching English as a Second Language Newfoundland and Labrador, the provincial affiliate of TESL Canada, when its co-leaders decided to resign without successors. The professional association was in limbo and I felt it was time for me to rejuvenate it. I spent a lot of time on this volunteer work.

Faculty expertise, which framed a sense of obligation, prevented individuals from stepping back from responsibilities during sabbatical. Jackie noted,

> I was just as involved with my program's group meetings and with thesis students as I would have been if I wasn't on leave. . . .

> I think that my failure to walk away from a number of university commitments had a significant impact on both my level of productivity during sabbatical as well as my feeling that I was even on sabbatical.

However, taking vacation time, even while on sabbatical, can be perceived as unacceptable. Cecile highlighted this:

> I manage an international listserv and I sent a message to the list well in advance to say the list would not be available for three weeks and couldn't believe how many people said this was unacceptable. Many others were supportive but I think this is an indication of the constant burden we are under where downtime is seen as being selfish and unprofessional.

Graduate supervision was also highlighted across narratives, particularly the sense of responsibility to students who were under pressure to complete their degrees. Sharon commented:

> I successfully processed six master's students through either a thesis or a research project. That included applying for ethics, collecting data, writing the thesis, examination of thesis, and final submission. . . . I took a cut in pay to have time to do my own work and my own professional and teaching development that did not transpire. Yet how could I have managed that many students and the tight project deadline and teaching responsibilities as well?

Some narratives portrayed workloads which did not remarkably differ from non-leave faculty workloads. Jackie said, "in some ways my sabbatical was just a continuation of my regular role at the university, minus the classroom teaching and a couple of service obligations."

Productivity: Anticipated and Unanticipated
Despite our narratives being full of lamentations about not achieving sabbatical goals, we found that we were highly productive during this leave. Although we may not have achieved what we set out to do, we completed new and different tasks as well as many of the goals we set ourselves. Cecile wrote:

> What surprised me was . . . I eventually started to really enjoy writing again. It was wonderful to feel that sense of focus without being pulled in a million different directions. Every day, I could just concentrate on writing. . . . I felt so focused and as a result I was very productive—research-wise. I really feel grateful that I was able to go on sabbatical.

Additionally, Jackie commented:

> Over the course of my sabbatical year, I was involved in the start up of six research projects, I wrote ethics and grant applications, and was an author on three manuscripts that were submitted for publication. I also submitted and had accepted a conference proposal.

Our sabbatical goals and intentions focused on research, and we did not account for the unanticipated research, teaching, and service commitments that emerged during the year of leave. Toni noted that, "we overestimate how productive we can be, with respect to how much [work] . . . can be produced that counts." When called to write these narratives and reflect on our goals and achievements, we were surprised at all the work we completed and noted the importance of this reflection, as well as the need to recognize all the work completed on one's sabbatical, not simply scholarship with measurable impact.

We found we all had sabbatical dreams. Dreams of time devoted to thinking, reflection, and rejuvenation. We were productive but not in the way we originally fantasized.

Recuperation from Burnout

Although sabbatical leave is not provided by the university to address burnout and well-being, renewal is an important aspect of this type of leave. Each of the narratives noted how desperately needed the sabbatical was to address issues of exhaustion and burnout. Burnout in the academy is a common phenomenon, and we all looked forward to our sabbatical year as a period to recuperate, reconnect with family, seek balance in life, and focus on physical and mental well-being. We recognize that this part of sabbatical time—recovery—is self-funded, but mentally it was important for all of us. Cecile wrote,

"I was really burnt-out physically and emotionally . . . I wanted to get healthy again without the incessant demands, to learn how to enjoy life." Xuemei was also looking for "recuperation from years of stressful work and the ensuing burnout." Jackie expressed, "the demands of my personal and work life over the course of the last number of years had worn me out and I think I was really hoping to find the energy and drive that had originally made me want to pursue an academic career." Gabrielle reflected, "My quest to attain tenure left me physically disconnected from family." For Heather and Xuemei, such trips were emotional. Heather's mother, who lived in British Columbia, chose to die with assistance during her sabbatical. Heather said:

> Those days were awful and life changing yet it seemed as if her final weeks were about as positive as anybody's might be. At least I could be there and care for her. I had the hours and the months to move through my process of grieving. I was grateful that I could, for once, plan for family needs as a priority rather than as something I needed to squeeze into a lifestyle oriented to professional achievements.

Xuemei travelled to China to visit her family, whom she is not able to see regularly. Her father had died two years before and she noted, "I had been grief-stricken . . . and hoped to unload the grief by reconnecting with my family." However, she "sank into deeper grief" while conversations about her father served as reminders of her loss. She felt prepared for the work she had planned to do, but not for "the emotional and psychological turmoil" she faced. As a result, "even the high-spirited, heart-warming family banquets only cheered me temporarily. My emotional state resembled a rollercoaster ride."

Some of us did find the time and space to recuperate, as Heather noted,

> I carved out time to apply for a major teaching award, as well as to apply for promotion to the rank of full professor, both of which were successful. . . . The leave period was worthwhile because I achieved some of my goals. Further, I undertook focused contemplation.

Cecile's sabbatical ultimately felt rejuvenating:

> I relished the last few months of my sabbatical where I set up a routine of writing in the morning, then exercising and walking in the late afternoon. It felt like a healthy, balanced way of working.

Gabrielle craved "the simplicity of routine and the needed solitude to work," and became more confident in the direction of her career.

Others felt time slipping away to ever-voracious work demands, with little left over for well-being, even on a sabbatical leave. For many of us, growing sabbatical workloads with new research projects while continuing to publish, supervise graduate students, develop courses, and serve our communities left little time for rejuvenation. The requests came steadily. Toni reflected, "Even if it involves saying 'no' there may be time and efforts exerted in pointing the inquirer to other human or material resources. This led to an increasing sense . . . that I might not meet my stated research goals." When we travelled on personal time, our work files were not only packed in our luggage but also in our minds. Indeed, we could not free ourselves from work. Gabrielle noted, "I found myself sneaking away from movies to check emails and follow up on my self-contrived to-do lists." Her family were baffled and her parents warned her that "life's not always about the rat race." Well-being became elusive, as Xuemei comments on the strong emotions, and unforeseen complexities, she experienced:

> I felt weak physically and mentally and had to go through many medical tests and exams, which lasted several months. I finished the course design under such a condition, feeling completely worn out and quite depressed by the end of summer.

For different reasons, Sharon also noted,

> I did not have time for self-reflection, self-rejuvenation, teaching improvement, or professional-development opportunities . . . I arrived back from sabbatical feeling as though I did not have a break. . . . I really struggled with establishing boundaries between my students, my colleagues, the faculty politics, my work, and my rejuvenation.

As Toni noted, as academics our identities have been shaped by both our own expectations and those of others, and finding the right balance remains a persistent challenge, especially during a sabbatical, where we feel we have more time.

Advice for Others

This was a first sabbatical for everyone, and we were somewhat hesitant about providing general advice. Further, the sabbatical experience is individually experienced. Cecile wrote, "how you approach a sabbatical depends on your personality," while Toni added "the sabbatical plan is different for every academic . . . I doubt there is any 'right answer' or 'best advice' in how to 'do a sabbatical.'"

Nevertheless, a primary recommendation involves setting realistic goals that focus on research and writing. As academics, we customarily aim to overachieve. Those going on sabbatical leave would be well-advised to consciously manage their personal expectations. Sharon advised, "think about what you truly have a chance of accomplishing," and Xuemei added, "make very realistic work plans, the bare minimum of work you are willing to do. Work will come piling up on its own." Removing oneself from the physical workplace is important, and Toni recommended "a conscious and daily effort to 'unplug' from the many demands that will come." Sharon noted: "Guard your time and stay out of faculty politics," and Jackie suggested "finding a way to ensure that you can completely extract yourself from any university obligations, including student supervision and program group meetings." Suggestions to meet sabbatical goals and to avoid getting side-tracked included refusing requests and avoiding email, while for a sense of rejuvenation one should focus on work one really wants to do. Being flexible and planning for the unexpected is advisable. Gabrielle wrote: "While some goals will remain unmet there can be unimagined accomplishments," and Heather added: "We should plan well, yet we should also predict that there will be unexpected events."

Many recommended strictly setting boundaries on ongoing faculty work, reducing supervision if possible, and informing administrative staff and colleagues that you are on sabbatical. Almost all the group suggested taking a shorter one-semester sabbatical or an alternative sabbatical format of multiple short leaves for the sole reason that it might be easier to set up boundaries and protect shorter amounts of time. Jackie wrote: "Combining a semester of sabbatical with a research semester every three years ... might be a better way."

Some suggested keeping a journal to allow us to recognize work completed and milestones achieved. This will enable reflection and an examination of the leave. Indeed, it was only through the process of reflection for this chapter that we realized how much we had achieved and the many successes we had overlooked. Finally, many advised taking time off, to protect physical and mental health, to seek and find balance, and to say "no" and do less.

Discussion

Much of the research on sabbatical leaves suggests advance planning and setting realistic goals and expectations for the sabbatical (Carr & Tang, 2005; Dunn & Halonen, 2018; Hubbard, 2002; Maranville, 2014; Smith et al. 2016; Yarmohammadian et al. 2018). Maranville (2014) recommended that, prior to taking a sabbatical, individuals should create an agenda and define their focus. We found it difficult to set realistic goals and define our focus and, instead, indulged in many fantasies about what we would achieve on sabbatical. We also found that many new projects emerged unexpectedly. We would suggest reducing sabbatical goals and anticipating the unexpected. Many academics view the sabbatical as an opportunity to re-energize and enhance their well-being (Carraher et al., 2014; Davidson et al., 2010). We feel that mental and physical well-being is an important part of sabbatical leave. Even if we did not all achieve it, we feel it is a crucial time to aim at re-establishing work-life balance.

Miller and colleagues (2012) suggested that individuals negotiate their sabbatical goals through a formal application process that clearly outlines a detailed workplan. However, Carraher et al. (2014) argue for "authenticity" in reference to sabbaticals, and that individuals taking sabbaticals should make choices that are right for them. While not everyone is able to leave or uproot their family to leave their home institution (Lundquist & Misra, 2017; Smith et al., 2016), many researchers note that distance is key to achieving sabbatical goals (Dunn & Halonen, 2018). That is, if you must take your sabbatical at home, then find a way to stay away from campus (Lundquist & Mrisa, 2017). Detach yourself from your institution either by working from home or finding an alternative office space (Quay, 2006). Additionally, individuals who perceive themselves with more control are better able to detach, and those with high levels of self-efficacy are better able to mitigate the stress and burnout that can occur after the six-year probationary period to achieve tenure (Davidson et al. 2010; Dunn & Halonen, 2018). Smith and colleagues (2016) suggest that women are less likely to take sabbaticals, tend to take shorter sabbaticals, and are more often affected by family roles. Additionally, individuals who take domestic sabbaticals are more likely to be called by their home institutions to perform duties even while on sabbatical. Our experiences align with these findings in the literature. Most of us found it difficult to detach and set boundaries even when we were on sabbatical. This could be because of the circumstances of our university as it underwent extensive cutbacks and resources were withdrawn, resulting in competition from units for positions. With increasing competition for resources, it was difficult to be "selfish" and take time for research, even during sabbatical leave. We often felt obligated to take on non-sabbatical work like teaching, committee work, and program development because of our responsibility to our units in these competitive times. Through this process of writing narratives, reflecting, and discussing, we also became aware of the gendered nature of our narratives in the sense that service to our units, programs, and students was often completed before our own work, and often at the cost of our own well-being. We recognize that, as Smith and colleagues suggest, we have recommended taking shorter sabbaticals. This is a direct consequence of the neoliberal pressures placed on us.

It is important to recognize the extent and impact of neoliberalism on our experiences of sabbatical leave. The fiscal cutbacks, and consequent insecurities, directly impacted on the decisions many of us made to continue regular duties. We are not the only ones to face the barrage of neoliberal policies and processes. Acker and Webber (2017) note that, in Canada, oversight and accountability requirements reduce the neoliberal influences to a greater degree than governments in other countries—such as those noted in the United Kingdom and Australia (Vidovich & Slee, 2001). Nonetheless, rigorous tenure processes in Canadian universities "have joined forces with the intensification of work and expectations of performativity that are identified with the neo-liberal university" (Acker & Webber, 2017, p. 550). New realities for faculty work life, characterized by increasingly challenging expectations, are driven in large part by neoliberal impacts on university reform. Vidovich and Slee (2001) argue that the rise of a globalized knowledge-based economy has brought universities in many countries under closer scrutiny for the economic contributions they make. They suggest governments have been particularly concerned that universities demonstrably serve "the national interest" in the global marketplace and the prospective contribution they make toward the economic well-being of the country. Acker and Webber (2017) argue these market-focused influences include greater emphasis within universities on corporatization, entrepreneurialism, managerialism, and marketization values. Academic subjectivities "are influenced by the changing academic environment, in particular how academics have been called upon not only to be more productive but also to display that productivity in measured, measurable and/or accountable forms" (p. 541). Stress resulting from increasing demands on faculty is reported to be particularly acute in junior faculty (Ghorpade et al., 2007; Watts & Robertson, 2011; Zábrodská et al., 2018). While research on market-model influences have not primarily focused on impact on sabbatical practices, we contend that these forces hold the potential to exert similar influences on faculty sabbatical plans, experiences, and activities. We can now see the structural and institutional impacts that the disciplining nature of the tenure process has on us, followed by a period of intense budgetary cutbacks, resulting in intensification of work. But it was only through this process of collaborative reflection that we have been able to draw these conclusions that are often invisible in the busyness of day-to-day life.

Conclusion

In reflecting on sabbatical experiences, our individual narratives portrayed a tension between the pursuit of unrealistic expectations for productivity and a striving for well-being. The illusion of having time on sabbatical was juxtaposed with a strong sense of obligation to others. Most narratives highlighted productive sabbatical experiences. We were all productive, more than we had anticipated. This was significant in the context of faculty tensions and the reality of how our time was spent addressing programming needs, graduate supervision, and requisite service commitments. We feel our sabbatical experiences are a commentary—a reflection—on the nature of contemporary academic work in neoliberal contexts, particularly for women.

Looking back, we see that our sabbatical goals were unrealistic in that the pursuit of research goals alongside competing ongoing work obligations, while continually striving for balance are practices which, at best, are at odds with one another. We had conjured images of having time to catch up on professional reading, to bond with our families, and to complete tasks that had been neglected. Nevertheless, realities proved to be different, highlighting the impact of a decreased salary and increased sabbatical-related expenses. Many of us self-funded a portion of our sabbatical but continued to perform regular duties. We found that our sabbaticals mirrored our regular professorial duties, with similar, if not increased, workloads. Our narratives particularly highlighted the importance of taking time to reflect as a community on the experience of sabbatical, to avail of opportunities to pursue group projects and work that is individually motivating.

References

Acker, S., & Webber, M. (2017). Made to measure: early career academics in the Canadian university workplace, *Higher Education Research & Development*, *36*(3), 541–554. https://doi.org/10.1080/07294360.2017.1288704

Carr, A. E., & Tang, T. L. (2005). Sabbaticals and employee motivations: Benefits, concerns, and implications. *Journal of Education for Business*, *80*(3), 160–164.

Carraher, S. M., Crocitto, M. M., & Sullivan, S. (2014). A kaleidoscope career perspective on faculty sabbaticals. *Career Development International*, *19*(3), 295–313. https://doi.org/10.1108/CDI-04-2013-0051

Davidson, O. B., Eden, D., Westman, M., Cohen-Charash, Y., Hammer, L. B., Kluger, A. N., Krausz, M., Maslach, C., O'Driscoll, M., Perrewé, P. L., Quick, J. C., Rosenblatt, Z., & Spector, P. E. (2010). Sabbatical leave: Who gains and how much? *Journal of Applied Psychology*, *95*(5), 953–964. https://doi.org/10.1037/a0020068

Dunn, D., & Halonen, J. S. (2018, January 18). Preventing post-tenure malaise. *The Chronicle of Higher Education*. https://www.chronicle.com/article/preventing-post-tenure-malaise/

Flaxman, P. E., Menard, J., Bond, F. W., & Kinman, G. (2012). Academics' experiences of a respite from work: Effects of self-critical perfectionism and perseverate cognition on post respite well-being. *Journal of Applied Psychology*, *97*(4), 854–865. https://doi.org/10.1037/a0028055

Ghorpade, J., Lackritz, J., & Singh, G. (2007). Burnout and personality: Evidence from academia. *Journal of Career Assessment*, *15*(2), 240–256. https://doi.org/10.1177/1069072706298156

Hubbard, M. (2002). Exploring the sabbatical or other leaves as a means of energizing a career. *Library Trends, 50*(4), 603–613.

Iravani, H. (2011). Analyzing impacts of sabbatical leaves of absence regarding faculty members, University of Tehran. *Procedia Social and Behavioral Sciences, 15*, 3608–3615.

Jarecky, R., & Sandifer, M. (1986). Faculty member's evaluation of sabbaticals. *Journal of Medical Education, 61*, 803–807.

Kang, B., & Miller, M. T. (1999). *An overview of the sabbatical leave in higher education: A synopsis of the literature base.* Research Gate: https://www.researchgate.net/publication/234657401_An_Overview_of_the_Sabbatical_Leave_in_Higher_Education_A_Synopsis_of_the_Literature_Base

Lundquist, J., & Misra, J. (2017). How to sabbatical. *Inside Higher Education.* https://www.insidehighered.com/advice/2017/05/11/making-most-your-sabbatical-year-essay.

Mamiseishvili, K., & Miller, M. T. (2010). Faculty sabbatical leaves: Evidence from NSOPF, 1999 and 2004. *Journal of Faculty Development, 24*(1), 11–18.

Maranville, S. (2014). Becoming a scholar: Everything I needed to know I learned on sabbatical. *Higher Learning Research Communication, 4*(1), 4–14.

Maslach, C., Schaufeli, W., & Leiter, M. (2001). Job burnout. *Annual Review of Psychology, 52*, 397–422.

Merriam, S. B., & Tisdell, E. J. (2016). *Qualitative research: A guide to design and implementation.* Jossey-Bass.

Miller, M. T., Bai, K., & Newman, R. E. (2012). A Critical Examination of Sabbatical Application Policies: Implications for Academic Leaders. *College Quarterly, 15*(2). http://collegequarterly.ca/2012-vol15-num02-spring/miller.html

MUNFA (2019). Memorial University and Memorial University Faculty Association, Newfoundland, Canada. http://munfa.ca/agreements_type/current-munmunfa-collective-agreement/

Quay, S. E. (2006). 5 Recommendations for Completing the Flexible Sabbatical: Notes from the Field. *Academic Leader, 22*(9), 1–2.

Riessman, C. (2008). *Narrative methods for the human sciences.* Sage.

Sima, C. (2000). The role and benefits of the sabbatical leave in faculty development and satisfaction. *New Directions for Institutional Research, 105*, 67–75.

Smith, D., Spronker-Smith, R., Stringerm R., & Wilson, A. (2016). Gender, academic careers and the sabbatical: a New Zealand case study. *Higher Education Research and Development, 35*(3), 589–603. https://doi.org/10.1080/07294360.2015.1107880

Vidovich, L., & Slee, R. (2001). Bringing universities to account? Exploring some global and local policy tensions, *Journal of Education Policy, 16*(5), 431–453. https://doi.org/10.1080/02680930110071039

Watts, J., & Robertson, N. (2011). Burnout in university teaching staff: a systematic literature review, *Educational Research, 53*(1), 33–50 https://doi.org/10.1080/00131881.2011.552235

Yarmohammadian, M. Y., Davidson, P., & Yeh, C. H. (2018). Sabbatical as a part of the academic excellence journey: A narrative qualitative study. *Journal of Education and Health Promotion, 7*. https://doi.org/10.4103/jehp.jehp_70_18

Zábrodská, K., Mudrák, J., Šolcová, I., Květon, P., Blatný, M., & Machovcová, K. (2018). Burnout among university faculty: the central role of work–family conflict. *Educational Psychology, 38*(6), 800–819. https://doi.org/10.1080/01443410.2017.1340590

Zahorski, K. J. (1994). *The sabbatical mentor: A practical guide to successful sabbaticals.* Anker Publishing.

CHAPTER 11

The Academic Sabbatical as a Voyage of Discovery: What *Really* Counts

Merridee Bujaki

Not everything that can be counted counts, and not everything that counts can be counted.
                                                    Albert Einstein

I present an autoethnographic look at my 2018–2019 sabbatical, situating it in comparison to two earlier sabbaticals. Autoethnographic research is self-reflexive and subjective (Chang, 2008). It "combines cultural analysis and interpretation with narrative details" (p. 46) in a manner that links personal experience to broader socio-cultural themes. In this chapter, I link my sabbatical experiences to neoliberalism, metricization, universities as gendered organizations, and gendered norms of care to make sense of my experiences and to encourage resistance to these concepts.

According to Chang (2008, pp. 48–49), autoethnography is "about searching for understanding of others (culture/society) through self." In this autoethnographic undertaking I have reflected on my 2018–2019 sabbatical experiences, consulted my curriculum vitae, my personal mission statement, my sabbatical plan, sabbatical report, and slides from my post-sabbatical presentation and endeavoured to apply "critical, analytical, and interpretive eyes" (Chang, 2008) to these data. I provide additional context by describing briefly two previous sabbaticals, in 2001–2002 and 2010–2011. My spouse has read my chapter drafts and commented, since in writing about my sabbaticals I necessarily divulge some information about him. For faculty members with spouses, dependent children, or other caregiving responsibilities, sabbaticals can have an impact on the whole family, given the potential for sabbaticals to substantially change the place and rhythm of work. In addition, asking my husband to read my draft provided a validity check for the family-related components of my sabbaticals. Writing and reading autoethnography frequently leads to self-reflection and self-examination, which can help transform individuals and their understandings of themselves and their connections to the broader world. My self-reflections have helped me to organize and structure my insights, as well as to inform and prioritize my actions. I hope my research supports and encourages others in their self-reflections and their future actions.

Currents in Recent Research

Neoliberalism and the Push to Quantify Academic Productivity
Sabbaticals contribute to research productivity and, thus, to decisions on career progress. In addition, reporting on sabbatical performance is mandated by many institutions. It is important to consider the neoliberal context, then, within which sabbaticals are embedded.

A recent focus in my research (Bujaki et al., 2017) has been the role of accounting as a disciplinary process, in which accounting makes some things visible and amenable to measurement or quantification (Miller & O'Leary, 1987). In addition, this process of counting and giving an account of one's work or productivity is implicated in identity work (Giddens, 1991) and the ways in which we come to see ourselves (Gendron & Spira, 2010; Robson, 1992), particularly in response to "fateful moments" (Giddens, 1991) in our lives. As such, these moments can provide "opportunities for self-reflection which can cause groups [or individuals] to question the taken for granted assumptions related to their identity and image" (Taylor & Scapens, 2016, p. 1078).

I experienced some of these effects myself in preparing my application for promotion to full professor in fall 2016. While confident I had a strong portfolio of scholarly work, I knew the various players involved in assessing my application (referees, peer committees, administrators, etc.) would be considering the "impact" of my work. Recently this has come to mean citation counts, journal rankings, journal impact factors, and the h-index (an indicator that a number of publications, h, for an individual author have each been cited at least h times). While no one insisted that I include these metrics in my application for promotion, they are readily available online, so I was aware they would be, in all likelihood, accessed and factored into the decision making, regardless of whether I provided them. Despite that my collective agreement explicitly states "with the exception of the external letters of reference nothing may be added to the [promotion] dossier without the candidate's knowledge and consent," I have seen these metrics referred to in letters submitted by external referees in response to the request that external referees "speak to the intellectual standing of the candidate within the discipline or field of expertise." Thus, these metrics often enter into career decisions. After much debate with myself, I concluded it was preferable I provide the metrics. Thus, I included a detailed table in my application that, for each publication, indicated citations, the rank of the journal in which the article appeared, and the journal's impact factor. As a scholar with an expertise in impression management (Bujaki & McConomy, 2012, 2015), I recognized creating the table allowed an opportunity to frame and explain the choices I had made, and thus to narrate my own understanding of my scholarship. At the same time, however, I recognized the contradiction in my "choosing" to represent myself using these metrics and my desire to actively resist these disciplinary practices.

Neoliberalism promotes market mechanisms as the means to guide social interactions (Mennicken & Miller, 2012; Chiapello, 2016) and is consistent with the notion of governmentality (Foucault, 1991), in which individuals are constructed as "governable persons" (Miller & O'Leary, 1987) and are taught to govern themselves and their activities (Viale et al., 2017). Accounting inscriptions (Miller & Rose, 1990; Graham, 2010)—such as *measures of productivity*—become part of the disciplinary mechanisms used by organizations to know an individual and by which the individual is both disciplined by their organization and by which they come to know and discipline themselves.

Mennicken and Miller (2012, p. 16) observe that accounting technologies help to operationalize neoliberal concepts and that these technologies, "whether through notation, computation, calculation, or the multitude of other mechanisms for rendering the decisions and actions of individuals, groups, organizations and populations amenable to regulation according to authoritative criteria," form part of the disciplinary practices enacted in neoliberal institutions. According to Dean (1995, p. 581), these technologies become "a frame in which questions of who we are or what we would like to become emerge." Such questions are particularly relevant in the context of work and how our identities are constructed and reconstructed through work (Miller & Rose, 1990). However, whenever there is discipline, including self-discipline, there are possibilities for resistance (Lamb, 2001; Viale et al., 2017).

In the neoliberal university context, there has been an increasing focus on the measurement and quantification of academic research. Introducing metrics to a process or field is termed "metricization." After twenty-five years as a full-time academic, this metricization is evident through my anecdotal experience but has also been observed by others. Muller (2018) writes about increasing pressures to measure and control the performance of post-secondary educational institutions, arguing this is evident in the growing trend toward management by performance metrics.

Performance metrics applied to universities include institutional rankings. Universities, in turn, attempt to measure the productivity of individual academics through metrics such as journal rankings, citation counts, the h-index, and impact factors (Parker & Guthrie, 2013). Muller (2018, pp. 78–79) argues, however, that "[w]hen individual faculty members, or whole departments, are judged by the *number* of publications, whether in the form of articles or books, the incentive is to produce *more* publications, rather than *better* ones . . . if the incentive system rewards speed and volume of output, the result is likely to be a decline in truly significant works." Muller also notes that once new measures are introduced, efforts to game the measures are inevitably introduced. Given the introduction of citation counts as an indicator of performance, Muller (p. 80) observes that "some scholars formed informal citation circles, the members of which made a point of citing one another's work as much as possible. Some lower-ranked journals actually requested that authors of accepted articles include additional citations to articles in the journal, in an attempt to improve its 'impact factor'." As an alternative to metrics, Muller advocates for returning to the use of professional judgment in assessing research quality.

Recent accounting research (including Bujaki & McConomy, 2017) also documents these recent trends and discusses their consequences. Wills and colleagues (2013) and Sangster (2015) link these trends directly to an increased focus by governments and institutions on accountability. While measures of productivity can be helpful in making decisions related to merit pay as well as tenure and promotion, the increased use of metrics may also have disadvantages. For example, innovative research may be less likely as researchers reorient their work to focus on the methodologies and topics of interest in "top" journals (Reinstein & Calderon, 2006; Hussain et al., 2015; Northcott and Linacre, 2010; McGuigan, 2015; Sangster, 2015). In addition, tensions or unhealthy competition among colleagues and game playing may arise in consequence of excessive reliance on metrics (Reinstein & Calderone, 2006; Malsch & Tessier, 2015; Moore, 2015). Further, McGuigan (2015, p. 195) notes that a focus on metrics and publications in leading journals "is changing the way individuals think about their work, the types of work undertaken, and the outlets in which it is disseminated," and in some cases emerging researchers are being encouraged to seek out research topics deemed to be safe and readily publishable (McGuigan, 2015), if not particularly innovative.

Other research has demonstrated the importance of considering the institutional context in which research is conducted (Sangster, 2015; Bujaki & McConomy, 2017) when interpreting metrics; that interdisciplinary or critical research is often not published in leading mainstream journals (Reinstein & Calderon, 2006; Moore, 2015; Sangster, 2015); and that assessments of productivity or merit should also take personal contexts, such as life-cycle stage (Wills et al., 2013), sex (Dwyer, 1994; Kirchmeyer et al., 2000; Rama et al., 1997), and care responsibilities (Ward & Wolf-Wendel, 2016; Thun, 2019), into consideration. Later in the chapter I touch on each of these personal contexts in describing my own sabbaticals.

Universities, Sabbaticals, and Care as Gendered
Universities have been socially constructed as masculine (Bailyn, 2003; Knights & Richards, 2003; Dany et al., 2011; Dubois-Shaik & Fusulier, 2017). That is, academia

> vehicles a "gendered order" in its structures, its principle of organization, its customs and ways of doing things . . . . This is notably connected to the old structure of the university built around a masculine figure . . . who is entirely engaged in his

work, freed from domestic necessities by the presence of an invisible carer (the person taking care), in order to devote himself entirely and unrestrainedly to his work. (Dubois-Shaik & Fusulier, 2017, p. 100)

As such, universities are gendered, masculinized institutions (DiGiorgio, 2010; Gonzales, 2014; Gander, 2019; Thun, 2019).

According to Acker (1990, p. 146): "To say that an organization . . . is gendered means that advantage and disadvantage, exploitation and control, action and emotion, meaning and identity, are patterned through and in terms of a distinction between male and female, masculine and feminine." Thus, it is important to consider gender and gender roles when discussing academic structures such as sabbatical leaves, and their impacts. To date, however, there is relatively limited research on the role of sabbaticals in women's academic careers (Carraher et al., 2014; Smith et al., 2016).

Sabbaticals allow for a period of renewal, reflection, and concentrated focus on research, generally without teaching responsibilities or administrative commitments (Carraher et al., 2014; Smith et al., 2016). For many academics, a sabbatical leave affords them an opportunity to travel to other institutions to collaborate and network with other academics (Smith, et al., 2016); to develop or advance their research activities, including grant writing, data collection, and academic writing or revising for publication. These activities are particularly important in terms of career progress because the work done on sabbatical can significantly enhance the sabbaticant's research productivity and aid them in building their network and extending their reputation, which are important factors in support of the academic's future career progress. In particular, sustained productivity and an international reputation are important considerations in career decisions, particularly promotion to full professor, which in many institutions requires the demonstration of an international reputation and being able to nominate other academics capable of attesting to the quality of one's body of scholarly work. The ability to take full advantage of opportunities during a sabbatical, however, may be impacted by gendered norms and expectations.

Given the masculine history of academic institutions, the ideal sabbatical is frequently thought to be one where the academic moves to another academic institution in a different geographic location, usually an international one, to spend a year immersed in the new environment. Generally, this would require the academic to relocate with their family for the year. In previous times, when academics were usually male and few women worked outside the home, the level of disruption this would have caused to home and family life would generally have been managed by the non-working spouse, who would have completed many of the tasks associated with packing up or renting out the family home, settling dependent children into new schools, arranging banking and medical appointments in the new locale, and then reversing the process on the family's return. The contributions of such unpaid support by a non-working spouse would allow the academic to focus exclusively on their research activities while on sabbatical. Even though work, social, and family roles and expectations have changed significantly in the last number of decades, this model of an "ideal" sabbatical persists. However, for many academics with working spouses, and particularly for female academics with care responsibilities, this ideal is rarely possible. In an unpublished working paper, Bujaki and colleagues (2020) document many of the challenges faced by women academics related to taking full advantage of their sabbaticals. Many limited their sabbatical travel to short trips in terms of both time and distance, especially when their children were young. The women interviewed also commented on the impact of these decisions on their career progress, recognizing that their career progress was delayed relative to many of their male peers. Dubois-Shaik and Fusulier (2017, p. 104) note that "university institutions are still quite far from having addressed the core issues that undermine women's career advancement . . . , [including a] logic and organization that does not take into consideration parenthood, family and personal spheres of life." Sabbatical leaves, while not intended to be gendered, frequently are, given that the assumption of an "unencumbered life" (Acker, 1990; Williams, 2001; Dinh, et al., 2017; Fodor & Glass, 2018; Huppatz, et al., 2018) is less applicable to female academics, given social norms and expectations that position women as primary caregivers.

Sabbaticals are an opportunity enjoyed by members of few professions. Academic work, generally, and sabbaticals, in particular, invite flexibility intellectually and in terms of time and location of work. For many academics, however, the benefits of this flexibility are tempered by assumptions of the ideal worker (Ward & Wolf-Wendel, 2016), one who devotes themselves wholly to work. While flexibility has some advantages in affording academics opportunities to navigate structural caregiving challenges (caring for children after school, accompanying family to medical appointments, being present for ill family members, etc.), the same flexibility leads to many academics working long hours in response to ideal worker norms.

Caregiving is also gendered (Chesley & Moen, 2006). Numerous studies have shown that women do more hours of childcare than fathers (Bujaki & McKeen, 1998; Buchanan et al., 2020), regardless of household type and country (Craig & Mullan, 2011), although this is becoming more egalitarian (Buchanan et al., 2020). Regarding caregiving for adult family members (usually parents or parents-in-law), most caregiving studies have focused on female caregivers (Chesley & Moen, 2006), as women "are typically the primary caregivers for their own and their husband's relatives" (Chesley & Moen, 2006, p. 1250). However, "among those [studies] that compared genders, most studies have found that female caregivers reported greater stress than male caregivers" (Kim et al., 2006, p. 1086). Male caregivers have been found to report lower levels of stress because they experience higher levels of esteem when they do provide care, given gendered socialization expectations for caregiving (Kim et al., 2006; Chesley & Moen, 2006). Kim and colleagues (2006) determined that this relationship was mediated by the type of support needed by the care recipient. Specifically, male caregivers reported more stress when the support needed by a care recipient was psychosocial, and less when the care recipient needed care to support their physical functioning. In addition, in examining gender differences in caregiving stress among caregivers of cancer survivors, Kim and colleagues found that 84 percent of "husband caregivers reported that they received help from family and friends . . . , whereas only half (51 percent) of the wife caregivers reported receiving such help" (p. 1089). Studies have found that the types of support provided by male and female caregivers differ, with women performing more routine and time-bound personal care and household tasks, while male caregivers were more likely to provide informational or tangible support (Yee & Schulz, 2000). Thus, regardless of whether caregiving is for children, parents, or spouses, women are most likely to provide this care.

I describe my own sabbaticals briefly in this chapter to illustrate the intersection of the masculinized nature of sabbaticals, gendered expectations of care, and neoliberal imperatives for ever greater productivity.

My Sabbaticals in Context

The academic year 2018–2019 was the third sabbatical in my career as an accounting professor, the first since beginning to work at my present institution, and the first since I was promoted to full professor. Based upon my previous sabbatical experiences, which had not allowed for a year-long relocation, I had planned four comparatively short research trips during this sabbatical. I anticipated attending three conferences. I had eight ongoing projects that I wanted to advance, and five additional ones that I hoped to commence, should time and funding permit. This sabbatical was to have been a time of undivided attention to my research: no teaching, no meetings, no pressing responsibilities caring for children—now 22, 24, 26, and 27 years of age at the beginning of the sabbatical—and no significant financial concerns. A time to travel, a time to write, a time to meet up with research colleagues, a time to develop new collaborations, and a time to explore new avenues of research. It was not to unfold as I had planned.

Early Career and First Sabbatical
Let me go back to the beginning. I married in the early 1980s while my husband and I were still both in university completing our undergraduate degrees. After graduating, we lived and worked in Toronto. I was a professional accountant for a Big Four accounting firm in the late 1980s and trying to figure out how I would combine a challenging career and family effectively in a city and a profession that seemed to expect total commitment to one's career. Having had a few female professors at university whose ability to combine career and family I admired, I concluded that an academic career would allow for meaningful work and the flexibility needed to raise a family. I began my PhD in the early 1990s, with an eleven-month old, and attended convocation to receive my degree five years later with four children—ages 6, 4, 2 and 1—cheering me on. Little did I realize at the time that both accounting firms and universities are "greedy organizations" (Coser, 1974), expecting undivided commitment from their members.

The period of my life pre-tenure is largely a blur. My family and I relocated closer to our hometowns so our children could know their grandparents while growing up. My husband and I re-established our careers. Between the flexibility my teaching and research permitted me, the flexibility allowed by my husband's decision to run his own business, and some trusted childcare providers, we managed. By the time I earned tenure and promotion to associate professor in 2000, our children ranged in age from five to ten, and I was looking forward to the type of break afforded by the opportunity to take a first sabbatical. I spent months researching options to relocate to Hungary, where my husband's family was from, for a year-long sabbatical. My husband was willing to close his business for the chance to live in his parents' home country for a year so that the whole family could experience their Hungarian heritage firsthand. Given my husband's ability to converse in Hungarian, and that he had several relatives living in Hungary, it seemed like a perfect plan. That is, until the reality of searching for educational opportunities for our unilingual English-speaking children set in. Although we were confident three of the four children could settle in effectively, the fourth was experiencing some challenges at school. We were concerned their social development might be adversely affected if they had to adapt to a new school in a new language in a foreign culture. We were particularly concerned about the possible effects on their self-esteem if a year away might mean they returned to school at home a year behind their classmates. When we discovered that the cost of English-language schooling for four children in Hungary would exceed my reduced salary on sabbatical (never mind covering living or research costs), and was only available in Budapest, not in the city where we hoped to live, the plan to take a "traditional" sabbatical was reluctantly set aside. Ultimately, I opted to focus on working from home on my first sabbatical in 2001–2002, to maintain a routine that avoided disruption for the rest of the family. We did, however, manage a month-long North American family vacation organized around key conferences I attended, and I did spend a month teaching overseas on my own.

Mid-Career and Second Sabbatical
After that first sabbatical, research became a somewhat secondary focus in my career as I took on additional overload teaching to contribute to supporting my growing family financially and as my husband returned to university to complete a second degree and reorient his career. At my former institution we had the option of delaying our sabbatical for two additional years (taking it after eight years, rather than six) and then taking it at 100 percent salary (versus

75 percent). I opted to take advantage of this arrangement and waited until 2010–2011 to take my second sabbatical. Given the costs of providing for a family with four children, with two in high school and two attending university, this seemed a prudent financial option. The cost of this arrangement for the academic, however, is the potential loss of a full sabbatical over the course of their academic career. For example, in a twenty-eight-year career a sabbatical taken every seventh year would allow for four sabbaticals in total. If sabbaticals were taken every ninth year, however, the same twenty-eight-year career would result in only three sabbaticals. In addition to financial considerations, my husband completed his second degree in 2006 and had worked his way into a highly valued job by 2008. He was unwilling to take a year off work to accompany me on an extended sabbatical trip, both as there was no guarantee that he would be able to return to his same position after a leave and as his father (aged ninety-two at the beginning of my sabbatical) was experiencing significant health concerns (he passed away during the sabbatical). Instead of a lengthy sabbatical trip, I began a new research project based geographically close to home and took a few international trips of short duration to gather data. This sabbatical rekindled my enjoyment of original research, and while on sabbatical I began considering a move to another institution where I would be encouraged to refocus my energy on research.

New University and Third Sabbatical

I changed institutions in 2012. The confluence of a lower teaching load, greater encouragement for research, and significantly reduced family responsibilities (children then aged seventeen to twenty-two) resulted in a highly productive period in my career, leading to promotion to full professor in 2017. Thus, when I applied for my third sabbatical, late in the fall of 2017, I was looking forward to being on sabbatical in 2018–2019. My two prior sabbaticals had been focused at home for family and financial reasons, and I now considered this a normal, if less than ideal, sabbatical. Recognizing that my husband could not easily interrupt his career to accompany me on an extended sabbatical trip, I planned for a series of short, unaccompanied one- to two-week trips that would allow me to attend conferences and visit with colleagues to advance a range of research and writing projects. The wisdom of a sabbatical plan based close to home was reinforced, first, when my mother had a stroke in the spring of 2018, and it became clear that she would need support from me on an ongoing basis and, second, when my husband was diagnosed with cancer that fall. Although my sabbatical ultimately had little travel, it gave me time to undertake a voyage of another kind—an academic sabbatical as a voyage of discovery—during which I had a chance to reflect on what *really* counts.

Plan Versus Reality: The 2018–2019 Sabbatical

The Approved Sabbatical Plan
My proposed sabbatical plan included a brief description of intended activities (divided into work on projects already in progress and new research projects I hoped to initiate), discussion of the anticipated location of my activities and travel plans, arrangements for my graduate students, my intended use of university facilities, anticipated expenses and research grants, and a brief discussion of additional expected income sources during the year. In terms of planned scholarly work, I listed eight projects for which my plan was to draft (in conjunction with various co-authors) new working papers. In addition, I noted five new projects that were possibilities, depending on the outcome of grant applications and available time.

Developing Personal Mission, Vision, and Values Statements
Despite my lengthy list of planned projects, my first sabbatical activity was to craft personal mission, vision, and values statements. I began my sabbatical with this self-reflective exercise in part because I realized I had too many distinct projects on the go, with too many distinct research teams, which I did not consider sustainable in the long run. The second reason was that I came to realize the key constraint in the balance of my career was never going to be having too few research ideas but having too little time. As I approached my fifty-fifth birthday, and realizing that several of my research projects had required eight to ten years to complete, I needed a touchstone for myself that would allow me to strategically select and commit to projects that fit my mission. After all, I had only ten years left until the typical retirement age of sixty-five. The career mission statement I crafted for myself is "to make a difference and foster success and inclusion in the lives and careers of individuals and groups of people who are disadvantaged in some way by their social identity/ ies, especially women and among accountants." I even went so far

as to categorize my current and planned projects in accordance with their fit with this mission, and I resolved to refocus on those best aligned with my stated priorities.

The Actual Sabbatical: First Six Months of Sabbatical
The first three months of my sabbatical went largely according to plan. Some writing, a vacation cruise to celebrate our thirty-fifth wedding anniversary, presentations of two papers—one in Ireland and one in Northern Ireland—and completion of reviews for several journals. In October, however, it became clear that my priorities were about to shift. Having previously accompanied my husband to some diagnostic medical procedures, while I was away at a week-long women's writing retreat it was confirmed that my fifty-eight-year-old husband had cancer. In fact, as further diagnostics soon revealed, he had two unrelated primary cancers, neither of which were causing him any pain but both of which required surgery. Initially, not much of my sabbatical changed. The timeline initially proposed for one major surgery to address both cancers was about eight weeks, to allow time for additional consultations with surgeons and oncologists. This would have taken us to mid-December, with a planned hospital stay of five to seven days. However, our daughter was getting married in late December, so a January surgery date was negotiated. Given this timeline, my husband and I agreed I would continue my planned week-long sabbatical trip in November, though I quietly cancelled my winter-term trips. I also ramped up my writing activities in the fall and submitted two conference papers in December, not sure what the winter would bring.

The Actual Sabbatical: Second Six Months of Sabbatical
It turns out postponing surgery until January was wise, at least in terms of making it to the December wedding. The hospital stay was nineteen days, rather than five to seven, and the resulting neurologic pain was both unexpected and unremitting. The hospital stay did not have much impact on my sabbatical plans; I wrote while at home and read academic articles sitting in the hospital room. The real impact, however, was when my husband was discharged from hospital and returned to our two-storey house, unexpectedly unable to walk and temporarily confined to a wheelchair. Recovery was a slow process, but by May 2019 we were able to dance together—this time at our son's wedding—and I was able to attend an out-of-town conference

and present two papers. But I have a new, lived appreciation for the mental-health impacts of stress and anxiety on productivity. Many days I was unable to write, not being able to summon the clarity of thinking and concentration required. Eventually, however, writing became an escape and my productivity ramped back up.

Insights and Reflections

The Actual Sabbatical: Reporting as Resistance

My institution requires a formal sabbatical report be submitted soon after the completion of a sabbatical. My formal report, submitted in July 2019, included the following statement:

> I did not travel as extensively as anticipated during my sabbatical as my plan was significantly impacted by the health status of two family members. Specifically, my mother had a stroke in April 2018 and required considerable support during the early months of my sabbatical. In addition, my spouse was diagnosed with two cancers in October 2018 and underwent extensive surgery in January 2019. He is continuing to receive treatment and requires support at this time.

In addition, my report included three two-column tables. The first table contrasted my planned sabbatical activities, related to the eight projects already in progress at the beginning of the sabbatical, with my sabbatical accomplishments/outcomes. I reported that six of the eight planned papers had been written and submitted to either a conference or a journal. Table two used the same structure to report on the five projects I had tentatively sought to undertake, two of which I had begun. The third table described significant additional activities during the course of my sabbatical, including five academic presentations and six article reviews; appointment to an editorial board; serving on the search committee for a new dean; attending forty-six governance meetings or events for a major research project and a research centre with which I am affiliated; serving as an advisory board member for a not-for-profit organization; reviewing two promotion-to-full-professor dossiers; serving as examiner for one PhD thesis, one PhD proposal, one PhD comprehensive examination, and one master's thesis; and holding sixteen virtual meetings with graduate students. Many of these activities were linked to research projects or graduate-student engagement, which continues regardless of being on sabbatical. Serving on the search committee for a new dean was a holdover from an ongoing search in the prior year, and my ongoing involvement with the research centre helped to support and mentor my successor as director of the centre, a condition of her accepting the role while I was on sabbatical.

In addition to the formal report to the university, my school also requires a post-sabbatical presentation to faculty colleagues. It was here that I actively chose to go off the formal, "objective" academic script. In a presentation titled "Sabbatical Reflections (and Resistance)" I described both the specific papers accepted or submitted for publication, a selection of presentations, and the other research and service activities noted above. I then provided a list of what, to my mind, really counts: the joy-filled celebrations of our thirty-fifth wedding anniversary and two children's weddings, and the emotional and physical demands of medical interactions and advocating on behalf of loved ones. These included supporting my mother during her stroke recovery at twenty speech-therapy sessions and at five medical appointments, as well as advocating on behalf of my husband with hospital personnel (surgeons, oncologists, pain specialists, social workers, physiotherapists, dieticians, and administrative and billing personnel, in addition to the roster of nurses) during his hospital stay, daily interactions with home-care nurses for several weeks following his discharge from hospital, and thirty-eight doctor, physiotherapy or laboratory appointments to which I accompanied my husband, until he was able to attend on his own, and the management and administration of too many prescription pills and group-insurance benefit claims to count.

For me, this informal accounting of my sabbatical activities was intended to be an act of resistance against neoliberalism's metricization of research and productivity in the university sector. Not only was this an act of resistance of my own, but I also hoped my presentation would empower others, especially women, to see their caregiving activities as legitimate, and to encourage them to resist increasing pressures for them and their work to be judged, and for their activities and their own identities to be governed, by external metrics. I also hoped to help others—men and women—recognize the gendered nature of post-secondary institutions and encourage them to resist pressures from these greedy organizations for ever more work.

Looking Forward with Optimism and Clarity of Purpose

I have been back from the sabbatical for over a year now. My husband's health is much improved, and after six months completely off work, followed by a year on a reduced work schedule, he has returned to full-time work. My mission, vision, and values statements have been tested, especially in the extraordinary times attendant with a global pandemic, but I find these statements have provided me with greater clarity of purpose and have helped me decline opportunities not fully aligned with my goals. Writing this autoethnographic chapter fits my mission to make a difference and foster success and inclusion, in part by exposing the pervasive effects of neoliberalism, gendered organizations, and gendered expectations of care on our work and our identities.

Sabbaticals are indeed voyages of discovery. The trips do not always take the intended path, and sometimes the destination turns out to be somewhere unanticipated. However, sabbaticals do offer a chance to relax, restore, and reflect on our research, our lives, our priorities. I am already looking forward to the next sabbatical. Along with everything else I did in this most recent sabbatical, I also spent four hours each week attending Hungarian-language classes, getting ready for my next sabbatical, which I hope will finally include an extended stay in Hungary. Perhaps sabbatical number four will be the "traditional" sabbatical at last: our children will be well established, my caregiving responsibilities should be reduced, my husband should be retired and free to travel, and I hope to be able to experience a sabbatical unencumbered by gendered norms for caregiving and neoliberal expectations for production.

In this ethnographic chapter, I explore how neoliberalism, metricization, universities as gendered organizations, and gendered norms of care have impacted my sabbatical experiences. I consider how these concepts may discipline and constrain sabbatical activities and academics' identities. At the same time, these reflections suggest possibilities for resistance and change. Ideally the insights and reflections included in this chapter serve as a catalyst for broad social and organizational changes to address the downsides of neoliberalism, the disciplinary effects of metricization, and the gendered nature of practices embedded in greedy organizations and norms for caregiving.

References

Acker, J. (1990). Hierarchies, jobs, and bodies: A theory of gendered organizations. *Gender & Society, 4*, 139–158.

Bailyn, L. (2003). Academic careers and gender equity: Lessons learned from MIT. *Gender, Work & Organization, 10*(2), 137–152.

Buchanan, T., Das, A. and McFarlane, A. (2020). Gender differences in within-couple influences on work–family balance satisfaction: when benefits become threats. *Journal of Family Studies, 26*(1), 106–125.

Bujaki, M. L., Bourgeault, I., & Gaudet, S. (2020). Academia as a Bourdieusian field: Masculine structures and their consequences for women [Unpublished manuscript].

Bujaki, M. L., Gaudet, S., & Iuliano, R. (2017). Governmentality and identity construction through 50 years of personal income tax returns: The case of an immigrant couple in Canada. *Critical Perspectives on Accounting, 46*, 54–74.

Bujaki, M. L., & McConomy, B. (2012). Metaphor in Nortel's letters to shareholders: 1997–2006. *Accounting, Auditing & Accountability Journal, 25*(7), 1113–1139. https://www.insidehighered.com/advice/2017/05/11/making-most-your-sabbatical-year-essay www.emeraldinsight.com/doi/abs/10.1108/09513571211263211?journalCode=aaaj

Bujaki, M. L., & McConomy, B. (2015). Responding to Accountability Predicaments: Impression Management in Voluntary Corporate Annual Report Disclosures. *The Accounting, Finance and Governance Review, 22*(1), 1–26.

Bujaki, M. L., & McConomy, B. (2017). Productivity in top-10 academic accounting journals by researchers at Canadian universities at the start of the 21st century. *Accounting Perspectives, 16*(4), 269–313.

Bujaki, M., & McKeen, C. (1998). Hours spent on household tasks by business school graduates. *Women in Management Review, 13*(3), 105–113. https://doi.org/10.1108/09649429810215848

Carraher, M., Crocitto, M., & Sullivan, S. (2014). A kaleidoscope career perspective on faculty sabbaticals. *Career Development International, 19*(3), 295–313.

Chang, H. (2008). *Autoethnography as method*. Left Coast Press.

Chesley, N., & Moen, P. (2006). When workers care: Dual-earner couples' caregiving strategies, benefit use, and psychological well-being. *American Behavioral Scientist, 49*(9), 1248–1269.

Chiapello, E. (2016sK. (2011). How mothers and fathers share childcare: A cross-national time-use comparison. *American Sociological Review, 76*(6), 834–861. https://doi.org/10.1177/0003122411427673

Dany F., Louvel, S., & Valette, A. (2011). Academic careers: The limits of the "boundaryless approach" and the power of promotion scripts. *Human Relations, 64*, 971–996.

Dean, M. (1995). Governing the unemployed self in an active society. *Economy and Society, 24*(4), 559–583.

DiGiorgio, C. (2010). Capital, power, and habitus: How does Bourdieu speak to the tenure process in universities? *The Journal of Educational Thought, 44*(1), 27–40.

Dinh, H., Strazdins, L., & Welsh, J. (2017). Hour-glass ceilings: Work-hour thresholds, gendered health inequities. *Social Science & Medicine, 176*, 42–51.

Dubois-Shaik, F., & Fusulier, B. (2017). Understanding gender inequality and the role of work/family interface in contemporary academia: An introduction. *European Educational Research Journal, 16*, 99–105.

Dwyer, P. (1994). Gender differences in the scholarly activities of accounting academics: An empirical investigation. *Issues in Accounting Education, 9*(2), 231–246.

Fodor, E., & Glass, C. (2018). Negotiating for entitlement: Accessing parental leave in Hungarian firms. *Gender, Work & Organization, 25*, 687–702.

Foucault, M. (1991). Governmentality. In G. Burchell, C. Gordon, & P. Miller (Eds.), *The Foucault effect: Studies in governmentality* (pp. 87–104). The University of Chicago Press.

Gander, M. (2019). Let the right one in: A Bourdieusian analysis of gender inequality in universities' senior management. *Gender, Work & Organization, 26*, 107–123.

Gendron, Y., & Spira, L. F. (2010). Identity narratives under threat: A study of former members of Arthur Andersen. *Accounting, Organizations and Society, 35*(3), 275–300.

Giddens, A. (1991). *Modernity and self-identity: Self and society in the late modern age.* Stanford University Press.

Gonzales, L. (2014). Framing faculty agency inside striving universities: An application of Bourdieu's theory of practice. *The Journal of Higher Education, 85*(2), 193–218.

Graham, C. (2010). Accounting and the construction of the retired person. *Accounting, Organizations and Society, 35*(1), 23–46.

Huppatz, K., Sang, K., & Napier, J. (2018). "If you put pressure on yourself to produce then that's your responsibility": Mothers' experiences of maternity leave and flexible work in the neoliberal university. *Gender, Work & Organization*, 1–17. https://doi.org/10.1111/gwao.12314

Hussain, S., Liu, L., Wang, Y., & Zuo, L. (2015). Journal rankings, collaborative research and publication strategies: Evidence from China. *Accounting Education, 24*(3), 233–55.

Kim, Y., Loscalzo, M., Wellisch, D., & Spillers, R. (2006). Gender differences in caregiving stress among caregivers of cancer survivors. *Psycho-Oncology, 15*, 1086–1092.

Kirchmeyer, C., Reinstein, A., & Hasselback, J. (2000). Relational demography and career outcomes among academic accountants. *Advances in Accounting Behavioral Research*, 3, 177–197.

Knights, D., & Richards, W. (2003). Sex discrimination in UK academia. *Gender, Work & Organization*, 19(2), 213–238.

Lamb, M. (2001). "Horrid appealing": Accounting for taxable profits in mid-nineteenth century England. *Accounting, Organizations and Society*, 26(3), 271–298.

Malsch, B., & Tessier, S. (2015). Journal ranking effects on junior academics: Identity fragmentation and politicization. *Critical Perspectives on Accounting*, 26(1), 84–98.

McGuigan, N. (2015). The impact of journal rankings on Australasian accounting education scholarship: A personal view. *Accounting Education*, 24(3), 187–207.

Mennicken, A., & Miller, P. (2012). Accounting, territorialization and power. *Foucault Studies*, 13, 4–24.

Miller, P., & O'Leary, T. (1987). Accounting and the construction of the governable person. *Accounting, Organizations and Society*, 12(3), 235–265.

Miller, P., & Rose, N. (1990). Governing economic life. *Economy and Society*, 19(1), 1–31.

Moore, L. (2015). Exploring the role of symbolic legitimation in voluntary journal list adoption. *Accounting Education*, 24(3), 256–273.

Muller, J. Z. (2018). *The tyranny of metrics*. Princeton University Press.

Northcott, D., & Linacre, S. (2010). Producing spaces for academic discourse: The impact of research assessment exercises and journal quality rankings. *Australian Accounting Review*, 20(1), 38–54.

Parker, L., & Guthrie, J. (2013). Accounting scholars and journals rating and benchmarking. *Accounting, Auditing & Accountability Journal*, 26(1), 4–15.

Rama, D., Raghunandan, K., Logan, L., & Barkman, B. (1997). Gender differences in publications by promoted faculty. *Issues in Accounting Education*, 12(3), 353–365.

Reinstein, A., & Calderon, T. (2006). Examining accounting departments' rankings of the quality of accounting journals. *Critical Perspectives on Accounting*, 17(4), 457–490.

Robson, K. (1992). Accounting numbers as "inscription": Action at a distance and the development of accounting. *Accounting, Organizations and Society*, 17(7), 685–708.

Sangster, A. (2015). You cannot judge a book by its cover: The problems with journal rankings. *Accounting Education*, 24(3), 175–186.

Smith, D., Spronken-Smith, R., Stringer, R., & Wilson, C. A. (2016). Gender, academic careers and the sabbatical: A New Zealand case study. *Higher Education Research & Development*, 35(3), 589–603.

Taylor, L., & Scapens, R. (2016). The role of identity and image in shaping management accounting change. *Accounting, Auditing & Accountability Journal, 29*(6), 1075–1099.

Thun, C. (2019). Excellent and gender equal? Academic motherhood and "gender blindness" in Norwegian academia. *Gender, Work & Organization, 27*(2), 166–180. https://doi.org/10.1111/gwao.12368

Viale, T., Gendron, Y., & Suddaby, R. (2017). From "Mad Men" to "Math Men": The rise of expertise in digital measurement and the shaping of online consumer freedom. *Accounting, Auditing and Accountability Journal, 30*(2), 270–305.

Ward, K., & Wolf-Wendel, L. (2016). Academic motherhood: Mid-career perspectives and the ideal worker norm. *New Directions for Higher Education, 176*, 11–23. https://doi.org/10.1002/he.20206

Williams, J. (2001). *Unbending gender: Why family and work conflict and what to do about it*. Oxford University Press.

Wills, D., Ridley, G., & Mitev, H. (2013). Research productivity of accounting academics in changing and challenging times. *Journal of Accounting & Organizational Change, 9*(1), 4–25.

Yee, J., & Schulz, R. (2000). Gender differences in psychiatric morbidity among family caregivers: A review and analysis. *Gerontologist, 40*, 147–164.

CHAPTER 12

Sabbaticals in a Research-Intensive University: Supports, Tensions, and Outcomes

Donald E. Scott and Shelleyann Scott

When we received an invitation to submit a chapter on our sabbatical experiences, we initially wondered what there was to write about, and what we could contribute, but this invitation led us to reflect on our sabbatical-application process, the actual sabbatical experiences, and the outcomes. Our reflection provided a useful opportunity to critically analyze the value of our different experiences and to provide advice to less-experienced academics about how to avoid the pitfalls into which we fell that could tarnish a sabbatical experience. We draw upon the literature review and analysis from our other chapter in this book to reflect on our sabbatical experiences (in this chapter). We present the policy framework under which we were operating when we applied for our leaves, and then we proceed to two narrative sections that outline each of our sabbatical experiences. Following these narratives, we include a discussion about the lessons we learned and present a set of recommendations that might enhance other academics' sabbatical experiences.

Literature Review

We undertook a systematic literature review, which appears here in chapter 1, in support of our autoethnographies. The review is augmented in this section with consideration of our—the Faculty Association of the University of Calgary—sabbatical regulations

(TUCFA, 2019, p. 27). Specifically, we explore who is eligible, what is the stated purpose, what is the qualifying period and remuneration details, and what is the application and/or appeal process.

At our university, academic sabbaticals are termed research and scholarship leaves (RSLs) and details about who can access these, when, application processes, the committee who review them, the appeal process, and accountability mechanisms are detailed within the collective agreement (TUCFA, 2019, p. 27). It is important to note that RSLs are different from administrative leaves (see TUCFA, 2019, Article 17, p. 36), which are for academics who have completed a term of five years in administration and are moving back into the faculty professoriate. RSLs only apply to academic staff, including both pre-tenure and tenure, as well as continuing-contract and part-time academics.

The purpose of RSL is "to enhance the quality of the academic staff member as a scholar and as a teacher, thereby assisting the university to achieve greater excellence in its basic areas of responsibility: effective teaching and the advancement of learning" (TUCFA, 2019, p. 27). We thought it was rather odd to include "as a teacher" in the explanatory descriptor given that this leave is about research and scholarship. However, the inclusion of teaching may be due to our university's more recent emphasis on messaging the importance of teaching, even though the University of Calgary is a research-intensive university. Alternatively, it may be to accommodate and legitimize the scholarship of teaching and learning (SOTL), a more contemporary focus in our university as a result of the implementation of recommendations made by the institutional learning and teaching plan task force (Sumara, 2011), underpinned by the scholarly research commissioned by the task force (Scott & Scott, 2012). Aside from SOTL, this means activities that support graduate students are legitimate aspects of a sabbatical.

A faculty member must have completed at least three years of full-time service to qualify for six months of RSL at the staff member's academic rank salary, or, alternatively, an academic can wait six years and have either six months at 100 percent salary or twelve months at 87.5 percent of salary. Unpaid leaves of absence may influence an academic's years of qualifying service (see TUCFA, 2019, section 16.3.1). Another useful condition is that of "First RSL," where a newly tenured faculty member (one who has successfully and recently achieved tenure at our university) will receive 100 percent of salary, rather than the usual 87.5 percent. Part-time faculty members can also access RSL; however, these qualification periods are pro rata.

In the education faculty, applying for RSL involves providing a "notice of intent to apply" to the dean between September 15 and October 15 in the year preceding the RSL term. The application includes a research proposal and timeline of activities. The proposal generally encompasses the purpose, research objectives, who you will be working or networking with, what you will be doing, and where. You are also required to identify the direct linkages between your proposed research and the university's research plan. If you plan to travel overseas to engage with research partners, or to attend conferences or university visits, you must provide a detailed travel plan, including a budget outlining flights, accommodation, per diem, car hires, and any equipment you will need to carry out your proposed research. These documents are submitted to the dean, who then convenes the RSL committee, which review all documentation and make recommendations for or against granting the RSL.

If a faculty member is denied RSL an appeal can be submitted, first to the head of department, then to the dean, and finally to the provost and vice-president academic. This appeal process must be commenced within one week of notification. This ensures that all parties involved in the decisions and appeals are kept informed. However, appeals can be a protracted process and the process can vary across different faculties. It is important to note that the dean holds the right to deny RSL based upon staffing issues or supervision concerns.

Upon completion of RSL, a report of activities and outcomes must be submitted to the dean within three months of their return. It appears that RSL reports vary according to each faculty's expectations and guidelines.

RSL is a significant benefit to academics in our university; however, there are notes of caution in the collective agreement. For example, a faculty member must return and render service equal to the number of months of the RSL. If a faculty member decides to leave or retire from the university upon completion of RSL, they may be required to pay back the assistance the university paid to them. Another cautionary note is that a faculty member cannot work or receive financial compensation from other sources while on RSL. This seems entirely reasonable given that the purpose is to promote research and/or teaching-related activities and outcomes; however, this is different to purposes described in the literature, where some were able to work in their field to increase the currency of their knowledge and skills (Gilbert et al., 2007).

Narrative 1: Shelley's International Research and Study Leave

My academic career commenced in Australia in 1995 as a sessional instructor teaching instructional strategies in my alma mater. For five years I juggled sessional university teaching, teaching high-school students, and leading instructional innovations in the school-district office all while undertaking my master's and doctoral research. It was mad but engaging, and intellectually challenging. I loved teaching science to high-school students, but I loved teaching adults more. Before I completed my doctorate, I was headhunted by a large business school to establish their quality-assurance and academic-development program at their Australian campus and across thirteen international campuses. This new challenge was exciting and offered me valuable time (one day/week for research activities) to dedicate to my doctoral completion, so I moved into academia full time. Within a year, I achieved tenure and my leadership role expanded. This position involved oversight of numerous professional staff, leading our academic-development department, providing teaching support to my academic colleagues (250+) across six faculties and to our overseas sessionals (500+), and oversight of our business-school "teaching and learning quality-assurance" reporting to thirteen governments.

As a tenured faculty member, my first sabbatical was due at the end of the sixth year; however, I postponed it because my research partner wanted to align her sabbatical period with mine to initiate a significant collaborative project. I really needed that sabbatical; I was tired of the politics, the constant emails, the emotional drain of working with underperforming faculty who were being targeted by their heads for performance management due to poor student evaluations, and the demands of quality-assurance reporting. I was fast approaching burnout and was avidly anticipating the time to engage in research, to enjoy the fun of collaborative scholarly activities, and to travel to conferences and networking with others in my field. Midway though my sixth year I successfully secured a tenured position at a research-intensive university in western Canada. As this represented a promotion to associate professor, better working conditions, and the opportunity to experience a new country and culture, my family and I were keen to make the move. Unfortunately, this meant I lost my first sabbatical. I was so disappointed as I had been looking forward to the rest and intellectual stimulation of this new project. Even so, the excitement of moving overseas and experiencing a new city, culture, and institution overrode my disappointment at losing my sabbatical.

My second sabbatical was due six years into my term at my Canadian university. However, around that time I was appointed as associate dean, so my sabbatical had to be postponed to take up this leadership role. The challenge of this new role overcame my disappointment of missing my sabbatical. This leadership role was stimulating, presented opportunities to network widely across the province, and offered considerable intellectual challenge in establishing new programs and engaging in entrepreneurial activities to improve the faculty's finances. I enjoyed two very successful years wherein the fee-for-service and cost-recovery programs I established largely supported the positive recovery of the faculty's finances, and we established a reputation for being the go-to faculty for unique and tailor-made programming design. Then the dean reorganized his executive team and I resumed my professorial role.

With the pressures of my leadership role, I was well and truly ready for my sabbatical. However, I was shocked to find that because I had not taken my first sabbatical before assuming my leadership role, I had stopped accruing qualifying years. Additionally, because I had not completed the full five-year term as associate dean, I was not due an administrative leave. I was confused and irritated that I had not been so informed. I had made incorrect assumptions, and I had not sought advice at the right time; indeed, I trusted where I should not have. I had no one to blame but myself; I had not read the collective agreement, I had not informed myself of my rights as either an academic or an administrator, and so I missed out.

After eight years of service I was eligible for six-month RSL on 100 percent pay, and there was no pro rata for a shorter term in administration. I could have chosen to take a year at 80 percent salary (in our current collective agreement, this salary reduction has been lifted to 87.5 percent salary), but I preferred to take six months at 80 percent pay and hold over qualifying time for my next leave (by taking the reduced time and reduced pay, but I could not recover my two lost years of accrued years while in administration). This would align my next sabbatical with Don, my husband, who would be due for RSL. Another stipulation was that I had to spend part of my leave outside of Canada, but I did not see this as a problem, rather as an exciting opportunity to forge useful international networks. Consequently, I set about planning my international sabbatical. I was ready to expand and promote the collaborative research project on university leadership development that Don and I had started a couple of years prior. Our project had not moved forward at the pace we preferred, largely because of my leadership responsibilities.

The Application Process and Documentation

My RSL application involved multiple sections that had to be completed:

1. A proposal with an itinerary and timeline of activities. I proposed to travel to New Zealand (for a week), Fiji (for two weeks), Australia (for three months), and the United Kingdom (for three weeks) to meet with collaborators, present to faculty and graduate students on our findings to date, and analyze our current data and draft at least one paper.
2. Letters of invitation from each university and organization (which specified the dates of my visit).
3. A complete itinerary and detailed budget.
4. Re-allocation of office space during the RSL agreement (this meant that I had to agree to allow others to use my office during my leave).
5. A statement of who was assuming my supervision, including emails of agreement from all eight of my students (to be lodged with the Faculty of Graduate Studies).
6. The RSL research grant application (which included the RSL application and budget) went to the central university research office.

I was fortunate because even though I had a heavy graduate-supervision load (seven EdDs and one PhD student), most of these students were co-supervised by Don, so I was able to get approval to have him assume their supervision during my absence. All students readily agreed to this change because they already had a positive relationship with him and this did not represent a disruption in support. My leave was approved, and I was advised to apply for the RSL research grant to supplement my reduced income and offset the costs of travel, accommodation, and so on. My grant application detailed all expenses, as well as a new laptop as mine was unreliable and heavy, which was a distinct disadvantage when undertaking six months of travel. The grant funding amounted to the 20 percent of my salary that I was losing. This was approved and I received the funding prior to departure.

New Zealand
My time in New Zealand was both productive and fascinating. I arranged a visit to the University of Auckland and met with the head of the academic-development unit. She organized my visit and was a wonderful host. She was deeply interested in our leadership-development project and indicated her desire to join the project. I presented to faculty and students, and met several faculty leaders. The highlight was gaining insights into how neoliberalism was influencing university policies and how this was impacting academic cultures. It also provided insights into their equity and diversity policies in support of Maori and Pacific Islanders students, faculty members, and staff, and enabled opportunities to compare and contrast New Zealand's truth-and-reconciliation approaches with Canada's (Canada, 2015). I was sad to leave but was delighted with the new collegial relationships that had been forged.

Fiji
The next stop was Fiji. Having been born in Fiji, it was great to reach out and network with people in the government and the university. I met with both the dean of the education faculty and the director of the Fiji Higher Education Commission in Suva, both of whom were gracious and hospitable hosts. The director indicated she wanted me to present on both our university leadership-development research and findings from an earlier K–12 assessment study. The government presentations included ministry personnel, school principals, university faculty, and lead teachers. We engaged in productive discussions and problem-solving sessions that focused on a wide range of K–12 and university issues and policies in Fiji. It was so interesting to see the similarities and differences in the education systems in Fiji and Canada. I also presented multiple sessions at the university to faculty members and graduate students on a range of topics related to our

research and to how education programs were structured in each other's universities. I made myself available to work with doctoral students to provide advice about their topics, potential educational-leadership literature, identified the key gurus in this field, and to simply be a listening ear about the trials and tribulations in their research activities. Faculty leaders and members were extremely welcoming and excellent hosts.

The other delight about my trip to Fiji was that I invited my eighty-some-year-old parents to accompany me so they could enjoy a holiday while I worked. My parents had lived in Fiji from 1958 through 1975 and were thrilled at the opportunity to travel there with me, to return to their old stomping grounds, and visit old friends. During my childhood, my dad had been first an industrial-arts teacher at Suva Grammar School and, later, was approached by government officials to design, oversee construction of, and lead the largest vocational/technical college—the Derrick Technical Institute (then the Fiji Institute of Technology, now the Fiji National University)—which served the entire South Pacific region. We not only spent quality time together revisiting favourite places from my childhood and visiting old family friends, but I also got to hear stories from the past that I had not been privy to as a child. It gave me such rich insights into the life and times of the last British colony and of colonial life, how education had been in the 1960s and 1970s in Fiji, and the diverse and colourful characters who populated the government and institutions of those times. I provided a useful taxi service and took Mum and Dad on visits to the high school and to the Fiji National University grounds. Highlights for Dad included invitations to visit the school workshops during his walking tour through the school. Dad regaled the teacher with stories about the machines he had built which were still in use. The teacher and his students were in equal measures curious and extremely gracious in listening to his stories of the school's start-up days, fifty years prior. His visit to the Fiji National University was fortuitous as there was a historian who interviewed him at length about his role in establishing the college and his decades-long leadership. Apparently, this historian had been trying to locate and contact Dad for years, only to have him walk into the staff room on his nostalgic tour. Our visit was extremely serendipitous for his research project. It was wonderful for Dad and Mum, who would not have made the trip by themselves, to have this opportunity to accompany me and share their wisdom while I was engaged in my own academic adventures. We then returned to Australia together.

Australia

The Australian leg of my sabbatical was largely based in Perth and Sydney and was equal parts catching up with family while establishing and reaffirming collegial networks. I met with several former colleagues keen to join our international project. Meetings with these colleagues linked our leadership-development project team with others across Europe, so our international team expanded significantly. I also presented on our current and past research to education and business faculty and graduate students. It was also enjoyable to re-establish linkages and to hear of the political, financial, and organizational culture changes to the university scene in Australia.

In addition to time spent networking and presenting, I engaged in serious writing time. I had the opportunity to look after my niece while her parents were away and, with a quiet place to work, I was afforded a number of weeks to analyze data and write up a paper, as well as to get to know her better. The other wonderful aspect of this time was to spend three months of quality time with my elderly parents. This time enabled me to not only write in a quiet place with no interruptions, but also to take on much of the household duties to give my Mum a break and to organize some necessary minor renovations. After four months away, I returned home to Canada for a couple of weeks before heading off to the United Kingdom.

United Kingdom

Don joined me for the UK leg of my "travel-batical." We initially went to London and Warwick to meet up with current collaborators, two of whom had already started their research work in the project and one who had taken a different role and was looking to explore the influence of unionization on leadership and university processes. While in London, Don and I presented on our early findings at a conference in Slough, which resulted in attracting a new collaborator in eastern Europe who was keen to join the project and mirror our approach in her national context. We also met potential new collaborators in Dundee, Scotland. The final stage led us to travelling into the Scottish Highlands, where we leased a rural property for two weeks for the purpose of engaging in a collaborative writing retreat. This retreat afforded us dedicated time to write, develop a grant application, and to discuss and reflect on the outcomes of the travel-batical. The advantage of this isolated retreat was the intermittent internet, which freed both of us from that constant expectation of email. Our retreat was both productive for our research but also enabled us to relax and unwind, and to plan the next steps in the project.

Accountability and Outcomes

Following our return, I submitted my report on the outcomes of my sabbatical. My report was six pages and included the original purpose and objectives of the RSL, and details of each outcome, and how these linked to the objectives. The feedback I received from my dean was that this was the most detailed and productive RSL report he had seen and he appreciated all my efforts.

One key outcome was that, in the following year, I achieved promotion to full professor. My promotion portfolio was greatly enriched by the outcomes of my RSL, and indeed the linkages I forged were highly advantageous, as one of my overseas contacts served as one of my promotion evaluators. From an affective perspective, I cannot describe how refreshing and delightful it was to have the opportunity to leave behind the constant demands of course-based teaching, unceasing emails, and doctoral supervision (as much as I enjoy working with my students) to engage in intellectually stimulating research activities. The gift of time to quietly sit and read, think, and write was immense and so productive. I love meeting new people, and the friendships and research collaborations I forged have been invaluable to the project and to my doctoral students, many of whom have now joined the project as full collaborators upon completion of their doctorates. Another unforeseen opportunity afforded by our new international networks has been the many invitations to serve as an external examiner for graduate students in Fiji, Australia, the United Kingdom, and South Africa.

Problems

One unforeseen problem was the financial implications of an overseas sabbatical. I noted that in our current collective agreement there is no stipulation regarding overseas travel. Indeed, the expense involved in travelling across multiple countries for five months exceeded the estimates made in the RSL grant application. Additionally, when it came time to submit my tax return, our accountant did not know how to conceptualize the grant funding.

When we contacted our university human-resources department, they were unable to provide clear and specific information about the tax implications of this income. They did supply a letter indicating that this was a grant, but the income created a significant tax issue. I am unsure if this grant was advantageous for the university, as a research metric, but the benefit to the faculty member remained unclear to me; the tax effect was certainly negative.

Narrative 2: Don and Shelley's Collaborative Research and Study Leave

I completed my doctorate in 2009 and pursued contract work and sessional teaching in 2010, as the university sector was suffering the strictures of an economic downturn. In 2011, I secured a tenure-track assistant-professor position, and for the next two years served as the EdD coordinator for the new Leadership in Post-Secondary Contexts program. Shelley served as my faculty mentor and we co-supervised seven wonderful doctoral students. As is common for most academics, my lead up to tenure and promotion was frenetic and challenging in ensuring my teaching, research, and service responsibilities were exemplary, and outputs were considerable as well as high quality. In addition to the work pressures, during my pre-tenure term I had been diagnosed with muscular dystrophy and I was also found to have an unrelated spinal stenosis. The spinal stenosis confined me to a wheelchair and left me in excruciating pain. I finally had surgery to correct the stenosis, but these medical issues created their own pressures in terms of loss of research productivity, which added psychological pressures in the lead up to applying for tenure and promotion. In 2016, I was fortunate enough to achieve both as an associate professor. I was more than ready for the break that RSL offers, but in consultation with Shelley we decided that I would be best to wait to align our RSL timing so we could undertake a collaborative one. Consequently, we submitted a joint RSL application to address both the collaborative nature of our project and my new need for assistance in international travel.

We planned a joint six-month travel-batical, to include two overseas trips, one to Australia and one to the United Kingdom, to work with our scholarly partners in each country. Even so, our major objective was to analyze data and complete at least one journal article. In our joint proposal, we ensured we linked our project and our RSL objectives to our university's research plan, specifically related to promoting collaborative research activities. We discussed RSL plans with our doctoral students, and asked two caring and conscientious colleagues if they would be prepared to assume our supervision loads during our RSL. Both our students and colleagues were happy with this shift of supervision.

Mirroring Shelley's earlier RSL application, we completed the requisite paperwork and submitted both applications to the RSL committee. Our first indication of problems emerged when we were invited to a meeting with a member of the executive team in our faculty, who informed us that the RSL committee had denied our applications. Naturally, we wanted to know why. An odd conversation unfolded; they were cagey and refused to provide the committee's rationale, but they indicated that there had been concerns about a husband and wife taking a joint leave. We questioned the committee's stance, as recently we had had to consult human-resources to obtain a ruling regarding various administrators' perceptions that Shelley and I working together (i.e., working together with our students, being collaborators in our joint-research, and even our involvement on doctoral committees) entailed a conflict of interest. We reminded the administrator that we had sought and received a clear directive from the university that, as our employer, they perceived us not as a married couple but as separate employees who happen to be in the same specialization; thus, our working together and/or being research partners did not constitute a conflict of interest. They hastily agreed and indicated that the decision to deny our leave was to be overturned, we would be granted our joint RSL. This contretemps left both of us feeling disturbed and disappointed, which was an inauspicious start to what should have been a much-anticipated sabbatical.

Further to the administrator's communication, the dean contacted me and said that the colleague who had kindly agreed to serve as supervisor for my graduate students was too junior and overloaded, and so I was required to maintain my supervisory responsibilities while on sabbatical. Given that our colleagues in the leadership specialization are overloaded all the time, with supervision loads rarely lower than five students per supervisor (some colleagues supervise nine or ten students), this rationale meant that it was unlikely that any of us would ever be able to take a sabbatical without a supervision load. Consequently, both Shelley and I had to continue our supervision with a combined group of fourteen students. Given that most of our students were in the same cohort and were fast approaching candidacy, retaining their supervision meant a significant additional load while on sabbatical. As our notification of approval came through, I received a further option from the dean that enabled me to extend my sabbatical from the initial six-months to a year because I had recently achieved tenure. Extensions to RSL for newly tenured faculty members was a new condition in the collective agreement in recognition of the stress involved in applying for tenure and promotion; hence, I readily took up this option to extend. Unfortunately, this was not available to Shelley, which did not leave her with feelings of joy or jubilation.

How Plans Go Awry
We commenced our sabbatical in January and started making plans to travel to Australia and the United Kingdom; however, it quickly became clear to us that the constant demands of our students were not likely to abate. We started meeting with them online. When we considered our finances at the time (our son had decided to get married mid-year), we came to the conclusion that a "travel-batical" was not financially viable; we opted for a "staybatical." We worked on two different papers, presented at two conferences, and met with our partners through synchronous technologies, but the vast majority of our time was taken up with meeting with students, running collaborative sessions for the students, and reviewing their proposals or final chapter drafts. A wonderful outcome was that all our students met their milestones in a timely manner and we maintained our close relationships with all of them; however, during the initial six months it was by no means either research productive or relaxing. Shelley returned to teaching more exhausted than she started. She was also deeply frustrated that we had made such little progress on our research-project objectives.

    I continued on in the second half of my sabbatical, and Shelley assumed most of my supervision load. This provided me with time to work on our project, but it remained difficult to have the time to collaborate and co-author with her; hence, my research productivity was deleteriously affected because so much of our planned analysis and writing was to be collaborative and she simply did not have the time. I did use the time to integrate much of the literature that I read into my course-based teaching, and I shared many papers I had found with my students as they pertained to their research topics; hence, I did engage in SOTL. I did make time to walk regularly, which aided my recovery from the spinal surgery, and I was able to take on more of the home duties to alleviate some of the pressure on Shelley, but I too found working alone, in our usually collaborative project, a little miserable and largely unproductive.

Highlights and Lowlights
Overall, the highlights of the sabbatical were the time we managed to carve out for our collaborative discussions and online meetings with our partners, and seeing the success of our incredible students. The non-academic outcomes for me included recovering from the frantic pre-tenure pace and getting time to aid my recovery from surgery. I enjoyed the dedicated time that Shelley and I had for our research, although simultaneously I resented the necessary interruptions we experienced due to the demands of supervision. The supervision dimension presents feelings of conflict for me. I enjoy working with my students, and revel in their success, but I remain aware of the time these supervisory activities demand and take away from my research. This lost research time ultimately impacts my performance-review metrics.

Shelley and I submitted a joint report when she returned and I submitted a further report at the completion of my RSL. We noted the deleterious impact that maintaining our students had had on our research, but we did not receive any comment other than "thanks for submitting your report." Upon reflection, the staybatical was an excellent option when finances were tight, but it must be noted that remaining at home can conversely result in too many distractions; students expect you to be constantly available to them because, from their perspective, "nothing has changed." Finally, the mental-health break generated by change in usual routines that is afforded by travelling does not occur.

Discussion and Lessons Learned

In this section, we discuss how our experiences compared to other published accounts about sabbaticals and provide advice regarding how to get the best out of this academic activity. We distilled seven key points, depicted in figure 12.1.

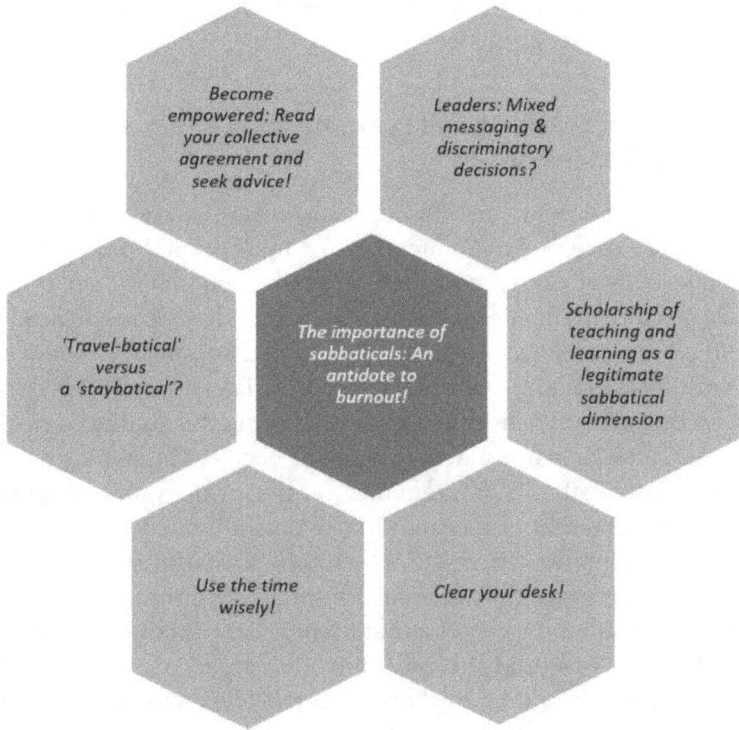

Figure 12.1. *Lessons learned.*

The Importance of Sabbaticals: An Antidote to Burnout!
Given the intensity of academic life, particularly for those who are working in research-intensive institutions, a sabbatical is a godsend to be released from the constant demands of teaching and service in order to concentrate solely on research activities (Davidson et al., 2010; Hedges, 1999). This was a common theme in the literature, and it highlighted the tensions between research and teaching in universities (Bai & Miller, 1999; Maranville, 2014; Marker, 1983) and how excellence in research does not necessarily translate into quality teaching and learning (Prosser, 2010; Prosser et al., 2008; Serow, 2000; Wernick, 2006). Therefore, we recommend new faculty members learn about, and take advantage of, their university's sabbatical policies (Else, 2015; Smith et al., 2016) to ensure their productivity remains high and they take a mental- and physical-health break. Given contemporary concerns with health and well-being, the value

of sabbaticals is greater than simply research (Blum, 2007; Lakkoju, 2020; Parkes & Langford, 2008).

Scholarship of Teaching and Learning as a Legitimate Sabbatical Dimension

We noted that for many institutions sabbaticals also encompass SOTL. This can produce positive outcomes for institutional programs and students (Gilbert et al., 2007; Miller & Bai, 2006; Sima, 2000). This broader conceptualization of research is important as many academics actively research teaching, learning, and assessment. To deny this as a valid research topic would be inappropriate, especially given the priority that all universities place on enhancing the quality of student outcomes. This is particularly important because in some research-intensive universities SOTL remains a lesser priority, or a secondary research area, to that of research in the discipline when considering tenure and promotion criteria (Parker, 2008); happily, this is starting to change (Subbaye & Vithal, 2016). Additionally, legitimizing presentations and workshops for graduate students is important (Delany, 2009; Halbert, 2015). We would also recommend that part of the accountability mechanism should be to share research outcomes with students, either through presentations or through integration into curriculum.

Become Empowered—Read Your Collective Agreement and Seek Advice!

One source of frustration for us was a lack of clarity surrounding RSL regulations. It was noted in the literature that many academics do not know they can take a sabbatical, or that they fear repercussions in stepping away from their role for a period and so forego one (for a deeper exploration, refer here to ch. 1; see also Friedman, 2018; Leung et al., 2020; Stelfox et al., 2015; Straus & Sackett, 2015). We would urge academics to empower themselves with the knowledge of their collective agreement, as these contain the rights and responsibilities of a faculty member. Human-resource partners are there to help with providing clarity and advice in this dimension of academic life. It is also important for universities to provide clear guidelines or academic workshops providing faculty members with detailed information about the processes, expectations, accountability, and tax implications of sabbaticals (Sima, 2000).

Clear Your Desk!
Few authors mentioned the complexity of maintaining doctoral students during a sabbatical (Gilbert et al., 2007). Indeed, our two different experiences of sabbatical pressed home the importance of transferring supervision of students to colleagues, when possible, in order to maximize the positive impacts of the sabbatical; that is, to have dedicated time for research and to have a rest from the constant demands of work and students. Of course, the risk in transferring your graduate students to a colleague is that students may feel rejected, or they may develop a greater affinity for your colleague and request to make the move permanent. If a faculty member loses students to their colleagues due to taking a sabbatical then all preceding supervision time and effort, and intellectual input invested to that point, is lost and is not recognized, particularly given that doctoral completions are the only metric of graduate-supervision activities. This is particularly important with students approaching the final stages of completion. Therefore, faculty members face an important dilemma: to maintain student supervision (and positive relationships) for the important metric and take the loss in sabbatical productivity or transfer their student with the associated risk of losing a supervision metric but gain sabbatical productivity (Burton, 2010; Halbert, 2015).

Travel-batical vs. Staybatical
There are pros and cons of a travel-batical compared with a staybatical (Smith, 2020). The advantages of a travel-batical are many. In terms of research it includes networking with colleagues in other institutions or organizations (Benshoff & Spruill, 2002; Sima, 2000), getting away from your home or work office, experiencing a change of pace, and intensively working with research partners with no distractions or interruptions. In terms of the personal dimensions it includes the opportunity to meet new people, see new places, eat different food, experience and appreciate other cultures, and identify the positive aspects of home (Friedman, 2018; Gallagher, 2018). The disadvantages relate to the expense of travel and accommodation, which can be significant if family accompany the sabbaticant, as well as the greater planning and documentation that is required.

The advantages involved in a staybatical include minimal financial impact; quality time spent with family, particularly aged parents if they are unable to travel with the sabbaticant; few disruptions to routines and work space; access to resources within the faculty; less requisite documentation; and with the COVID-19 pandemic, it is a considerably safer option to that of taking flights and living in a country that may not have a sound healthcare system (Marshall, 2014; Smith, 2020). The disadvantage to a staybatical is the temptation and/or expectation to continue juggling usual academic responsibilities, maintain timely email responses, and not secure your freedom from faculty meetings and other duties because you are present. Additionally, a staybatical will mean forgoing an enriching cultural experience, which promotes greater understanding of international literature and the value of international networking, crucial for promotion to the full-professor ranks. Therefore, faculty members need to weigh the pros and cons and decide what is right for them.

Use the Time Wisely!
While the literature highlights the advantages of slowing down, resting, and deriving intellectual stimulation and revitalization from changing mental gears (Swenty et al., 2011; Wilson, 2016), there is a danger that a sabbatical may become derailed or wasted if a faculty member is not disciplined in using this precious time to write and engage in associated research activities. Consequently, it is important to remain mindful of your university's accountability mechanisms, wherein you will be required to report on your sabbatical outcomes (Industrial Relations News, 1963). As Miller et al. (2012), Spencer and Kent (2007), and Gilbert et al. (2007) indicated, university leaders should ensure they follow through with clear accountability processes so a response can be made to critics of sabbaticals as an unwarranted "perk" within the academy (Sima, 2000).

Leaders: Mixed Messaging and Discriminatory Decisions
In our situation, which we admit may be a rarity, it is important for leaders to consider the alignment between the university's research missions and goals and approval of sabbatical objectives. Our research proposal overtly articulated our sabbatical application's alignment with the university's mission for increased collaboration in research as well as the desirability for international research, and yet when it came to the approval process, collaborative activities were not perceived as appropriate. Additionally, the literature highlighted gender discrimination as prevalent. In our case, there may have been discrimination related to marital status. Therefore, faculty members

should challenge decisions that appear to be discriminatory (Smith et al., 2016) or incongruous with university priorities. This links to the point about empowering yourself through knowledge of the collective agreement and university policies, and being prepared to push back on flawed decisions.

Conclusion

This chapter explores two academics' narratives of their sabbatical experiences. One was an international sabbatical and involved travel to four countries, collaboration with existing research partners, forging new partnerships and networks, and presentations and workshops with faculty, students, and government personnel. The second sabbatical was a staybatical designed to get data analysis and writing completed. The pros and cons of each type of sabbatical were analyzed and compared in relation to the literature. Seven key points were revealed as the lessons learned, which are highlighted in figure 12.1 and discussed in the "lessons learned section." These seven lessons outline key considerations that are crucial to maximize the impact of a sabbatical while avoiding the pitfalls we encountered in our own sabbatical experiences.

Overall, we strongly advocate for sabbaticals as crucial opportunities for research and to progress international projects. Given the intensity of academic life and work, we refute the claim that sabbaticals are a perk, which is largely undeserved, for academics who enjoy cushy positions in the ivory tower. Indeed, we contend that sabbaticals are essential antidotes to the depredations of managerialist universities, that they are a way for faculty members to achieve intellectual revitalization and to remain academically productive, pedagogically innovative, research active, and—probably most important—emotionally and physically well balanced.

References

Bai, K., & Miller, M. T. (1999). *An overview of the sabbatical leave in higher education: A synopsis of the literature base*. ERIC. https://files.eric.ed.gov/fulltext/ED430471.pdf

Benshoff, J. M., & Spruill, D. A. (2002). Sabbaticals for counselor educators: Purposes, benefits, and outcomes. *Counselor Education and Supervision*, 42(2), 131–144. https://doi.org/10.1002/j.1556-6978.2002.tb01805.x

Blum, S. (2007). Sleep and the sabbatical. *The Chronicle of Higher Education, 53*(25), C.2.
Burton, L. D. (2010). Sabbatical. *Journal of Research on Christian Education, 19*(1), 1–6. https://doi.org/10.1080/10656211003641106
Canada. (2015). *Truth and Reconciliation Commission of Canada*. Queen's Printer. See https://nctr.ca/about/history-of-the-trc/trc-website/
Davidson, O. B., Eden, D., Westman, M., Cohen-Charash, Y., Hammer, L. B., Kluger, A. N., Krausz, M., Maslach, C., O'Driscoll, M., Perrewé, P. L., Quick, J. C., Rosenblatt, Z., & Spector, P. E. (2010). Sabbatical leave: Who gains and how much? *Journal of Applied Psychology, 95*(5), 953–964. https://doi.org/10.1037/a0020068
Delany, D. (2009). *A review of the literature on effective PhD supervision*. https://www.tcd.ie/CAPSL/assets/pdf/Academic%20Practice%20Resources/Effective_Supervision_Literature_Review.pdf
Else, H. (2015, April 16). Recharge, refocus, relax. *Times Higher Education*, 42–49.
Friedman, S. L. (2018). A sabbatical: The gift that keeps on giving. *Cellular and Molecular Gastroenterology and Hepatology, 5*(4), 656–658.
Gallagher, A. (2018). The value of a sabbatical: Four countries, three conferences and two homecomings. *Nursing Ethics, 25*(8), 953–954. https://doi.org/10.1177/0969733018811260
Gilbert, G., Day, B., Murillo, A., Patton, J., Sibley-Smith, A., & Smith, B. (2007). *Sabbaticals: Benefitting faculty, the institution, and students*. The Academic Senate for California Community Colleges. ERIC. https://files.eric.ed.gov/fulltext/ED510576.pdf
Halbert, K. (2015). Students' perceptions of a "quality" advisory relationship. *Quality in Higher Education, 21*(1), 26–37. https://doi.org/10.1080/13538322.2015.1049439
Hedges, J. R. (1999). Sabbaticals: What's the big deal?! *Academic Emergency Medicine, 6*(9), 877–879. https://doi.org/10.1111/j.1553-2712.1999.tb01233.x
Industrial Relations News. (1963). The pros and cons of executive sabbaticals. *Management Review, 52*(10), 47.
Lakkoju, S. (2020). Work–life satisfaction in academia: Myth or reality? *Decision, 47*(2), 153–176. https://doi.org/10.1007/s40622-020-00243-9
Leung, J. G., Barreto, E. F., Nelson, S., Hassett, L. C., & Cunningham, J. L. (2020). The professional sabbatical: A systematic review and considerations for the health-system pharmacist. *Research in Social and Administrative Pharmacy, 16*(12), 1632–1644. https://doi.org/10.1016/j.sapharm.2020.02.011
Maranville, S. (2014). Becoming a scholar: Everything I needed to know I learned on sabbatical. *Higher Learning Research Communications, 4*(1), 4–14.
Marker, D. G. (1983). Faculty leaves. *New Directions for Higher Education, 41*, 37–46. https://doi.org/10.1002/he.36919834105

Marshall, S. M. (2014). Sabbatical reflections from an academic mother. *Women in Higher Education, 21*(12), 33–34. https://doi.org/10.1002/whe.10407

Miller, M. T., & Bai, K. (2006). Sabbatical leave programs as form of faculty development. *Academic Leadership: The Online Journal, 4*(1), n.p.

Miller, M. T., Bai, K., & Newman, R. E. (2012). A critical examination of sabbatical application policies: Implications for academic leaders. *College Quarterly, 15*(2), n.p. http://collegequarterly.ca/2012-vol15-num02-spring/miller.html

Parker, J. (2008). Comparing research and teaching in university promotion criteria. *Higher Education Quarterly, 62*(3), 237–251. https://doi.org/10.1111/j.1468-2273.2008.00393.x

Parkes, L. P., & Langford, P. H. (2008). Work-life balance or work-life alignment? A test of the importance of work-life balance for employee engagement and intention to stay in organisations. *Journal of Management and Organization, 14*(3), 267–284.

Prosser, M. (2010). Faculty research and teaching approaches: Exploring the relationship. In J. Christensen Hughes & J. Mighty (Eds.), *Taking stock. Research on teaching and learning in higher education* (pp. 129–137). McGill-Queen's University Press.

Prosser, M., Martin, E., Trigwell, K., Ramsden, P., & Middleton, H. (2008). University academics' experience of research and its relationship to their experience of teaching. *Instructional Science: An International Journal of the Learning Sciences, 36*(1), 3–16. https://doi.org/10.1016/j.learninstruc.2007.01.004

Scott, D. E., & Scott, S. (2012). Multi-faceted professional development models designed to enhance teaching and learning within universities. In J. O. Lindberg & A. D. Olofsson (Eds.), *Informed design of educational technologies in higher education: Enhanced learning and teaching* (pp. 412–437). IGI Global.

Serow, R. C. (2000). Research and teaching at a research university. *Higher Education, 40*(4), 449–463. https://doi.org/10.1023/a:1004154512833

Sima, C. M. (2000). The role and benefits of the sabbatical leave in faculty development and satisfaction. *New Directions for Institutional Research, 2000*(105), 67–75. https://doi.org/10.1002/ir.10506

Smith, D. R. (2020). Is sabbatical a dirty word? *EMBO reports, 21*(7), e50886. https://doi.org/10.15252/embr.202050886

Smith, D., Spronken-Smith, R., Stringer, R., & Wilson, C. A. (2016). Gender, academic careers and the sabbatical: A New Zealand case study. *Higher Education Research and Development, 35*(3), 589–603. https://doi.org/10.1080/07294360.2015.1107880

Spencer, M., & Kent, P. (2007). Perpetuating difference? Law school sabbaticals in the era of performativity. *Legal Studies, 27*(4), 649–677. https://doi.org/10.1111/j.1748-121X.2007.00064.x

Stelfox, H. T., Straus, S. E., & Sackett, D. L. (2015). Clinician-trialist rounds: 27. Sabbaticals. Part 2: I'm taking a sabbatical! How should I prepare for it? *Clinical Trials, 12*(3), 287–290. https://doi.org/10.1177/1740774514567970

Straus, S. E., & Sackett, D. L. (2015). Clinician-trialist rounds: 26. Sabbaticals. Part 1: Should I take a sabbatical? *Clinical Trials, 12*(2), 174–176. https://doi.org/10.1177/1740774514562917

Subbaye, R., & Vithal, R. (2016). Gender, teaching and academic promotions in higher education. *Gender and Education, 29*(7), 926–951. https://doi.org/10.1080/09540253.2016.1184237

Sumara, D. (2011). *Systemic, specialized and sustained University of Calgary integrated framework for teaching and learning. A report and recommendations of the Institutional Learning and Teaching Plan Task Force.* https://live-provost.ucalgary.ca/provost/sites/default/files/teams/1/iltp_forgfc_june2011.pdf

Swenty, C. F., Schaar, G. L., Phillips, L. A., Embree, J. L., McCool, I. A., & Shirey, M. R. (2011). Nursing sabbatical in the acute care setting: What is the evidence? *Nursing Forum, 46*(3), 195–204. https://doi.org/10.1111/j.1744-6198.2011.00225.x

The Faculty Association of the University of Calgary (TUCFA). (2019). *The collective agreement between the faculty association of the University of Calgary and the Governors of the University of Calgary. July 1, 2019 to June 30, 2020.* (pp. 1–178). https://www.ucalgary.ca/hr/sites/default/files/teams/239/tucfa-ca.pdf

Wernick, A. (2006). University. *Theory, Culture & Society, 23*(2–3), 557–563. https://doi.org/10.1177/0263276406062810

Wilson, A. K. (2016). Mini-sabbaticals: Routes to reenergize chairs and their departments. *The Department Chair, 26*(4), 13–14. https://doi.org/10.1002/dch.30076

Conclusion

The sabbatical, as the chapters in this book highlight, is a remarkable experience. It should be clear that it is an earned privilege that reaps benefits for the academic and the institution, and includes benefits that extend beyond both. Despite the positive impact of sabbaticals, one must be cautious about hidden details and negative effects. We found both but concluded that they did not outweigh the benefits.

As an example of hidden details, we mentioned finding a tension when we were seeking chapter submissions. The cause of the tension gained some definition along the way. We found a perception of the sabbatical as a guilty pleasure. This idea is not one we had found in the literature, but the sense of guilt, or of an embarrassment of riches, is one we believe should be investigated among faculty who have had sabbaticals. The perception seems to be rooted in a lack of clarity of how to talk about the sabbatical, particularly in an academic sense, of not knowing how to frame such an unusual experience. It may be that we have experiences throughout our lives talking about work, about holidays, about many things, but we have no experience describing great lengths of unstructured work time. As a result, we fumble this discussion. It also fits with the suspicion mentioned in the introduction that sabbatical planning aims for the stars and then, regardless of how realistic that is, leads to feelings of guilt if the result does not fulfill what was likely wishful thinking, or some difficulty naming the successes, of which there is evidence of many, paired with the inability to achieve everything imagined. An honest interpretation is challenging. Given the general lack of understanding, often little is said. It also fits a second interpretation, where there is guilt tied to receipt of such a remarkable opportunity. As one example, on a sabbatical one can watch neighbours leave for work because of the flexible, self-directed opportunity a sabbatical provides. Human nature is complicated and multiple possible interpretations are legitimate. There is an opportunity for specific research in this area.

We did find our chapters are consistent with Davidson et al. (2010), who found that sabbaticals promote well-being. However, they also found no enduring evidence of well-being after the sabbatical, and hypothesized that it may replenish coping skills, a value that they did not investigate. The interplay of well-being, coping skills, and work ethic are clearly visible in Elliott-Johns's chapter here. However, the chapter by Handford challenges one to consider how a change of pace, whether for better or worse, might be more broadly applicable than well-being. The observations are consistent with evidence of minimal to no change in productivity, while also offering evidence of feelings of intellectual renewal and a sense of improved teaching (Kang & Miller, 1999). However, it has been suggested that important benefits may include evidence that the university is engaged in providing corporate social responsibility and serving the public good (Spencer et al., 2012). Evidence of this can be found among the chapters here but is problematic because of a perception that it is service as opposed to research. For example, Rodriguez addressed a societal need identified in the Truth and Reconciliation Commission of Canada's final report (Canada, 2015), but she raises concerns of whether it aligned with research. Some challenges observed in this book support seeking clarification of this aspect of sabbaticals.

While we used a narrative approach, the outcome should be consistent with Iravani (2011), who surveyed 120 faculty members and used factor analysis to derive five categories of impact from sabbaticals. The categories (with the percentage of variance provided in brackets) are professionalism (32 percent), psychological/cultural effects (19 percent), capacity building (18 percent), institutional productivity (10 percent), and individual motivation (9 percent). We consider these in terms of the chapters in this book.

Professionalism, in cognitive terms, includes developing new knowledge, learning new skills, gaining new insights, and updating existing knowledge. An example is Kelley (2016) visiting companies that could infuse his teaching and research knowledge. Lin writes of working at a foreign research lab with a technology that was not available at her institution. Another example is Stright (1964), who held a postdoctoral position during his sabbatical. Since there are disciplinary variations around what constitutes research, there is an issue with the interpretation of this dimension and the strategic importance placed on sabbaticals (Spencer et al., 2012). However, there is substantial supporting evidence of this dimension within the book. What this book adds to the literature is the tangible diversity that reveals itself from the self-directed feature of the sabbatical. Consider Rodriguez updating existing knowledge *of others*, a form of dissemination, so that they can address identified societal needs. She is acting professionally, but generally the interpretation of an updating of knowledge is updating the academic's knowledge. By contrast, Elliott-Johns addresses professional identity and self-study. Perhaps bridging these two seemingly disparate positions is Sibbald, who remarks that a role as a journal editor was simultaneously both service and professional development. Virtually all the authors show evidence of professionalism, but no two are alike.

Psychological effects are oriented to work-life balance, stress, and peace of mind. These issues are abundantly clear in the chapter by Elliott-Johns, and perhaps contrasted by Handford. Armenakyan provides a unique work-life balance, where the enjoyment of cultures while travelling to fulfill her academic goals has a personal fulfillment. Kornelsen appears to have had life-balance dominate a practitioner leave, but it was a lesser component of an academic sabbatical. Cohan (2018) speaks of sabbaticals as being "anti-climactic" and admits to struggling with her own impending sabbatical. She describes it as "a chance to shift my perspective on how I relate to creativity, time, space, place and self—and the interconnectedness of these things" (p. 3). This is consistent with Hubbard suggesting the sabbatical is for "taking stock" (Hubbard, 2002, p. 604) and Stine (1987), a "break from routine." Pragmatically, this category is also consistent with sabbaticals addressing declines in faculty satisfaction and the related increases in their potential for burnout (Kang & Miller, 1999). This is particularly notable in Kornelsen's account of his practitioner leave. These notions are concordant with the chapters in this book, but the prevalence is less pronounced than professionalism, consistent with Iravani's (2011) quantitative assessment.

Capacity building is oriented to an alteration of personal attitudes, improved quality of teaching, and self-efficacy. It includes social capital that may develop new opportunities and allow the person to take on new roles in the institution, such as supervision of graduate students. Institutional productivity is oriented to the organizational impact of the sabbatical and may reflect details of the research methodology. A prospective example is the possibility that Lin, having worked with a new research technology, could bring those methods to her home institution. There is considerable additional evidence of capacity building, and, like professionalism, it shows an abundant diversity of experience among the authors of this book.

The final factor, individual motivation, entails engaging an international community. It is oriented toward extension beyond the institution and the immediate context of the institution. It seems to emphasize travel for sabbaticals, which is contrary to sabbatical accounts during the pandemic. Bujaki also argues that this is a gendered vision that can be contrary to family responsibilities. Apart from that caveat, there is evidence of considerable travel and interactions by the chapter authors. A notable example is Armenakyan, who spent signficant time in different countries teaching, conducting research, and enaging in conferences. Block too shows an international connection, but also an effort to subsequently use that engagement within an immediate community. For those considering the option, it is worth considering the unanticipated financial repurcussions of the choice that S. Scott experienced.

Iravani's (2011) work shows considerable promise but needs extending to other domains to show how factors influencing sabbatical vary with jurisdiction. While capacity building, institutional productivity, and individual motivation are not unreasonable conceptually, the definitions and interpretations are discordant with the Canadian context. It is also revealing that some facets of sabbaticals, such as taking courses, do not clearly fit in the framework.

Hutchins et al. (2005) found 72 percent of medical faculty used sabbaticals for part-time study, with 51 percent of the study occurring at the master's level or above. Sibbald is an example in this book of one who used sabbatical time in pursuit of a master's degree in mathematics (his focal area is the preparation of mathematics teachers, for which he has master's and doctoral degrees in education). Kornelsen also mentions being at the beginning of a master's in his practitioner leave. There is some discrepancy, however, regarding the use of sabbaticals to complete work toward a degree. On one hand, Thompson and Louth (2003) say "sabbatical leaves may not be used for work toward an advanced degree" (p. 147), but Kang and Miller (1999) list it as a specific sabbatical activity for faculty whose highest attained degree is a master's. Fundamentally, the issue is whether taking a course to advance one's skill set is treated the same as or differently than advancing the credentials for the role one is occupying. We are aware of two faculty members at one institution wherein one took courses in direct support of their research but another pursued general coursework that would support broadening their overall research scope, who was told this did not "count" as they already held a terminal degree.

Sabbaticals allow revitalization, opportunities for growth, and a means for preparing for future retirement (Spencer et al., 2012; Weintraub, 2008), which are all mentioned in Elliott-Johns's chapter. Carraher et al. (2014) say sabbaticals have a positive benefit for scholarly production, influence well-being, tend to reward past performance, and have little impact on teaching. Block demonstrates revitalization and well-being with her transformative experiences in distant place-based learning. Sabbaticals address dips in productivity that may occur after a tenure decision (Kang & Miller, 1999). The mechanism for improving productivity is likely due to the extent of choice (Hubbard, 2002) that one may pursue during a sabbatical. This may account for Stine (1987) finding few faculty members would change their sabbaticals. However, Stine also observed that the primary change that would be sought was to "find more time for self." Kornelsen offers a notable instance when he compares his practitioner sabbatical (that found time for self) and his academic sabbatical. We certainly found evidence of these considerations and, unlike other areas of the academic literature, the details seem to be quite accurate in this area.

Generally, there is little in the way of negative remarks about sabbaticals. As Kang and Miller (1999) noted: "When disparaging comments are issued toward sabbaticals, they are usually viewed within the context of administrators taking, or more appropriately, abusing sabbaticals as they depart senior positions and 'return' to faculty status" (p. 16). There is a hint of these sorts of challenges where S. Scott found sabbaticals delayed and lost in the early development of her career, while not due to abuses, do signal a communication gap. In a similar vein, in the early thinking about this book Sibbald (2020) recounts being told "sabbaticals can be a shock as you learn how replaceable you are" (p. 171). It has been reported that 10 percent of medical doctors do not have positive experiences (Hutchins et al., 2005), though they generally report "a sense of personal satisfaction and development" (p. 63). The impact of the COVID-19 pandemic, as witnessed in Handford's chapter, is something we are not aware of arising in the literature. The negative impacts of world events are not constrained to pandemics, though it is the only one directly observed in this book. Armenakyan speaks of the importance of connecting to her other home, Armenia, and the fighting that erupted there after the submission of her chapter is indicative of how her sabbatical plans could have been disrupted if the timing had been different.

Stine (1987) includes recommendations to mitigate "post-sabbatical depression," which may simply be a severe form of a common difficulty returning to an imposed work schedule that Reynolds (1990) recounts in a personal account. We did not observe these specific examples because they do not fit the scope of this book. However, we did observe some negative impacts that left us wondering. In several cases, initial submissions of chapters seemed to lack substantial details. We again wondered about the relationship of this with the tension around a guilty-pleasure perception, and a general lack of experience describing substantial time spent in an alternative, and changed, work setting. We addressed the issue, and chapters infused with details populate this book, but there was a sense of authors holding back in early drafts. Otherwise, many accounts are positive, which is not surprising because academics with negative accounts would be unlikely to propose a chapter in the first place.

The existing literature has emphasized the outcomes of sabbaticals (Carraher et al., 2014). We propose studying the lived experiences during sabbaticals to focus on the process, and how this contributes to the ultimate outcomes. As an example, Rodriguez was very successful, judging by the many presentations she reported giving. However, without examining the process one would not be overly aware of the issue of whether there was a misalignment between the defining research aspect and her emphasis on addressing a societal need. Sibbald also encourages examination of the process by using the passage of time in his analysis. Bujaki draws in neoliberal considerations and provides resistance through the provision of sabbatical events that go beyond the academy walls.

There are instances arising in this book that can benefit from further research. For example, there was only one mention of collegiality during sabbaticals aligned with: "I have seen faculty on sabbatical being chided on those days they do show up (e.g., 'What are you doing here? Go home.')" (Endres, 2001, p. 36). Is this an issue? There is also an assumption that faculty on sabbaticals enact proportional changes on all dimensions of their role. However, it is possible that different faculty members emphasize different facets of their roles and that this obfuscates research approaches from establishing benefits of sabbaticals. We asked our authors about their experiences going to their campuses during sabbatical. The experiences ranged from chiding to an expectation they would attend key meetings pertaining to their academic unit. There were mentions of engaging the campus in different ways, such as spending lengthy amounts of time in the library. We did not find a singular image but rather a diversity reflecting individual choice and, perhaps, a diversity of workplace cultures.

The development of this book had several chapter authors include appendices of what they achieved during their sabbaticals. It seemed defensive; that they felt a need to provide demonstrable proof of accomplishments. It was likely due to revisiting sabbatical reports, but it also made us wonder about the perception of the sabbatical as a guilty pleasure—the sense that one cannot simply speak about a sabbatical without explaining the productivity that warrants receiving it.

We did not entertain this information as part of the chapters because we did not want the narratives diminished by an assessment of accomplishments. As we have said about tenure, we question the measuring of academic accomplishments (Sibbald & Handford, 2017), and sabbaticals are not that different. What we decided to do by way of acknowledging accomplishments is to provide details of accomplishments that we requested from the authors after submission of the vast majority of chapters. We kept the information separate and collated it so that we could speak to the collective productivity of the authors. This reveals that during a sabbatical the "average" academic in our group accomplished this tally:

- wrote 4.5 papers,
- wrote one book chapter,
- wrote one course development,
- gave seven presentations,
- gave three workshops, and
- engaged with two thesis supervisions.

Additionally, within the group:

- 25 percent published books,
- just under 25 percent produced a report, and
- 70 percent developed funding proposals.

Our query also allowed authors to identify other endeavours they engaged in during their sabbaticals. However, we did not ask the authors as a group about their engagement in these activities, and the extent may be under-represented. On average, the additional details per author were:

- edited a journal issue,
- attended a meeting for networking purposes,
- 70 percent visited a university other than their own,
- 60 percent completed a peer review for a journal or book,
- 50 percent were involved in conference planning or chairing a research group,
- 50 percent engaged in a professional-development course,
- 30 percent were external doctoral examiners,
- 15 percent taught overseas, and
- 23 percent attended a conference where they did not present (if they did present, the entire conference is included as a presentation).

There were mentions, by individuals, of many other activities, including preparing a video, engaging in a government task force, applying for research awards, book reviews, book proposals, a personal thesis, and a writing retreat.

To put the level of effort into context, imagine an "average" academic proposing a sabbatical. If the proposal is to be accurate for the "average," then that means that they must include all the items with a fixed count (i.e., write 4.5 papers, write a chapter, supervise two theses). When the item has a percentage that is the probability of that item. For example, conference planning and professional development are each 50 percent, so the average academic must pick one of the two. Continuing in this manner makes it clear that this is a significant outcome. Add to that the preparation and effort that goes into making these items happen; a paper, for example, uses research that must be completed.

We did not include the productivity for each individual because it is not the place of this book to give oversight to individuals. The details of activities cannot be compared easily. We feel that using the "average" academic is evidence of amazing productivity. What this does not include is any indication of recuperation or burnout avoidance. Those intangibles are something we did not inquire about, though we are aware of a sense of reduced stress that comes through in talking to academics who have had sabbaticals.

Through the process of developing this book, we became aware of challenges faced by some faculty. These were not something they necessarily wanted to reveal for fear of repercussions. However, good editing that asks questions sometimes leads to private conversations, revealing details. We offer a few without names because of the importance of the issues.

We learned of conditional acceptance of sabbatical proposals. The conditions required the faculty member to take specific actions and made the sabbatical dependent on the outcome. One condition included an application for funding, for example, with the sabbatical approval dependent on receipt of the funding.

There was also an instance where two members of the same university received very different responses to a similar aspect of their sabbatical proposals. This may be due to differences in the way the proposals portrayed the activity, but it could also reflect differences in the administrative handling of sabbatical proposals.

This conclusion brings together "findings" and relates these to the literature. There are, however, experiences that are intangible and tend to be silenced by the lack of opportunity to discuss them. We now wonder how the sabbatical influences views of collegial governance, and of higher education in general. When we step out of the familiar into unknown territory, we often return to the familiar with quite profound insight. Consider, as an example, a colleague who worked in Niger, Africa, for an extended period. Upon her return to Canada, she found grocery stores profoundly offensive; the over-abundance of food and choice a gross violation of the valuing of human existence in other parts of the world. It left an indelible mark on her view of inequity and the effects this has on human dignity.

When a faculty member returns to their department and their institution, they have spent considerable time outside the institution, away from their daily colleagues. When they return they are changed. They see themselves as much more autonomous. They see their colleagues in new light; they may be more generous, more valuing of their colleagues' autonomy. In the end, this may be a greater embracing of the diversity of knowledge, passions, and pathways that exist within departments and faculties, and within the academy overall. What if sabbatical actually builds both collective and self-efficacy—those core cognitive resources that may be the foundation of collegial governance?

It has been fascinating to engage with the entire collection of academics in this book and learn how remarkable and diverse sabbaticals are. We encourage further research about sabbaticals and the choices scholars make when given the opportunity. It clearly is reflective of their efforts to address everything from specific research goals to societal needs with their own needs for restoration coinciding.

References

Canada. (2015). *Truth and Reconciliation Commission of Canada*. Queen's Printer. See https://nctr.ca/about/history-of-the-trc/trc-website/

Carraher, S. M., Crocitto, M. M., & Sullivan, S. (2014). A kaleidoscope career perspective on faculty sabbaticals. *Career Development International*, 19(3), 295–313.

Cohan, D. J. (2018, October 23). Releasing oneself from the pressure of having a perfect sabbatical. *Inside Higher Ed*.

Davidson, O. B., Eden, D., Westman, M., Cohen-Charash, Y., Hammer, L. B., Kluger, A. N., Krausz, M., Maslach, C., O'Driscoll, M., Perrewe, P. L., Quick, J., Rosenblatt, Z. & Spector, P. E. (2010). Sabbatical leave: who gains and how much? *Journal of Applied Psychology*, 95(5), 953–964.

Endres, T. G. (2001). An examination of the sabbatical year in Leviticus 25 and its implications for academic practice. *Journal of the Association for Communication Administration*, 30(1), 29–38.

Hubbard, M. (2002). Exploring the sabbatical or other leave as a means of energizing a career. *Library Trends 50*(4), 603–613.

Hutchins, A., Hastie, A., Starkey, C., Hilton, S., & Clark, R. (2005). An investigation into the benefits of prolonged study leave undertaken by general practitioners. *Education for Primary Care, 16*(1), 57–65.

Iravani, H. (2011). Analyzing impacts of sabbatical leaves of absence regarding faculty members, University of Tehran. *Procedia Social and Behavioral Sciences, 15,* 3608–3615.

Kang, B., & Miller, M. T. (1999). *An overview of the sabbatical leave in higher education: A synopsis of the literature base.* ERIC. https://files.eric.ed.gov/fulltext/ED430471.pdf

Kelley, T. R. (2016, November). Postcards from a road trip to innovation: One professor's saga. *Technology and Engineering Teacher,* 26–30.

Reynolds, S. J. (1990). Sabbatical: The pause that refreshes. *The Journal of Academic Librarianship, 16*(2), 90–93.

Sibbald, T. M. (2020). Establishing balance to define a new normal. In T. M. Sibbald & V. Handford (Eds.), *Beyond the academic gateway* (pp. 155–172). University of Ottawa Press.

Sibbald, T., & Handford, V. (2017). Is there a metric for measuring tenure? *Academic Matters* (Winter), 9–13.

Spencer, M., Clay, H., Hearne, G., & James, P. (2012). A comparative examination of the use of academic sabbaticals. *The International Journal of Management Education, 10*(3), 147–154.

Stine, R. L. (1987). *The sabbatical leave in higher education: The view of the recipient* [Abstract from unpublished doctoral dissertation]. University of Kansas.

Stright, L. (1964). Sabbatical leave: A critique. *Journal of Higher Education, 35*(7), 388–390.

Thompson, T. C., & Louth, R. (2003). Radical sabbaticals: Putting yourself in danger. *College Composition and Communication, 55*(1), 147–171.

Weintraub, T. (2008). Sabbatical in paradise. *Community & Junior College Libraries, 14*(3), 153–160.

Contributors

Anahit Armenakyan is an associate professor of marketing in the School of Business at Nipissing University. Armenakyan has published research in the areas of country image, sport mega-events, sport marketing, and wine marketing. She is also exploring marketing issues around ecotourism, tourism destination, immigrant housing, organic-produce purchasing behaviour, and international business partnerships. Dr. Armenakyan teaches a wide range of marketing courses in consumer behaviour, advertising and promotions, digital marketing, and social marketing. Her practical experience in Armenian, American, and international companies has proven useful in tailoring her course materials and expanding her research interests. She is an adjunct research professor at Carleton University.

Cecile Badenhorst, MA (UBC), PhD (Queen's), is a professor in the adult-education/post-secondary program, Faculty of Education, at Memorial University of Newfoundland. She has conducted research and published in the areas of doctoral education, doctoral writing, graduate writing, thesis/publication writing pedagogies, academic literacies, and faculty writing. She engages in qualitative, arts-based and post-structural research methodologies. She has written three books in the area of graduate-student writing: *Research writing* (2007), *Dissertation writing* (2008), and *Productive writing* (2010). She is a co-editor of *Research literacies and writing pedagogies for masters and doctoral writers* (2016) and *Re-imagining doctoral writing* (2021).

Lee Anne Block is an associate professor in the Faculty of Education, University of Winnipeg. Her research and teaching are focused on how we name and engage with difference in educational locations. In her first study leave, place-based learning evolved into place making, which includes taking action. Her second study leave led to a consideration of reconciliation through healing as significant to cultural sustainability. She was a classroom teacher for twenty years.

Merridee Bujaki is a full professor of accounting at the Sprott School of Business, Carleton University. She has an undergraduate degree in psychology, an MBA, and a PhD in management, all from Queen's University. Merridee is a Fellow of the Chartered Professional Accountants of Ontario (FCPA, FCA). Merridee serves as co-director of the Centre for Research on Inclusion at Work at Carleton's Sprott School of Business. Merridee's research addresses voluntary corporate reporting by Canadian publicly traded corporations, the accounting history of the construction of the Rideau Canal, and the careers of public accountants. More recently, Merridee has been researching the careers of women academics, board diversity disclosures by Canadian public companies, and the mental health of accounting professionals.

Antoinette Doyle is an associate professor in the Faculty of Education, Memorial University of Newfoundland. Her research interests lie in the areas of developmental reading and writing of preschool and school-aged children, and reading and writing instruction, including spelling and its relation to reading.

Susan E. Elliott-Johns, PhD, is an associate professor in the Schulich School of Education, Nipissing University, where she works with preservice teachers and graduate students (PhD), and she also teaches in the MEd in educational leadership program at Yorkville University. Susan holds degrees in curriculum and instruction from McGill University (PhD, MEd) and the University of London (BEd). Her career as an educator spans over forty years as teacher, consultant, school administrator, and university professor. Her research interests continue to focus on narrative self-study, informed by reflexive inquiry, to uncover ways of making sense of our authentic selves and our teaching lives in relational spaces.

Victoria Handford is an associate professor in education (leadership) at Thompson Rivers University. She teaches in person, online, and blended, and has developed courses in all three delivery modes. Tory held multiple roles in education prior to moving to her university position. She was a teacher, vice-principal, principal, an education officer for the Ontario Ministry of Education, and a program officer for the Ontario College of Teachers. Her research interests are school and school-district leadership and trust. She is currently serving as coordinator of graduate programs as well as acting chair of the School of Education.

Jackie Hesson is an associate professor with the counselling psychology program in the Faculty of Education at Memorial University of Newfoundland. She is also a registered clinical psychologist, with a research and clinical practice focused on adults with attention-deficit hyperactivity disorder.

Lloyd Kornelsen is an associate professor in the Faculty of Education, director of the human-rights program, and acting executive of the Global College at the University of Winnipeg. Lloyd's research interests derive from twenty-five years of teaching high-school social studies and his current work with social studies teachers. Dr. Kornelsen has been granted the Manitoba Education Research Network Award for outstanding achievement in education research and the University of Winnipeg's Clifford J. Robson Memorial Award for teaching excellence.

Xuemei Li is an associate professor at the Faculty of Education, Memorial University of Newfoundland. Her research interests include TESL/TEFL curriculum and methodology, second/additional language writing, ESL support in schools and communities, migration and newcomer integration, and identity issues in additional language contexts. She teaches, supervises, and publishes in these areas. Dr Li's research projects investigate language and social support for newcomers (immigrant, refugee, and international students) in Canada, and particularly in Newfoundland. She also explores

English-for-academic-purposes writing instruction and teacher education in Chinese universities.

Pei-Ying Lin, an associate professor at the Department of Educational Psychology and Special Education of the University of Saskatchewan, works with diverse populations of children, youth, parents, in-service and pre-service teachers, university faculty members and staff, as well as testing agencies. Her research interests include the use of different research methods and approaches for studying classroom and large-scale assessment policies and practices for students with special needs and English-language learners. Her recent research also explores the use of educational neuroscience methods to better understand the cognitive development and processing of children with special needs.

Heather McLeod (PhD, University of Victoria), a professor at Memorial University of Newfoundland, has won national, university, and faculty awards for teaching and curriculum development. She has served as associate dean (undergraduate). Heather uses qualitative and arts-based research approaches. Her current research initiatives include an Art Hive community project, a poetry project, and an exploration of becoming a researcher/developing an academic identity. Before coming to the academy she taught in public schools in British Columbia and in Nunavut. She has worked in policy advising for government and in communications and training for a teachers' organization.

Sharon Penney, PhD, is an associate professor in the Faculty of Education at Memorial University of Newfoundland. She is a certified teacher and a registered psychologist with the Newfoundland and Labrador Psychology Board. Sharon is Mi'Kmaw from Benoit First Nations, a community on the west coast of Newfoundland and Labrador. Sharon holds a PhD from the University of Alberta in educational psychology (special education). She has worked in a variety of positions in both clinical and school settings for over twenty years. Her research is focused on inclusive education, autism spectrum disorders, and home and school partnerships, as well as positive mental health. She works primarily with qualitative methodologies and mixed-methods research.

María del Carmen Rodríguez de France's career in education spans thirty-seven years. She acknowledges the responsibility and the privilege of living and working on the land of the W̱SÁNEĆ and with the SENĆOTEN- and Lekwungen-speaking people for over twenty-two years. Born and raised in Monterrey, Mexico, Carmen is a faculty member of the Department of Indigenous Education in the Faculty of Education at the University of Victoria. She facilitates courses on Indigenous education and contributes to social-justice and Latin American studies. Carmen's work with Indigenous children, youth, and adults has been documented in academic publications, poetry, and stories.

Donald Ernest Scott is an associate professor in leadership, policy, and governance at the Werklund School of Education, University of Calgary. Don has thirty years of K–12 teaching and administration experience, as well as close to a decade of post-secondary teaching and program-leadership experience. Don's research focuses on professional and academic development, as well as leadership development, in both schools and the higher-education sectors. His research has explored the influence and potential of information and communications technology in supporting the capacity building of teachers, academics, and leaders; student assessment; quality teaching and learning; and supporting students who are at risk.

Shelleyann Scott is a professor in the leadership, policy, and governance specialization at the Werklund School of Education, University of Calgary. Shelleyann has experience as an educator and leader in K–12 and universities. She has experience as a professional and academic developer in Australia, Canada, and internationally. Her research interests include leadership and professional development of leaders and educators, quality teaching and learning, instructional and assessment strategies, and inclusion. Shelley has served as vice-president, president, and is the current past president of the Canadian Association for the Studies of Educational Administration.

Timothy Sibbald is an associate professor in the Schulich School of Education at Nipissing University. His focus is primarily on mathematics education, which was founded in experiences as a high-school math teacher and prior experience in remote-sensing research. While his current research focuses on mathematics education, he also studies his educator experiences that arise as his career progresses. He is the editor of the *Ontario Mathematics Gazette*, published by the Ontario Association of Mathematics Educators.

Gabrielle D. Young, PhD, is an associate professor at Memorial University of Newfoundland, where she teaches undergraduate and graduate courses surrounding understanding and supporting students with specific learning disorders, as well as a practicum in special education. Gabrielle's research interests surround the use of assistive and instructional technology in inclusive classrooms, applying the principles of universal design for learning to support students with exceptionalities in the general education classroom, and pre-service teachers' efficacy to support students in inclusive classrooms and facilitate positive mental health.

Index

A
accountability, 7, 15, 25, 44, 180, 189, 214, 222
agenda, 17, 21, 77, 83, 141, 179
    hidden, 89, 92
agricultural, 2

B
balance, work-life, 31, 65, 92, 98
burnout prevention, 18, 26, 160, 175, 180, 208, 219

C
caregiving, 84, 186, 192, 199, 200
children, 29, 50, 96, 130, 149, 160, 186, 192, 199
climate change, 71
curriculum development, 17, 19, 31, 150, 161

D
discrimination, 20, 72, 222

E
editor, 50–51, 59, 96, 170, 229
examiner, 76, 157, 198, 214, 234
expectations (vision), 13, 44, 87, 166, 172, 196, 200, 230

F
farm, 139, 140, 142, 144–145
farmer, 2, 4, 144
    farmers' market, 135
functional near-infrared spectroscopy (fNIRS), 130–133
funding, 21, 83, 91, 114, 193, 211, 235

G
Gates. *See* university gates
gender, 27, 180, 185, 190, 230
gendered, 154, 180, 185, 189–192, 199, 200, 230
goals, 39, 53, 83, 93, 153, 170–172, 178, 182
graduate students. *See* supervision
grants, 21, 42, 149, 171, 190, 196,
guilty pleasure, 227, 232, 233

H
healing forest, 139, 148–151

I
identity, 47–49, 66, 73, 114, 121, 186

M
masculine, 189, 190
metricization, 185, 188, 199, 200
multitasking, 60
    task switching, 90, 94, 97, 98, 100

N
neoliberal, 25, 154, 180, 186, 199, 211
networking, 19, 31, 113, 118, 207, 208, 213, 221, 222, 234
neuroscience, 130, 137

P
pandemic (COVID-19), 66, 72, 76, 84, 123, 200, 222
parents, 78, 108, 115, 136, 177, 193, 212
peers, 21, 122, 191
place-based, 139, 141, 143–144, 231
planning, 63, 112, 136, 178, 221, 235
practicum, 51, 56, 61, 63, 156–157, 158

R
reflective (reflexive), 17, 22, 48, 65, 66, 71, 77, 105, 147, 155, 172, 177, 185
rejuvenation (recuperation, renewal, revitalization), 2, 3, 74, 77, 83, 87, 93, 155, 167, 171, 175, 223, 228, 231, 235
religion, 2–4, 81
retirement, 39, 67, 100, 196, 231

S
sabbatical rates, 6
shrjapat, 118, 122–123
special education, 130, 133, 134, 135
spouse, 75, 93, 96, 97, 98, 115, 185, 186, 191–192, 194, 198
"staybatical", 28, 154, 217, 218, 221–222, 223
stress, 14, 18, 23, 31, 89, 112, 137, 168, 176, 180, 181, 192, 198, 217, 229, 235
study leave, 16, 17, 139, 140, 141, 143, 148, 151, 153, 155–156, 157, 158, 160, 161, 162, 208, 215

T
tensions, 9, 57, 170, 171, 172, 173, 181, 189, 219
tenure, 27, 194, 206, 208, 215, 217
time, 42, 53, 71, 93, 177, 196
"travel-batical", 213–214, 215, 217, 221
truth and reconciliation, 39, 43, 148, 211, 228

U
university gates, 81, 82–83

W
well-being, 14, 22, 24, 31, 40, 115, 118, 136, 142, 158, 167, 168, 175, 177, 179, 180, 181, 219, 228, 231

Education

Series Editors: Nicholas Ng-A-Fook and Carole Fleuret

Our *Education* series seeks to advance thought-provoking research within the broader field of education. Scholarly works in this series examine educational research from a multidisciplinary perspective and address a variety of issues in the field, including curriculum studies, arts-based education, educational philosophy, life writing, foundations in education, teacher education, evaluation, and counselling.

Previous titles in the *Education* Series

Joël Thibeault and Carole Fleuret, eds., *Didactique du français en contextes minoritaires : entre normes scolaires et plurilinguismes*, 2020

Timothy M. Sibbald and Victoria Handford, eds., *Beyond the Academic Gateway: Looking Back on the Tenure-Track Journey*, 2020.

Anne M. Phelan, William F. Pinar, Nicholas Ng-A-Fook, and Ruth Kane, eds., *Reconceptualizing Teacher Education: A Canadian Contribution to a Global Challenge*, 2020.

Michelle Forrest and Linda Wheeldon, *Scripting Feminist Ethics in Teacher Education*, 2019.

William F. Pinar, *Moving Images of Eternity: George Grant's Critique of Time, Teaching, and Technology*, 2019.

Pierre Jean, *Planification de formations en santé : guide des bonnes pratiques*, 2019.

Thomas R. Klassen and John A. Dwyer, *Décrocher son diplôme (et l'emploi de ses rêves !) : comment maîtriser les compétences essentielles menant au succès à l'école, au travail et dans la vie*, 2018.

Timothy M. Sibbald and Victoria Handford, eds., *The Academic Gateway: Understanding the Journey to Tenure*, 2017.

Lise Gremion, Serge Ramel, Valérie Angelucci, and Jean-Claude Kalubi, eds., *Vers une école inclusive : regards croisés sur les défis actuels*, 2017.

For a complete list of the University of Ottawa Press titles, visit:
www.press.uOttawa.ca

www.ingramcontent.com/pod-product-compliance
Lightning Source LLC
Chambersburg PA
CBHW061346300426
44116CB00011B/2009